125

In the early 1880s, William D. Longstaff wrote a poem that later became a hymn called "Take Time to Be Holy." Becoming a holy person is intentional; you have to work at it. Samuel Logan Brengle embodies for me everything I could imagine a holy person to be. What I see is a man who knew lots about life in the streets but saw it from the perspective of knowing lots about life in the Lord's presence. Bob Hostetler has done us a service by arranging Brengle's holiness writings into bite-size pieces, one for each day of the year, to help us spend time in secret with Jesus.

**GORDON MACDONALD**
Author, speaker, and pastor for more than 40 years

This daily diet of wisdom from Brengle's life affords a wonderful opportunity to deepen the health of your own journey toward wholeness. The simplicity of a day-to-day dose of wisdom from such a godly man is a gift that will multiply in effect each day. Holiness, in its generous and transforming nature, perfectly reflects the deep complexity of God's own heart. The Holy Spirit will work its restoring way in your heart as you walk this path of daily devotions. God's holy nature will become a new and fresh breeze each day.

**KEVIN MANNOIA**
Founder and chair of the Wesleyan Holiness Consortium and professor of ministry at Azusa Pacific University

*Take Time to Be Holy* is a splendid book. The richness of its devotional selections from the writings of Samuel Logan Brengle reveals the depth of his insights into the doctrine of the Holy Spirit and a subtle delineation of biblical holiness. The diligent unraveling of this multi-faced subject discloses a multifaceted character who deserves to be rediscovered as a twenty-first century "prophet of holiness."

**LEONARD SWEET**
Bestselling author, professor (Drew University, George Fox University), and chief contributor to Sermons.com

# TAKE TIME TO BE
# HOLY

## 365 DAILY INSPIRATIONS
## TO BRING YOU CLOSER TO GOD

### Samuel Logan Brengle
*Edited by Bob Hostetler*

**TYNDALE™
MOMENTUM**

*An Imprint of
Tyndale House Publishers, Inc.*

*Dedicated to*

*Miles, Mia, Calleigh, and Ryder*

Visit Tyndale online at www.tyndale.com.

Visit Tyndale Momentum online at www.tyndalemomentum.com.

*TYNDALE* is a registered trademark of Tyndale House Publishers, Inc.
*Tyndale Momentum* and the Tyndale Momentum logo are trademarks
of Tyndale House Publishers, Inc. Tyndale Momentum is an imprint of
Tyndale House Publishers, Inc.

*Take Time to Be Holy: 365 Daily Inspirations to Bring You Closer to God*

Copyright © 2013 by The Salvation Army and Bob Hostetler. All rights
reserved.

No portion of this book may be reproduced in any manner without
written permission.

Cover photograph of sun copyright © Roman Sakhno/Veer. All rights
reserved.

Cover photograph of fog copyright © David M. Schrader/Veer. All
rights reserved.

Designed by Beth Sparkman

Published in association with the literary agency of Steve Laube
Agency, LLC, 5025 N. Central Ave., #635, Phoenix, AZ 85012.

ISBN 978-1-4143-7906-7

Printed in China

19   18   17   16   15   14   13
 7    6    5    4    3    2    1

# INTRODUCTION

I met Commissioner Samuel Logan Brengle when I was a young man.

The Salvation Army's greatest exponent of holiness died twenty-two years before I was born, but when I was a teenager, I read Clarence Hall's inspiring biography of Brengle, *Portrait of a Prophet*. As a result, I began systematically reading Brengle's own works, and by the time I was twenty, I had read them all: *Helps to Holiness*, *Heart Talks on Holiness*, *The Way of Holiness*, *The Soul-Winner's Secret*, *When the Holy Ghost Is Come*, *Love-Slaves*, *Resurrection Life and Power*, *Ancient Prophets and Modern Problems*, and *The Guest of the Soul*. Perhaps more than any other person, living or dead, Commissioner Brengle taught and guided me as a young man, and his influence remains with me to this day.

Brengle's thinking, preaching, and writing sailed comfortably on the current of nineteenth-century holiness teaching, building on the tradition of John Wesley, Charles Finney, Asa Mahan, James Caughey, Phoebe Palmer, and William and Catherine Booth. As an officer in The Salvation Army, Samuel Logan Brengle made it his central mission to serve others and tell them of salvation through Jesus Christ and new life through His Holy Spirit. "His articulation of entire sanctification . . . served as the basis for Salvation Army holiness self-understanding through most of the twentieth century."[1] Brengle espoused a doctrine of full sanctification that was often misunderstood even in his own time, and the conversation continues in the church today. Brengle made it clear that he did not mean Christians can achieve heavenly perfection in this life or be free from sin and temptation, but that moment-by-moment deliverance from sin by the power of the Holy Spirit is possible for everyone who believes.

It is my hope that *Take Time to Be Holy* will enhance and enlarge Brengle's influence and broaden the conversation on the transforming work of the Holy Spirit in every believer's life. The selections in this volume have been drawn from his books, and I have taken care to preserve the integrity, impact, and voice of the original writing while making a few necessary changes. These include:

- editing for length, to fit the devotional format;
- revising archaic terms and updating the language to reflect more contemporary usage;
- shortening and simplifying sentence structure to conform more closely to contemporary practice;
- explaining specific Salvation Army references that may be unfamiliar to some readers;
- updating Scripture references (at times retaining the King James Version—used exclusively in Brengle's writings—while frequently incorporating modern translations, especially when doing so will aid comprehension and enjoyment);
- citing Scripture quotes not referenced in the

original and noting the sources for quotes, lines from hymns, etc.;

- adding introductory, transitional, and concluding phrases when necessary.

It is my hope and prayer that even the most devoted reader of Brengle's writings will find his or her enjoyment and blessing not only unimpeded by such changes, but heightened.

Finally, the words of General Bramwell Booth in the preface to Commissioner Brengle's first book apply equally to the volume you hold in your hands:

This book is intended to help every reader of its pages into the immediate enjoyment of Bible holiness. Its writer is an officer of The Salvation Army who, having a gracious experience of the things whereof he writes, has been signally used of God, both in life and testimony, to the sanctifying of the Lord's people, as well as in the salvation of sinners. I commend him and what he has here written down to every lover of God and His Kingdom on the earth.

To which I will add, only: Amen.

*Bob Hostetler*

# SAMUEL LOGAN BRENGLE

Born on June 1, 1860, in Fredericksburg, Indiana, Samuel Logan Brengle became a follower of Jesus Christ as a teenage boy. After serving four rural Indiana churches as a circuit preacher, he enrolled in Boston University School of Theology. There he encountered such influences as Dr. Daniel Steele, a professor and leading proponent of the doctrine of holiness, and the writings of Hannah Whitall Smith (*The Christian's Secret of a Happy Life*) and Catherine Booth (*Popular Christianity*). He also described the impact of a sermon by Dwight L. Moody:

> God searched me. I saw the corruptions of my heart as never before. I was humbled into the dust. . . . Day and night for weeks I asked, I sought, I knocked. . . . Then one glad, sweet January morning suddenly the door opened at which I had knocked so importunately; I received, I found what I so earnestly sought. It was far beyond what I received when I was saved as a boy. That was the day, dawn; this the broad day with the sun risen in my soul. That was "peace with God"; this was "the peace of God." That was forgiveness and the new birth; this was cleansing from all sin, heart purity, and fullness of love and joy and peace and long-suffering. That was accompanied by the witness of the Spirit; this by the fullness of His

indwelling. It was the fulfillment of that great group of promises and assurances of Jesus in John 14:15-23. He had fulfilled His promise and the Father had given me the "Other Comforter." . . . Christ was revealed in me, and, oh, how I loved it! It seemed I would nearly die of love. . . . My whole inner being was transformed.[2]

Before long, Brengle felt God calling him into service with The Salvation Army. In May 1887, he sailed to London, where he presented himself to General William Booth, who told him, "You belong to the 'dangerous classes.' You've been your own boss for so long that I don't think you will want to submit to Salvation Army discipline."[3]

Nonetheless, Brengle was accepted into the Salvation Army's training school in London. There, the first assignment given to this scholar and accomplished orator was to black the boots of his fellow cadets (Salvation Army seminarians). Though at first he inwardly disdained the task, he soon remembered the biblical example of Jesus washing His disciples' feet, whereupon he prayerfully and joyfully submitted to the work.

Brengle was commissioned a Salvation Army officer and returned to the United States to serve in Boston. One night, a brick hurled by an angry drunkard struck Brengle in the head. The blow nearly killed him, and sidelined him from preaching for eighteen months. But during that time, Brengle wrote a series of articles on holiness. These were later gathered and published as a little red book entitled *Helps to Holiness*. That book would become an international success, and the first of nine by Samuel Logan Brengle, causing him later to remark, "If there had been no little brick, there would have been no little book!"[4]

By the time of his death in 1936, Commissioner Brengle was an internationally renowned preacher and worldwide ambassador of holiness. His influence continues today, perhaps more than that of any Salvationist in history other than the founders, William and Catherine Booth.

# SOURCE MATERIAL

Each daily reading includes an abbreviation and a chapter number to denote the original source of the excerpt.

## The Future Before You

*Behold, I am doing a new thing.* (Isaiah 43:19)

Don't underestimate the power of God in you. Paul tells us not to think too highly of ourselves (Romans 12:3). Yet he said of himself, "I can do all things through him who strengthens me" (Philippians 4:13). He thought of himself linked to the illimitable strength of Christ, and therefore omnipotent for any work Christ set him to do.

The future before you is big with opportunities and possibilities. Open doors on every hand invite you to enter and do service for the Master and for others, and the strength that worked in Paul works in you, if you do not hinder it by selfishness and unbelief.

Keep the fire of love and faith and hope burning in your heart, and you may start a blaze that will someday sweep the world. Seek the Lord. Seek Him daily, constantly, with your whole heart.

If honor comes, thank God and lay it at the torn feet of Jesus, and forget it, lest it ruin you. If honor comes not, still thank God and go on. Seek only the honor of walking in the footsteps of Jesus, of loving, serving, sacrificing, suffering for others, and you shall have your reward. You surely shall, and it will be great, exceeding abundantly above all you ask or think, given by the Master's own hand.

*LS*, 17

## Redeem the Time

*Walk circumspectly, not as fools but as wise, redeeming the time, because the days are evil.* (Ephesians 5:15-16, NKJV)

Value time. Diamonds and gold nuggets are not so precious as minutes. Eternity is made up of moments, and "lost time is lost eternity."

"Believe me," said William Gladstone, "when I tell you that . . . the waste of [time] will make you dwindle, alike in intellectual and in moral stature, beyond your darkest reckonings."[5]

What is life but a glad, present consciousness of God and self and duty, and a hearty obedience thereto? And yet thoughtless idlers try to "kill time," and thus destroy their most valuable possession.

If you would redeem the time, begin the moment your eyes open in the morning. Let no idle, foolish, hurtful thoughts be harbored for an instant, but begin at once to pray and praise God and to meditate on His glories, His goodness and faithfulness and truth, and your heart will soon burn within you and bubble over with joy. Bounce out of bed at once and get the start of your work and push it, else *it* will get the start and push *you*.

*SWS, 6*

## The Work of the Spirit

*When the Spirit of truth comes, he will guide you into all the truth.* (John 16:13)

All lovers of Jesus should in these days seek fresh renewings and a greater fullness of the Holy Spirit. We should study what the Bible says about Him as a Person. He is not a mere influence, passing over us like a wind or warming us like a fire. He is a Person, seeking entrance into our hearts that He may comfort us, instruct us, empower us, guide us, give us heavenly wisdom, and fit us for holy and triumphant service.

If we will seek His presence and yield ourselves to Him in secret prayer, He will make the Bible a new book to us. He will make Jesus precious to us. He will make God the Father ever real to us. We shall not walk in darkness, but shall have the light of life. We shall not be weak in the presence of duty or temptation, but "strong in the Lord and in the power of His might" (Ephesians 6:10, NKJV). We shall be "ready for every good work" (Titus 3:1).

God has greater things for all His people than the world has ever yet seen, if we but believe on the Lord Jesus Christ and permit the Spirit to lead us.

*GS*, 2

## The Blessing of the Holy Spirit

*John baptized with water, but you will be baptized with the Holy Spirit not many days from now.* (Acts 1:5)

Do you want to know what the blessing of the Holy Spirit is? It is not a mere sentiment. It is not a happy sensation that passes away in a night. It is a whelming flood of love that brings every thought into captivity to the Lord Jesus (2 Corinthians 10:5); that casts out all fear (1 John 4:18); that burns up doubt and unbelief as fire burns flax; that makes one "meek and lowly in heart" (Matthew 11:29, KJV); that makes one hate uncleanness, lying and deceit, a flattering tongue, and every evil way with a perfect hatred; that makes heaven and hell eternal realities; that makes one patient and gentle with the disobedient and sinful; that makes one "pure . . . peaceable . . . open to reason, full of mercy and good fruits, impartial and sincere" (James 3:17); that brings one into perfect and unbroken sympathy with the Lord Jesus Christ in His toil and travail to bring a lost and rebel world back to God.

Oh, how I had longed to be pure! Oh, how I had hungered and thirsted for God—the living God! And He gave me the desire of my heart. He satisfied me—I weigh my words—He satisfied me!

*HH*, Introduction

## A Perfection God Requires

*Let steadfastness have its full effect, that you may be*
*perfect and complete, lacking in nothing.* (James 1:4)

God alone is absolutely perfect in all His attributes, and to such perfection we can never hope to attain.

There is, however, a perfection which we are given to understand God requires in us. It is a perfection not of head but of heart; not of knowledge, but of goodness, of humility, of love, of faith. Such a perfection God desires us to have, and such a perfection we may have. I am proclaiming only the plain, simple truth as it is revealed in God's Word, and we ought to desire to rise up to all the privileges God has conferred upon us.

If we go down before Him in complete humility and say, "Lord, I am willing to have my heart changed. Though it may mean that I shall be despised and hated and persecuted, I will take up my cross; I will crucify myself. I am willing that my selfishness and pride and hate and uncleanness shall be taken from me, and that You shall reign in me and create in me a clean heart, perfect in its love, submission, loyalty, trust, and obedience"—if we will say that to Him, He will answer our prayer today, now, this moment, if we will but believe.

*GS, 5*

# A Good Tree

*A good tree produces good fruit.* (Matthew 7:17, NLT)

Holiness is not absolute perfection, which belongs to God only; nor is it angelic perfection; nor is it Adamic perfection—for, no doubt, Adam had a perfect head as well as a perfect heart before he sinned against God. But it is Christian perfection—such perfection and obedience of the heart as a poor fallen creature, aided by almighty power and boundless grace, can give.

It is that state of heart and life which consists in being and doing all the time—not by fits and starts, but steadily—just what God wants us to be and do.

Jesus said, "Make the tree good and its fruit good" (Matthew 12:33). Now, an apple tree is an apple tree all the time, and can bring forth nothing but apples. So holiness is that perfect renewal of our nature that makes us essentially good, so that we continually bring forth fruit unto God, with never a single work of the flesh grafted in among this heavenly fruit.

It is possible for the Son of God thus to transform us. It is as easy for me to be and to do what God wants me to be and to do in this life, every day, as it is for the archangel Gabriel to be and do what God wants of him.

*HH, 1*

## A Perfect Heart

*The blood of Jesus his Son cleanses us from all sin.*
(1 John 1:7)

The Bible tells us that holiness is perfect deliverance from sin. "The blood of Jesus . . . cleanses us from *all* sin" (1 John 1:7, italics added). Not one bit of sin is left, for your old self is crucified with Him, "that the body of sin might be brought to nothing, so that we would no longer be enslaved to sin" (Romans 6:6), for we have "been set free from sin" (Romans 6:18).

The Bible also tells us that it is "perfect love" which must expel from the heart all hatred and every evil disposition contrary to love (1 John 4:18), just as you must first empty a cup of all oil that may be in it before you can fill it with water.

Thus, holiness is a state in which there is no anger, malice, blasphemy, hypocrisy, envy, love of ease, selfish desire for good opinion of others, shame of the Cross, worldliness, deceit, debate, contention, covetousness, nor any evil tendency in the heart.

It is a state in which there is no longer any doubt or fear.

It is a state in which God is loved and trusted with a perfect heart.

*HH, 1*

## A Perfect-Hearted People

*Let your heart therefore be perfect with the LORD our God.*
(1 Kings 8:61, KJV)

God is looking for people whose hearts are perfect towards Him. This perfection of heart, of purity, of goodness, was seen in Jesus, and we are to follow His example.

1. We are to be perfectly submitted to God. We are to come to the place where we no longer complain, nor talk back, nor resist, but yield in perfect submission to all His will.

2. Like Jesus, we may perfectly trust God. We may possess a confidence in God that holds out in ways we do not understand.

3. God desires His people to be perfect in love, to love Him perfectly with all our hearts—with all our power to love.

4. There must be perfect loyalty. Love is not an emotion, a happy feeling. It is not something on the surface. It is a deep principle, revealing itself in perfect loyalty to God.

5. God also requires of us perfect obedience. Our performance may not always be perfect, but our spirit may be perfect.

How can I do this? How can I put away things that seem to be a part of my very being? I cannot! Work as I will, I shall always fail to change my moral nature. But God can. It is His work.

*GS, 5*

## The Arithmetic of Holiness

*Wash me, and I shall be whiter than snow.* (Psalm 51:7)

Entire sanctification is at once a process of subtraction and addition.

The Bible says, "Put off all these: anger, wrath, malice, blasphemy, filthy language out of your mouth" (Colossians 3:8, NKJV). The apostle Paul talks as though we were to put these off in much the same way as we would a coat. It is not by growth that a person puts off a coat, but by an active, voluntary, and immediate effort of the whole body. This is subtraction.

But the apostle adds, "Clothe yourselves with compassion, kindness, humility, gentleness and patience" (Colossians 3:12, NIV). No more does a person put *on* clothing by growth, but by a similar effort of the whole body.

You may grow *in* your coat, but not *into* your coat; you must first get it on. Just so, we may "grow in grace" (2 Peter 3:18, KJV), but not into grace. We may swim in water, but not into water.

It is not by growth that you get weeds out of your garden, but by pulling them up. It is not by growth that you expect a dirty little boy to get clean. He might grow to manhood and get dirtier every day. It is by washing with much pure water that you expect to make him at all presentable. And so it is with us.

*HH, 2*

# JANUARY 10

## Sharing the Divine Nature

*He has given us great and precious promises . . . that enable you to share his divine nature.* (2 Peter 1:4, NLT)

Many years ago, a young woman asked me, "What is this sanctification?"

I asked, "Do you have a bad temper?"

"Oh, yes," she said. "I have a temper like a volcano."

"Sanctification," I replied, "is to have that bad temper taken out." That definition set her thinking and did her good; but it was too narrow. If I had said, "Sanctification is to have that bad temper and all sin taken away, and the heart filled with love to God and others," that would have done, for that is sanctification. That is holiness. It is to be made a partaker of the divine nature (2 Peter 1:4, KJV).

A spark from the fire is like the fire. The tiniest twig on the giant oak, or the smallest branch of the vine, has the nature of the oak or the vine. A drop of water from the ocean is like the ocean: not in its size, of course, but in its essence. Just so, a holy person is like God. That person is not infinite, does not know everything, has not all power and wisdom as God has, but is like God in nature—good and pure, loving and just.

Holiness, then, is conformity to the nature of God. It is likeness to God, as He is revealed in Jesus.

*WH, 1*

## Pure Love

*God's love has been poured into our hearts through the Holy Spirit.* (Romans 5:5)

On January 9, 1885, at about nine in the morning, God sanctified my soul. God used a friend to encourage me to confess it everywhere, so the following day I preached on the subject as clearly and forcibly as I could, and ended with my testimony.

God blessed the Word mightily to others, but I think He blessed it most to myself. That confession put me on record. It cut the bridges down behind me. Those who knew me were now looking at me as one who professed that God had given him a clean heart. I could not go back now. I had to go forward. God saw that I meant to be true till death. So two mornings after that, He gave me such a blessing as I never had dreamed a man could have this side of heaven. It was a heaven of love that came into my heart. Oh, how I loved! In that hour I knew Jesus and I loved Him till it seemed my heart would break with love. I loved the sparrows, I loved the dogs, I loved the little urchins on the streets, I loved the strangers who hurried past—I loved the whole world.

Do you want to know what holiness is? It is pure love.

*HH,* Introduction

## Love Slaves

*Paul, a slave of God and an apostle of Jesus Christ.*
(Titus 1:1, NLT)

There was a law among the Hebrews that one man might become the slave of another, but at the end of six years he must be allowed to go free (Deuteronomy 15:12-17). But if he loved his master and preferred to remain with him as his slave, then he was marked as his master's forever. This was not the slavery of compulsion and law, but the willing and glad slavery of love.

This also is the true freedom and service of the Christian. The love slave is altogether at the Master's service. The slave's mind is willing. The slave's hands are ready. The slave's feet are swift. To sit at the Master's feet and look into His loved face, to listen to His voice, to run His errands and do His bidding, to share His privations and sorrows, to watch at His door, to guard His honor, praise His name, defend His person, to seek and promote His interests, and if necessary, to die for His dear sake—this is the joy of the slave of love, and is counted as perfect freedom.

To the sinner, Christ's yoke looks intolerable, His burden unbearable. But to those who have entered into the secret of the Master, His yoke is the badge of freedom, and His burden gives wings to the soul.

*LS, 1*

## What Holiness Is and Is Not

*Put on your new nature, created to be like God—truly righteous and holy.* (Ephesians 4:24, NLT)

*Holiness is not necessarily a state in which there is perpetual rapturous joy.* Jesus Himself was "a man of sorrows, and acquainted with grief" (Isaiah 53:3).

*Holiness is not a state of freedom from temptation.* Our Lord was tried and tempted by the devil.

*Holiness is not a state of freedom from infirmities.* The saints' infirmities have always proved a source of great trial and great blessing.

*Holiness is not a state of freedom from affliction.* Job and Jeremiah and Daniel and Paul and all the martyrs have, and shall always, come up through great tribulations.

*Holiness is not a state in which there is no further development.* It would be as wise to say that corn would grow no more when the weeds were destroyed. When the heart is purified, it develops more rapidly than ever before.

*Holiness is not a state from which we cannot fall.* "If you think you are standing firm you had better be careful that you do not fall" (1 Corinthians 10:12, GNT). But while we may fall, we need not fall.

*But holiness is a state of conformity to the divine nature.* It is an indescribable blessing, received through a complete renunciation of all sin, an uttermost consecration to all the known will of God, importunate prayer, and childlike faith.

*HTH, 2*

JANUARY 14

## Being Emptied to Be Filled

*Stay here in the city until the Holy Spirit comes and fills you with power from heaven.* (Luke 24:49, NLT)

Waiting on God empties us that we may be filled. Few wait until they are emptied, and hence few are filled. It is far easier to plunge madly at this thing and that, and do, do, do, till life and heart are exhausted in joyless and comparatively fruitless toil, than it is to wait on God in patient faith until He comes and fills you with the power of the Holy Spirit.

Jesus commanded the disciples, saying, "Tarry in the city of Jerusalem until you are endued with power from on high" (Luke 24:49, NKJV). So they cried to God, and searched their hearts, and forgot their fears and jealousies and selfish ambitions and childish differences, and had but one desire: a mighty, consuming hunger for God. Then suddenly God came—in power, with fire, to purge, cleanse, and sanctify them through and through, and dwell in their hearts, and make them bold in the presence of their enemies, humble in the midst of success, patient in fiery conflicts, steadfast in spite of persecution, joyful in loneliness and misrepresentations, and fearless and triumphant in the face of death. God made them wise to win souls, and filled them with the very Spirit of their Master, till they turned the world upside down.

*HH*, 26

## Help to Interpret My Own Times

*Long ago, at many times and in many ways, God spoke to our fathers by the prophets.* (Hebrews 1:1)

Many students of prophecy think the prophets have put into our hands a God-given telescope, through which we can peer into the future and foresee the course of all coming history to the utmost bounds of time, and they prepare elaborate charts and write no end of books. But their value to me ever since God sanctified me has appeared to consist not in the light they throw upon generations yet unborn, but the light they throw upon my own generation. I want help to interpret my own times.

Have we problems? Are we confronted by vice and sin in our city? Is evil triumphant and injustice and wickedness entrenched in high places in the State? We shall find light on every problem in the messages of the prophets, and we shall find help and strength in company with them, for they walked with God and lived and spoke and suffered and died for Him.

With my open Bible I live with prophets, priests, and kings; I walk and hold communion with apostles, saints, and martyrs, and with Jesus, and mine eyes see the King in His beauty and the land that is afar off.

*AP, 1*

## Filled with the Fullness

*Be filled with all the fullness of God.* (Ephesians 3:19)

Do you want to really know the Lord? If your whole soul desires it, you may. This revelation of the Lord Jesus is more than salvation—it is the positive side of that experience which we call a "clean heart" or "holiness."

First, be sure your sins are forgiven. If you have wronged anybody, undo the wrong so far as you can. Submit to God, confess your sins, then trust Jesus, and all your sins shall be forgiven, and He will remember them no more (Jeremiah 31:34).

Second, come to Him with your will, your affection, your very self, and ask Him to cleanse you from every evil desire, from every selfish wish, from every secret doubt, and to come and dwell in your heart and keep you pure, and use you for His own glory. Then struggle no more, but walk in the light He gives you, and trust Him to answer your prayer; as sure as you live you shall soon "be filled with all the fullness of God" (Ephesians 3:19).

At this point, do not become impatient and yield to secret doubts and fears. God will come to you! And when He comes, He will satisfy the uttermost longings of your heart.

*HH, 19*

## Why Be Holy?

*You shall be holy, for I the LORD your God am holy.*
(Leviticus 19:2)

We should be holy because God wants us to be holy. "As he who called you is holy, you also be holy in all your conduct, since it is written, 'You shall be holy, for I am holy'" (1 Peter 1:15-16). It is God's will, and it cannot be evaded.

To many, the command seems harsh. But "God is love" (1 John 4:8), and His commands are not harsh, but kind. They come from the fullness of an infinitely loving and all-wise heart. They are meant for our good. A railway train might argue that running over the same two rails year after year was very commonplace. But if it insisted on larger liberty and jumped the track, it would certainly ruin itself. So anyone who wants freedom, and refuses to obey God's commands to be holy, is headed for destruction.

Oh, how tender are His words! "What does the LORD your God require of you, but to fear the LORD your God, to walk in all his ways, to love him, . . . and to keep the commandments and statutes of the LORD, which I am commanding you today for your good?" (Deuteronomy 10:12-13).

For your good! Do you not see it? Nothing harsh, nothing selfish in our dear Lord's command. It is "your good" He is seeking.

*WH, 2*

## Holy and Useful

*If you keep yourself pure, you will be a special utensil
for honorable use. Your life will be clean, and you will
be ready for the Master to use you for every good work.*
(2 Timothy 2:21, NLT)

So long as there are any roots of sin in the heart, the Holy
Spirit cannot have all His way in us, and our usefulness is
hindered. But when our hearts are clean, the Holy Spirit
dwells within, and we have power for service.

A plain, humble young man fell on his knees before the
Lord and cried to Him for a clean heart. Another man,
overhearing him, wrote about it, saying, "I shall never
forget his petition. 'O God, I plead for this blessing! My
Father, I will give up every known sin, only I plead with
Thee for power.' As if his sins were passing before him,
he said again and again, 'I will give them up; I will give
them up.'

"Then, without any emotion, he rose, turned his face
heavenward, and simply said, 'Now, I claim the blessing.'
With a shining face he reached out his hand to clasp mine.
You could feel the presence of the Spirit as he said, 'I have
received Him; I have received Him!'

"And I believe he had. In the next few months he led
more than sixty men into the Kingdom of God. His whole
life was transformed."[6]

*WH, 2*

## Let Not His Blood Be Spent in Vain

*Christ loved the church and gave himself up for her, that he might sanctify her.* (Ephesians 5:25-26)

We should be holy because Jesus died to make us holy. He gave Himself to stripes, and spitting, and cruel mockings, and the crown of thorns, and death on the cross "to redeem us from all lawlessness and to purify for himself a people for his own possession who are zealous for good works" (Titus 2:14). Let us not disappoint Him. Let not His precious blood be spent in vain.

We should be holy in order that we may be safe. Sin in the heart is more dangerous than gunpowder in the cellar.

Finally, we should be holy because we are most solemnly assured that without holiness "no one will see the Lord" (Hebrews 12:14), and God has made all things ready so that we may have the blessing if we will.

*O Savior, I dare to believe,*
*Thy blood for my cleansing I see;*
*And, asking in faith, I receive*
*Salvation, full, present, and free.*[7]

WH, 2

## A Present Privilege

*Although I want to do good, evil is right there with me.*
(Romans 7:21, NIV)

A bright young man in one of my meetings said, "Since the Lord converted me, I never wanted any bad thing, but something in me did."

One day a boy who had been blessedly saved came to his mother and said, "Mama, I'm tired of living this way. You tell me to go and do things, and I do them; but I feel angry inside, and I want to be good all the time."

Both the young man and the boy wanted to be good, but each found he was not holy. However correct the outward life might be, the heart was not clean. This is the experience of every true follower of Jesus who has not pressed on into holiness, and it corresponds to the Scripture in which Paul says, "When I would do good, evil is present with me" (Romans 7:21, KJV).

Some say that we cannot get rid of this evil nature until we die. But the Bible certainly teaches that we can be made holy in this life. The Bible says, "Be holy" (1 Peter 1:16, NIV), and that means now, not after death. Just as God gave this great blessing to the early Christians (Acts 2:4; 15:9), He will surely give it to us, when we give ourselves fully to Him.

*WH, 4*

## Preparing His House

*The Spirit of truth . . . dwells with you and will be in you.*
(John 14:17)

When a man is building a house, he is in and out of it and round about it. But we do not say he *lives in* it. And so Jesus said of the Holy Spirit, "He lives *with* you" (John 14:17, NIV, emphasis added). When the house is finished, the owner moves in with his family. Then he is, in the fullest sense, *within* it. He abides there.

Every child of God knows that the Holy Spirit is with him or her, working, striving to set the house in order. And with many, this work is done quickly.

But often this work is slow, for He can only work effectually as we work with Him, practicing intelligent and obedient faith, as the Spirit seeks to bring every thought into "captivity to the obedience of Christ" (2 Corinthians 10:5, NKJV). This will lead the soul to that point of glad, wholehearted consecration to its Lord, and that simple, perfect faith in the merits of His blood which shall enable Him to cast out the old nature and, making the heart His temple, enthrone Christ within.

What is your experience? Are you filled with the Spirit? Or is the old nature still warring against Him in your heart? Oh, that you may receive Him fully by faith just now!

*HGC, 2*

## The Second Blessing

*Open their eyes . . . that they may receive forgiveness of sins and a place among those who are sanctified by faith in me.* (Acts 26:18)

The advocates of entire sanctification often call it "the second blessing." Many object to the term, saying they have received the first, second, third, and fiftieth blessing. No doubt they have; and yet the people who speak of "the second blessing" are right, in the sense in which they use the term.

Suppose a man asks a woman to become his wife, and after due consideration and prayer, she consents. That is the first blessing, and it fills him with great peace and joy. Many blessings follow. Every letter, every tender look, every fresh assurance of affection is a blessing; but not the second blessing.

Then, after patient waiting, they come together and, in the most solemn and irrevocable manner, give themselves to each other as man and wife. That is the second blessing, unlike anything that preceded or anything to follow. And now their peace and joy and rest are full.

The first blessing in Jesus Christ is salvation, with its negative side of remission of sins and forgiveness, and its positive side of renewal or regeneration. And the second blessing is entire sanctification, with its negative side of cleansing, and its positive side of filling with the Holy Spirit. And when time is no more, then in eternity we shall have the third blessing—we shall be glorified.

*HGC, 3*

## Burn with Holy Fire

*He will baptize you with the Holy Spirit and fire.*
(Luke 3:16)

How plainly is the work of the Holy Spirit taught in the Bible! And yet many of God's dear children do not believe it is their privilege to be free from sin and pure in heart in this life. But may we not?

1. It is certainly *desirable*. Every sincere Christian wants to be like Christ: free from sin, pure in heart.

2. It is *necessary*, for without holiness "no one will see the Lord" (Hebrews 12:14). Sin must go out of our hearts—all sin—or we cannot go into heaven.

3. This purification from sin is *promised*. "I will sprinkle clean water on you, and you shall be clean from all your uncleannesses" (Ezekiel 36:25). When all is removed, nothing remains.

4. And that deliverance is *possible*. Jesus Christ came and suffered and died that He might "save his people from their sins" (Matthew 1:21). The promises of God's Word were given "so that through them [we] may become partakers of the divine nature, having escaped from the corruption that is in the world because of sinful desire" (2 Peter 1:4).

If you will look unto Jesus just now and receive the Holy Spirit, you shall be made free from sin. It "will have no dominion over you" (Romans 6:14). And you will burn like the bush Moses saw, with holy fire.

*HGC, 5*

## Feed Your Own Soul

*Solid food is for adults—that is, for those who through
constant practice have their spiritual faculties carefully
trained.* (Hebrews 5:14, WNT)

Can you feed your own soul, or must you still be fed? Do
you prepare your own soul food, or do others prepare it
for you?

One Salvation Army divisional commander said, "I will
guarantee I can send the worst kind of a backslidden officer to a certain corps [church], and in three months the
soldiers [members] will have prayed for him and helped
him and loved him and gotten him so blessed that he will
be on fire for God and souls."

Those soldiers were no longer spiritual babies that had
to be fed with a spoon. They were independent. They had
exercised their senses (Hebrews 5:14, KJV) and become
spiritual men and women—able to feed themselves, able
to find their own food and prepare their own food.

And not only so, but they were able to feed others. If
their officers did not give them suitable soul food, then
they fed the officers. If nobody blessed them, then they
rose up and blessed somebody else, and so blessed themselves. Like the widow of Zarephath (1 Kings 17), who
divided her meager flour and oil with Elijah, and found
both flour and oil unwasting through months of famine, so
they gave of their spiritual food to more needy souls, and
found themselves enriched from God's unfailing supplies.

*AP, 9*

## In the Furnace of Fire

*Though he slay me, yet will I trust in him.* (Job 13:15, KJV)

It is not God's purpose to take us to heaven on flowery beds of ease, clothe us in purple and fine linen, and keep a sugarplum in our mouths all the time. That would not develop strength of character, nor cultivate simplicity and purity of heart; nor in that case could we really know Jesus and the fellowship of His sufferings. It is in the furnace of fire, the lions' den, and the dungeon cell that God most freely reveals Himself to His people.

We must not presume that we will get through the world without heavy trials, sore temptations, and afflictions. Job was a perfect man, yet in a day he lost all his property and his children. But he looked up from his ash heap, and out of his awful sorrow and desolation and fierce pain, cried out, "Though he slay me, yet will I trust in him" (Job 13:15, KJV). Joseph is one of the few men in the Bible against whom nothing is recorded, yet like Daniel his very holiness and righteousness led to the terrible trials he endured in Egypt.

While we may be afflicted, yet we can comfort ourselves with David's assurance, "The righteous may have many troubles, but the LORD delivers them from them all" (Psalm 34:19, TNIV).

*HTH, 2*

## Consecration and Sanctification

*Then the fire of the Lord fell and consumed the burnt offering and the wood and the stones and the dust, and licked up the water that was in the trench.* (1 Kings 18:38)

One day a woman said to me, "Brother Brengle, I wish you would call it 'consecration' instead of 'sanctification.' We could all agree on that."

Her mistake is a common one. There is as big a difference between consecration and sanctification as between our work and God's work. She wanted to rob religion of its supernatural element and rest in her own works.

Elijah piled his altar on Mount Carmel, slew his bullock, and placed it on the altar. That was consecration. But Baal's priests had done that. They had spent the day in the most earnest religious devotions, and so far as anyone could see, their zeal far exceeded that of Elijah.

What did Elijah more than they? Nothing, except to pour water on his sacrifice—a big venture of faith. If he had stopped there, the world would never have heard of him. What power had cold stones and water and a dead bullock to glorify God and convert an apostate nation? But Elijah believed for *God* to do something. He expected it, he prayed for it, and God split the heavens and poured down fire. That was sanctification! It is God *in* us that enables us to glorify Him, and work together with Him for the salvation of the world.

*HH, 26*

## Count the Work Done

*Count yourselves dead to sin but alive to God in Christ
Jesus.* (Romans 6:11, NIV)

Some time ago in one of my meetings a woman claimed
the blessing. She did not get any special witness that the
work was done, but soon she came again and testified,
and her testimony threw light on the difficulty with many
people.

She said that for several days she did not feel any different, but a thought came to her mind that her sanctification
was a part of her Father's will, offered on the simple conditions of full consecration and childlike faith in Him. Then
it dawned upon her that she had met these conditions, and
that now instead of waiting for any unusual feelings, she
must just act as though it were done.

When she began to count it done and to act as though
it *were* done, she began to realize and feel that God *was*
doing His part.

It is just at this point that many people fail. They wait
for feeling, and hesitate and doubt and repine, and maybe
throw away their confidence. Instead, they should reck-
lessly but intelligently give themselves over to Jesus, to do
His will unto death. They should step out on the promise
with humility and faith, and with a shout of defiance to the
devil and all their fears, count the work done.

*HTH, 3*

## Where Hindrances Lie

*People harvest only what they plant.* (Galatians 6:7, NCV)

There are hindrances in the way of holiness with most people; but if you are seeking the experience, you must put from you, forever, the thought that any of these hindrances are in God, or in your circumstances, for they are altogether in yourself. It is extreme folly to sit down with indifference and quietly wait, with folded hands, for the blessed experience to come to you. Be sure of this, it will not come, any more than a crop of potatoes will come to the lazy farmer who never lifts a hoe, nor does a stroke of labor. The rule in the spiritual world is this: "If you don't work, you don't eat" (2 Thessalonians 3:10, CEV), and "People harvest only what they plant" (Galatians 6:7, NCV).

Therefore, the way of wisdom is to begin at once, by a diligent study of God's Word, much secret prayer, unflinching self-examination, rigid self-denial, hearty obedience to all present light, and faithful attendance at the meetings of God's people, to find out what these hindrances are. Then by the grace of God, we must put them away, though it cost as much pain as to cut off a right hand or to pluck out a right eye (Matthew 5:29-30).

*HH, 3*

## Imperfect Consecration

*Offer yourselves as a living sacrifice to God, dedicated to his service and pleasing to him.* (Romans 12:1, GNT)

One great practical hindrance to holiness is imperfect consecration. Before a watchmaker can clean and regulate my watch, I must give it into her hands. Before a captain can navigate me across the ocean, I must board his ship and stay there. Just so, if I would have God cleanse and regulate my heart, if I would have Him take me safely across the ocean of time, I must put myself fully into His hands and stay there. I must be perfectly consecrated to Him.

A Salvation Army captain knelt and sang, "Anywhere with Jesus I will go," adding, "Anywhere but to _____, Lord." Her consecration was imperfect. There were some things she would not do for Jesus, and therefore Jesus would not cleanse or keep her.

Perfect consecration consists in putting off your own disposition, desires, likes and dislikes, and putting on Christ's—giving up your own will in all things and accepting the will of Jesus instead. This may seem impossible and disagreeable to your unsanctified heart. But if you mean business for eternity, the Holy Spirit will soon show you that it is not only possible, but easy and delightful thus to yield to God.

*HH, 3*

## Imperfect Faith

*May the God of peace himself sanctify you completely.*
(1 Thessalonians 5:23)

The second hindrance in the way of the person who would be holy is imperfect faith.

All who are born of God and have the witness of His Spirit to their justification know full well that it was not through any good works of their own, nor by growing into it, that they were saved, but it was "by grace . . . through faith" (Ephesians 2:8). But very many of these dear people seem to think that we are to grow into sanctification, or are to get it by our own works. The Lord settled that question, and made it as plain as words can make it, when He told Paul that He sent him to the Gentiles to "open their eyes, so that they may turn from darkness to light and from the power of Satan to God, that they may receive forgiveness of sins and a place among those who are sanctified by faith in me" (Acts 26:18). Not by works, nor by growth, but by faith were they to be made holy.

If you will be holy, you must come to God "with a true heart in full assurance of faith" (Hebrews 10:22), and then, if you will wait patiently before Him, the wonderwork shall be done.

*HH, 3*

## Too Small a Blessing

*It is a great word the prophet has spoken to you; will you not do it?* (2 Kings 5:13)

There are some people who fail to get the blessing because they are seeking something altogether too small. Some claim the blessing of holiness because they have given up tobacco, or something of that sort, while they are still impatient, unkind, or absorbed with the cares of this life. Thus, they soon get discouraged and conclude there is no such blessing. Their trouble is in seeking too small a blessing. They have given up certain outward things, but the inward self-life is still uncrucified. The gold miner washes the dirt off the ore, but cannot wash the dross out of it. The fire must do that, and then the gold will be pure.

Holiness is a great blessing. It is the renewal of the whole heart and life in the image of Jesus, the utter destruction of all envy, malice, impatience, pride, lust, love of ease, love of human recognition, shame of the Cross, self-will, and the like. It makes its possessors "gentle and lowly in heart" (Matthew 11:29), patient, kind, full of compassion and love, full of faith and zeal.

Come to the Lord with simple faith; lay your case before Him, ask Him to take away all uncleanness and to perfect you in love, and then believe that He does it.

*HH, 3*

## Seeking Something Else

*The aim of our charge is love that issues from a pure heart and a good conscience and a sincere faith.* (1 Timothy 1:5)

Some people fail to obtain holiness because they are seeking something altogether different. They want a vision of heaven; or deliverance from all trials and temptations, all mistakes and infirmities; or a power that will make sinners fall as if dead when they speak.

But "the purpose of the commandment is love from a pure heart, from a good conscience, and from sincere faith" (1 Timothy 1:5, NKJV). Holiness is nothing more than a pure heart filled with perfect love toward God and others. Purity and perfect love are so Christlike and so rare in this world that they are in themselves a great, great blessing.

Do you want to be like Jesus? Are you prepared to suffer, to be hated by all for His name's sake (Matthew 10:22)? Then "lay aside every weight, and the sin which so easily ensnares" you (Hebrews 12:1, NKJV); present your body "a living sacrifice, holy, acceptable unto God, which is your reasonable service" (Romans 12:1, KJV); and "run with patience the race that is set before [you], looking unto Jesus the author and finisher of [your] faith" (Hebrews 12:1-2, KJV). Resist all of Satan's temptations to doubt, and you will soon find your hindrances gone, and yourself rejoicing "with joy that is inexpressible and filled with glory" (1 Peter 1:8).

*HH, 3*

## The Radicalism of Holiness

*Christ in you, the hope of glory.* (Colossians 1:27)

Do not think you can make holiness popular. It cannot be done. There is no such thing as holiness separate from "Christ in you," and it is impossible to make Christ Jesus popular. "Christ in you" is "the same yesterday and today and forever" (Hebrews 13:8)—hated, reviled, persecuted, crucified.

"Christ in you" came not to bring peace on earth, but a sword; came "to set a man against his father, and a daughter against her mother, and a daughter-in-law against her mother-in-law" (Matthew 10:34-35). "Christ in you" will not quench the smoking flax, nor break the bruised reed of penitence and humility (Isaiah 42:3, KJV); but He will pronounce the most terrible, yet tearful, maledictions against hypocritical formalists and lukewarm Christians who are friends of the world and, consequently, enemies of God (James 4:4, NIV).

Do you not see the impossibility of making such a radical gospel as this popular? Fire and water will consort together as quickly as the "Christ in you" and the spirit of the world.

Do not waste your time trying to fix up a popular holiness. Just be holy because the Lord God is holy. Seek to please Him without regard to the likes or dislikes of others.

*HH, 20*

## The Home of the Soul

*I know a man in Christ who fourteen years ago was caught up to the third heaven.* (2 Corinthians 12:2)

"I know a man in Christ," wrote Paul. Imagine someone writing, "I know a man in Napoleon, in Buddha, in Caesar," and we shall see at once how striking, how startling is this expression. We should be not only startled but shocked to hear this of any but Christ Jesus. But the Christian consciousness is not offended by hearing of "a man in Christ." It recognizes Him as the home of the soul, its hiding place and shelter from the storm, its school, its fortress and defense from every foe.

Do you know any man or woman in Christ? How many people do you know who live in Him and walk in the unbroken fellowship that being "in Christ" must imply? Do you know twenty? Ten?

But let us not judge others. Paul was not doing so. He reckoned his brothers and sisters to be in Christ. But this man whom he knew "in Christ" was not one of them, but himself. He was the man. There was no doubt about his being in Christ. He wrote with complete assurance.

Can you speak with such assurance? Do you know yourself to be in Christ? What a profound fellowship and union!

*LS, 2*

## The Sin against the Holy Spirit

*Whoever speaks a word against the Son of Man will be forgiven, but whoever speaks against the Holy Spirit will not be forgiven, either in this age or in the age to come.*
(Matthew 12:32)

All the people I ever met who thought they had committed the unpardonable sin were full of contrition. However, they refused to believe that the Savior's mercies were still offered to them. The vast ocean of His love had become a burning desert to them.

Not so with those of whom Jesus spoke in Matthew 12:32. They were not anxious. They shed no tears. They refused to humble themselves, confess their sins, put away their evil doings, sacrifice their pride, and follow Him. They declared that His miracles were wrought, not by the Holy Spirit, but by the prince of devils.

Their sin was unpardonable because it hardened their hearts against those evidences and gifts and tender graces which alone could produce repentance and faith, and without which there can be no pardon.

I have never seen anyone who I could truly say had committed such a sin. And I have always been able to say to those weeping, anxious, penitent souls who mourned because they thought they had sinned the unpardonable sin that I was fully convinced that they had not. No one whose heart is broken with sorrow for sin, and who is willing to come to Jesus and trust His atoning love, has committed that sin.

*RLP,* 24

## Not Death, but Love

*For our light and momentary troubles are achieving*
*for us an eternal glory that far outweighs them all.*
(2 Corinthians 4:17, NIV)

Bewildering as life may seem, with its commingling of joy and sorrow, health and sickness, pleasure and agony, pain and loss, life and death, it is nevertheless all working for good to them that love God (Romans 8:28), and preparing us all for the painless, tearless life that shall endless be (Revelation 21:4).

*Behind, a Presence did move*
*And grasp me by the hair;*
*And a voice in mastery asked, as I strove,*
*"Guess now who holds thee." "Death," I said, and there*
*The silver answer rang out, "Not Death, but Love."* [8]

God has not promised us freedom from affliction, but He has assured us that "this light momentary affliction is preparing for us an eternal weight of glory beyond all comparison" (2 Corinthians 4:17). It is Love Who holds us.

*RLP, 28*

## Keep On Seeking

*Beloved, building yourselves up in your most holy faith and praying in the Holy Spirit, keep yourselves in the love of God.* (Jude 1:20-21)

A Salvation Army soldier [member] recently wrote:

*I have entered into a new experience with Jesus: more light, more love, more peace, more joy, and a better victory.*

*It was God's will that I should go through such dark experiences as I wrote you about before. The Lord did not leave me, but He showed me the reality of the devil and his tricks (Ephesians 6:11). I came out more than conqueror!*

*The devil is never discouraged. If he can't get the big things, he will try for the small ones, but what can he do? The more I fight, the stronger I become. I can't describe to you my experience with Jesus—sometimes in shouting and jumping and the overflowing of the Spirit; and sometimes in calmness with a shower of tears.*

*My heart is flooded with light, love, peace, and joy. The best is yet to come. Hallelujah!*

When I first met this writer, he was full of doubts and seemed almost hopelessly in the dark. Again and again he seemed ready to give up entirely, but with help and encouragement he kept on praying, reading, seeking, and now he has found, and his joy is almost too big for utterance.

*AP, 7*

## Pray Through

*Ask, and it will be given to you; seek, and you will find; knock, and it will be opened to you.* (Luke 11:9)

If people who are not satisfied in their experience would take time to "pray through," they would find their dark tunnels leading out into broad day. Jesus still lives and keeps "watch above His own"[9] and pours out the Holy Spirit. But before we can be filled, we must be emptied. Before we can have the life more abundant, we must die to sin. The "old self" must be crucified and put off before Jesus can abide in our hearts and satisfy the hunger of our souls.

Are you satisfied? If not, begin right now and stir yourself up to seek until you have found. Rouse yourself. Find a secret place and pray, and pray again, and yet again, and you shall "pray through" and be satisfied. I know, for I have prayed through. Say to Him as did Charles Wesley, "*Wrestling, I will not let Thee go, Till I Thy name, Thy nature know.*" And you will soon be crying out, as did Wesley:

> 'Tis Love! 'tis Love! Thou diedst for me;
> I hear Thy whisper in my heart
> The morning breaks, the shadows flee,
> Pure, universal Love Thou art. . . .[10]

*AP, 7*

## Labor for Spiritual Food

*Let us go forward, then, to mature teaching and leave behind us the first lessons.* (Hebrews 6:1, GNT)

I knew a man sodden with drink, who within a few days was saved and sanctified. Shortly after, he became a Salvation Army officer. He would sit up till after midnight reading, praying, and meditating, until in a short time I marveled. His mind was all alert, his soul on fire, and his mental and spiritual equipment a joy to those who knew him. He labored for spiritual food and was soon able to feed others.

Whenever I met this man, he wanted to talk on spiritual things. His grasp of doctrine, his knowledge of Scripture and the literature of holiness, and his intimate acquaintance and communion with God delighted and refreshed me. He was an ordinary country boy, but he became extraordinary through diligence in seeking fellowship with God, eagerness in hunting for truth, and loving zeal in imparting the truth to other souls about him.

Officers should feed their soldiers; pastors should feed their flocks. But all should learn to find spiritual food and to feed themselves, and not only so, but to share their soul food with yet needier souls. And so they shall know no soul famine, but be "fat and flourishing" (Psalm 92:14, KJV).

*AP, 9*

## But What a Difference!

*I the Lord search the heart and examine the mind, to reward each person according to their conduct, according to what their deeds deserve.* (Jeremiah 17:10, NIV)

Nero and Marcus Aurelius both ruled Rome with absolute power. But what a difference! Nero, a monster of iniquity, execrated of all; Aurelius, writing meditations which the wise and learned still delight to ponder as guides to safe and useful living.

Napoleon and Washington—both great statesmen and generals. But what a difference! One a ruthless conqueror, building a glittering empire on an ocean of blood, dying an exile on a lonely isle. The other refusing a crown and dying at last honored by his former foes, with a character above reproach.

John and Judas were both apostles. But what a difference! One betrayed his Master and made for himself a name synonymous with infamy and treachery. The other pillowed his head on the Master's bosom, and was permitted to look deep into heaven, to behold the great white throne and Him that sat upon it, the innumerable multitudes of the redeemed, the glory of the Lamb that was slain, and the face of the everlasting Father.

History cares not an iota for rank or office, but only for the quality of one's deeds and the character of one's mind and heart. And if this be so of the judgment of history, how much more must it be so of the judgment of God.

*AP, 10*

## First Things First

*I count everything as loss because of the surpassing worth of knowing Christ Jesus my Lord.* (Philippians 3:8)

What shall have primacy with us? What shall have our last thoughts when falling asleep and our first thoughts on awaking?

Many things make so subtle, so reasonable an appeal as to usurp first place:

1. Our work. Is it not to build God's Kingdom on earth, to rescue men and women from sin? Yes, it is all that. But it must not have first place.

2. Our position. "Searching for honor is not honorable" (Proverbs 25:27, GW). Those who overlook such truths, while they may attain the desire of their heart, miss the glory that God gives.

3. Our family. This may become a deadly snare. "Whoever loves son or daughter more than me is not worthy of me" (Matthew 10:37), said Jesus.

4. Our education. The better informed and wiser we are, provided we are dedicated wholly to God, the more effectually can we glorify Him. But woe to those who put this first.

What, then, shall be first? That must be first, the loss of which is the loss of all. To lose God is the sum of all loss. If we lose Him, we lose all. If we lose all and still have Him, we shall in Him again find all.

*AP, 10*

## The Word of the Lord Came

*Then he fell to the ground, and heard a voice.*
(Acts 9:4, NKJV)

*Where one heard noise, and one saw flame,*
*I only knew he named my name.*[11]

This happened to Paul on the road to Damascus (Acts 9). His spiritual eyes were opened. He saw God in Christ, and the old Scriptures took on new meaning.

It happened to Martin Luther. As on his knees he painfully climbed the stairway in St. Peter's in Rome, a voice sounded in his soul: "The righteous shall live by faith" (Romans 1:17). He saw God's kindly purpose and way of salvation by faith.

It happened to Augustine, deeply convicted of sin and spiritual impotence, upon reading, "The night is far gone; the day is at hand. So then let us cast off the works of darkness and put on the armor of light. Let us walk properly as in the daytime, not in orgies and drunkenness, not in sexual immorality and sensuality, not in quarreling and jealousy. But put on the Lord Jesus Christ, and make no provision for the flesh, to gratify its desires" (Romans 13:12-14). Instantly Augustine's inner being flamed with spiritual light.

The word of the Lord came in searching experiences and travailings of spirit as God drew nigh and revealed His will, His name, and His nature.

*AP, 12*

## Searching Questions

*One who is faithful in a very little is also faithful in much,
and one who is dishonest in a very little is also dishonest
in much.* (Luke 16:10)

Are we faithful in the use of our money? A distinguished
Christian leader said to me one day, "You have given yourself to God, why give Him your money?" I confess I was
deeply surprised, if not shocked. I ask others to give, and
I should feel myself utterly faithless if I did not give freely
to my Master's cause.

Are we faithful in the use of our time? Do we gather up
the minutes for useful employment, for prayer, for reading, for studying, rejoicing, and attending to the duties of
the day?

Are we faithful in our speech? Little words are slipping
out through the portals of our lips continually. Are they
words we would say in the presence of Jesus? For every idle
word we shall have to give an account (Matthew 12:36).

Are we faithful in the use of eye and ear and hand and
foot? Are we faithful with ourselves, with our hearts, our
consciences, our imaginations? Do we live as in God's
sight, seeking always to please Him, so that someday the
Master will say to us, "Well done, good and faithful servant. You have been faithful over a little; I will set you over
much. Enter into the joy of your master" (Matthew 25:23).

*AP*, 11

## The Unbreakable Bondage of Love

*Paul and Timothy, slaves of Christ Jesus.*
(Philippians 1:1, CEB)

James, Jude, Peter, and Paul counted themselves slaves of God and of Christ.

The word and the relationship seem harsh and forbidding, but not so when we realize their meaning to these apostles. They were love slaves. The bondage that enthralled them was the unbreakable bondage of love.

A slave of love cares nothing for his or her own life (Acts 20:24), because it belongs to the master. The slave has no other interests than those of the master, wants no other, will have no other. The love slave would rather suffer and starve for the master than feast at another's table.

Do you ask, "How shall I enter into this sweet and gentle and yet all-powerful bondage of love?" By your own choice and by God's revelation of Himself. The choice must be complete, and it must be final. Then, as a love slave, you must wait upon the Master. If He is silent to you, watch. When He speaks to you, listen. What He says to you, do. Take time, find time, make time to seek the Lord, and He will be found of you. He will reveal Himself to your soul, and you shall know the sweet compulsions of the slavery that is love.

*LS, 1*

## Where There Is No Whisperer

*I have said nothing in secret.* (John 18:20)

There was nothing dark and hidden about Jesus. He was and is the Light of the world, and He welcomed the light. He stood upright, looked people squarely and kindly in the eye, and spoke what He had to say. He entered into no secret cabals and councils. He belonged to no party faction. Jesus belonged to the world. He was the "Son of Man," of humanity. He said, "I have said nothing in secret" (John 18:20).

If we "follow in his steps" (1 Peter 2:21), we shall not be talebearers; we shall not listen to nor pass on gossip. "A whisperer separates close friends," said Solomon (Proverbs 16:28); and again he said, "Where there is no whisperer, quarreling ceases" (Proverbs 26:20). And Paul linked up whisperers—people who go about saying things in secret that they are afraid to say to everybody—with fornicators, murderers, backbiters, and haters of God (Romans 1:29-30, KJV).

Whisperers openly wrong their own souls, weaken their own character, and corrupt themselves, while those who listen are filled with suspicions and dislikes, destroying the beautiful spirit of brotherly love. This quenches the spirit of prayer, and faith in God and in others languishes and possibly dies, for faith can live and flourish only in an atmosphere of frankness, kindness, and goodwill.

*AP, 20*

## How Jesus Trained Paul

*The gospel I preach is not of human origin. I did not receive it from any human being, nor did anyone teach it to me. It was Jesus Christ himself who revealed it to me.* (Galatians 1:11-12, GNT)

A strange, glorious, divine experience had come to Paul on the road to Damascus and in the street called Straight. For three years he wrestled with his problems and the Lord illumined him, and he began to see new meanings in the ancient Scriptures. The risen Jesus spoke to him and appointed him the apostle to the Gentiles.

Little did Paul know what lay before him in the untrodden future. That was graciously hidden from him. His Lord did not spare him, but He never failed him. And so out of wide experience and intimate knowledge, Paul could write letters that were the revelation of the plan, the purpose, the mind, the character of God in Christ—letters that have come down across two thousand years and are still as sweet and fresh and life giving as clear waters from everlasting springs, bubbling up in deep, cool valleys, fed by eternal snows from great mountains.

I see Your school is not an easy one, O Christ, but I would learn from You. Train me, teach me. Do You reply to me as to James and John, "You do not know what you are asking" (Matthew 20:22)? Still, O Lord, train me, discipline me, teach me, that I may know You.

*AP, 22*

## Holiness Obtained

*Put off your old self, which belongs to your former*
*manner of life and . . . put on the new self, created after*
*the likeness of God in true righteousness and holiness.*
(Ephesians 4:22, 24)

How is holiness obtained? Not by purgatorial fires, but by Holy Spirit fire. Not by works; that would make you your own savior and sanctifier. Not by growth. Growth adds to us, but takes nothing from us; neither does it change the nature and disposition. Holiness consists in having something taken from us and in having our spiritual nature made over into the image of Jesus. To be holy we must have every unclean desire and inclination and passion removed. We are told to put off the "old self" (Ephesians 4:22), just as we put off an old coat, "and to put on the new self, created to be like God in true righteousness and holiness" (Ephesians 4:24, NIV), just as we put on a new coat. It would be nonsense to talk of growing out of an old coat into a new one!

Well, how can you get it? From Jesus, who saved you and spoke peace to your troubled conscience when you feared you were sinking into hell. Jesus, who died for you. But how? By asking. By giving yourself freely and forever to Him, that He might be not only your Savior, but also your Lord and Master; to do and suffer all His blessed, wise, tender will.

*HTH, 3*

## Put Yourself on Record

*With the mouth confession is made unto salvation.*
(Romans 10:10, KJV)

At one of our services, a man knelt, seeking a clean heart. Having prayed, he said, "I give myself to God, and now I am going to live and work for Him with what power I have, and let Him give me the blessing and power just when He chooses. He has promised to give it to me, and He will do it, will He not?" Just then light shot through his soul, and his next words were, "Glory to God!" He reasoned with God and, looking to the promise, was delivered. Others around him reasoned with the devil, looked to their feelings, and were not sanctified.

After you have taken the step of faith, you must talk your faith. Those who are not afraid to announce their convictions to the world and defend them will have true stability. It is so in politics, in business, in all moral reforms, and in salvation. A universal law underlies the declaration, "With the mouth confession is made unto salvation" (Romans 10:10, KJV). If you would remain sanctified, you must put yourself on record before the devils in hell, your acquaintances on earth, and the angels in heaven. You must stand before the world professing and possessing heart purity. Only in this way can you burn the bridges behind you. Until all are destroyed, you are not safe.

*HH, 24*

## The Testimony of Holiness

*All were amazed and perplexed, saying to one another,
"What does this mean?" But others mocking said, "They
are filled with new wine."* (Acts 2:12-13)

A seventeen-year-old girl got the blessing of holiness. Her
brother had laughed and made fun of her religion, but now
she had the Comforter abiding with her. Peace and love
and power were in her heart, and a few days afterward,
her brother came to her and burst into tears. "I've been
watching you these few days and I want to get saved." She
gladly prayed with him. The last I heard of him, he had
been used in the salvation of six of the clerks in his work-
place. He said he was going to try to win them all for the
service of God.

When the Holy Spirit comes, a certainty and confidence enter the heart, and these are felt in the testimony.
The fire of the Comforter's blessed presence is felt in it.
And people take notice of what is said. As at Pentecost,
some will be glad and some will be mad, but none will be
indifferent.

Such testimony makes people feel the sweetness of the
Spirit, the reality of sin, the possibility of righteousness,
and the certainty of a coming judgment. The simplest
Holy Spirit testimony has something of this power in it.
Reality is in it, eternity is in it, God is in it, and so it has
power.

*RLP, 20*

## Throw Yourself Away for Jesus

*I have fully proclaimed the gospel of Christ.*
(Romans 15:19, NIV)

Satan nearly entrapped me after I received the blessing of holiness. I felt I ought to preach it, but I shrank from the odium and conflict I saw it would surely bring, and I hesitated to declare publicly that I was sanctified. But I had promised God I would preach it if He would give me the experience. He cleansed me on Friday, and I determined to preach about it on Sunday. But I felt weak and faint.

On Saturday morning, however, I met a coachman on the street who had the blessing, and I told him what God had done. He shouted and praised God. "Now, Brother Brengle, you preach it. The Church is dying for this."

We walked across Boston Common and Garden, and talked about the matter, and my heart burned within me. In my inmost soul I determined I would teach holiness, if it banished me forever from the pulpit, and made me a byword to all my acquaintances. Then I felt strong. The way to get strength is to throw yourself away for Jesus.

The next day I preached from "Let us go on unto perfection" (Hebrews 6:1, KJV). I closed with my experience, and the people wept, and some said afterward that they wanted the same experience. Bless God, some of them got it!

*HH, 28*

## No Little Salvation

*The blood of Jesus his Son cleanses us from all sin.*
(1 John 1:7)

It is no little salvation that Jesus Christ came to work out for us. It is a "great salvation" (Hebrews 2:3), and it saves from all sin and uncleanness, all doubt and fear, all guile and hypocrisy, all malice and wrath.

While I have been perplexed by human teachings and theories regarding the sinful nature, God's teachings are plain as day. God does not admit that we get rid of the sin nature at conversion, for all His teachings and exhortations concerning it are addressed to Christians. God's Word does exhort us to grow in grace, but that simply means to grow in favor with God, by obedience and faith. Corn may grow beautifully and delight the farmer, but all its growth will not rid the field of weeds.

Neither does God anywhere teach that the sinful nature need bother us till death, or that death will destroy it. Nor do I find any warrant in the whole Bible for purgatorial fires being the deliverer from this evil. But I do find that John says, "the blood of Jesus his Son cleanses us from all sin" (1 John 1:7)—not part or some, but *all* sin. I proved this fifteen years ago, and ever since I have been walking in a day with no setting sun, and everlasting joy and gladness have been mine.

*HTH, 1*

## One Blazing Fire

*Let those who love Him be like the rising of the sun in its might.* (Judges 5:31, NASB)

One of the blessed things about a holy life is its supernatural, constant, and often unconscious influence for good. A holy person does not have to resolve and struggle to be a blessing. Without conscious effort, his or her life and talk and looks inspire the fainthearted, encourage the timid, instruct the ignorant, feed the hungry, and rebuke the proud, selfish, and wayward. A holy person blesses others in all sorts of ways, and is often surprised to learn of it.

Luke says of Jesus that "all the crowd sought to touch him, for power came out from him and healed them all" (Luke 6:19). Just so, virtue goes out from holy people, as perfume floats from a rose, or warmth from fire.

After the overthrow of Sisera, Deborah and Barak sang a song of triumph and thanksgiving, and closed it with these words: "Let those who love Him be like the rising of the sun in its might" (Judges 5:31, NASB). Think of it! How mighty the sun is! How it floods the world with light! How it warms the whole earth and quickens and gladdens every living thing! None can stop the sun in its course, and such is God's plan for holy men and women.

*WH, 7*

## Hindrances to Holiness

*Let us throw off everything that hinders.*
(Hebrews 12:1, NIV)

God's perfect salvation satisfies the heart and the mind. It makes its possessors "more than conquerors" (Romans 8:37) over the world, the flesh, and the devil, and enables them to do the will of God on earth as it is done in heaven. It is a full, joyous life, the abundant life Jesus promised in John 10:10. Then why do so few, comparatively, have it?

*1. Ignorance.* Multitudes of Christians have never heard of the Holy Spirit's second work that purifies the heart and perfects it in love. It is, strange to say, an unpopular and uncommon theme. God's Word is so plain that a fool need not err; but many religious folk prefer to take their standard from the people round about them rather than from God's book.

*2. Unbelief.* Many are familiar with the Scriptures, but they have not an appropriating faith. They have read the exceeding great and precious promises, but as the Bible says, "The promises didn't do them a bit of good because they didn't receive the promises with faith" (Hebrews 4:2, *The Message*).

*3. Misguided desires.* Some expect the blessing of full salvation to bring deliverance from temptations, infirmities, natural consequences, and the like. Full salvation delivers always from impurity, but not always from infirmities. Indeed, we should "count it all joy" when we "meet trials of various kinds" (James 1:2).

*HTH, 4*

## Clouds and Fog

*I know a man in Christ who fourteen years ago was caught up to the third heaven—whether in the body or out of the body I do not know, God knows.* (2 Corinthians 12:2)

Truly, the revelation Jesus gave me of Himself is unutterable, but I got this revelation not by seeking some marvelous "third heaven" experience, similar to what Paul had, but by humbling myself to walk with Him, wait for His counsel, do His will, and believe what He said. Then He came to me, took up His abode in my heart, and gave me His joy. He has shown me that holiness does not consist so much in rapturous, sublimated experiences, as in lowly, humble, patient, trustful love.

While some put the experience up among the clouds, others leave it down in the fog, and so fail to get it. For instance, a man has been convicted about the use of tobacco or a woman about the styles she wears and, after a struggle with pride and habit, yields and casts away the offending thing. Of course there is now no condemnation, and that soul feels justified. But it may not yet be sanctified. It is not, until the Holy Spirit comes in, destroying every root of bitterness and sin out of the heart. Holiness is a thing of the heart. It is the purging away of the dross of the soul, the renewing of our whole nature so that we are made "partakers of the divine nature" (2 Peter 1:4).

*HTH, 4*

## The Hard Work of Prayer

*I discipline my body and keep it under control, lest after preaching to others I myself should be disqualified.*
(1 Corinthians 9:27)

Let no one imagine that prayer is easy work. It is difficult and amounts sometimes to an agony, but it will turn to an agony of joy in union and fellowship with Jesus.

The other day a Salvation Army captain, very faithful in prayer, was lamenting to me that he often has to force himself to secret prayer. But all men and women of much prayer have suffered the same.

The Reverend William Bramwell, who used to see hundreds of people converted and sanctified everywhere he went, prayed six hours a day, and yet he always went to secret prayer reluctantly. He had to pull himself up to it. And he would often have dry seasons, but he persevered in faith, and he would wrestle with God until the victory came. Then, when he preached, the clouds would break and rain down blessings on the people. Why was Bramwell able to say such new and wonderful things that brought blessings to so many? "Because he lives so near the throne that God tells him His secrets, and then he tells them to us," one man said.

We should promptly respond to the inward call to prayer. "Resist the devil, and he will flee from you" (James 4:7). We must discipline our bodies and our wills, lest we become disqualified (1 Corinthians 9:27).

*HH, 18*

## As Fire Purges Gold

*Let us cast off the works of darkness and put on the armor of light.* (Romans 13:12)

If you knew you had to die tonight, what would you do? You would give yourself to God. You would give up any grudges and, if you had the opportunity, ask forgiveness. If you had any selfish plans or ambitions, they would sink into molehills before the mighty mountains of eternity, and you would give them up quickly. If you had stolen, cheated, or been unfaithful in the discharge of any duty, you would confess it, mourn over it, and do all in the limited time left to make the matter right. Then you would throw up your hands in helplessness, and ask God to forgive you. And if you really trusted, you would receive forgiveness, and be at peace.

Now you would be a candidate for holiness. If the Holy Spirit should reveal hatred, selfishness, lies, adulteries, murders, and suchlike, you would cry to God to cleanse you and entirely change your heart. You would ask God to do it for Jesus' sake, trust Him to do it, and wait with full expectation until He did it.

And He would do it. He would purge your heart of all unholy conditions by the Holy Spirit, as surely as fire purges gold of dross. This is just what He wants to do.

*HTH, 3*

## The Outcome of a Clean Heart

*Create in me a clean heart, O God.* (Psalm 51:10)

David prayed, "Create in me a clean heart, O God. . . .
Then I will teach transgressors your ways, and sinners
will return to you" (Psalm 51:10, 13). It is the same truth
Jesus expressed when He said, "First, take the log out of
your own eye. Then you can see how to take the speck
out of your friend's eye" (Matthew 7:5, CEV). The log is
inbred sin; the speck is the transgressions that result from
inbred sin.

The following are some of the results of a clean heart:
(1) the person who receives the blessing becomes a soul-
winner, (2) there is constancy of spirit, perfect peace, perfect joy, perfect love, (3) the Bible becomes a new book,
(4) a shepherd spirit replaces the spirit of lordship over
God's people, (5) temptation is quickly recognized and
easily overcome through faith in Jesus, (6) divine courage
possesses the heart, (7) there is a sense of the weakness of
the flesh and of utter dependence on God, (8) the cleansed
person is careful of what he or she looks at, and (9) the
one who is thus cleansed lives to glorify God, without any
desire for honor or reward other than the "well done" of
the Lord (Matthew 25:23).

*HTH, 5*

## So Walk in Him

*As you received Christ Jesus the Lord, so walk in him.*
(Colossians 2:6)

Colossians 2:6 is one of the simplest and most complete statements of how to keep the blessing that can be given. The conditions of getting it are the conditions of keeping it.

It took faith unmixed with doubt to grasp the blessing. Unbelief was banished. The assurance of God's love in Jesus was heartily believed. His ability and willingness to save to the uttermost was fully accepted, and His Word simply trusted. This same steadfast, childlike faith must be maintained. God cannot require less of the sanctified man or woman to keep the blessing than He did of that person to get it. Peter said we "are kept by the power of God through faith" (1 Peter 1:5, KJV). Notice it is the power of God that keeps us, but it is faith that links us to the power as the coupling links the railway carriage to the locomotive.

We may suffer prolonged trials, great perplexities, and fierce temptations—they are a part of the discipline of life—but we must

*Keep on believing, this is the way;*
*Faith in the night as well as the day.*[12]

*HTH, 6*

## Keeping the Blessing

*They overcame him by the blood of the Lamb, and by the word of their testimony.* (Revelation 12:11, KJV)

To keep the blessing of holiness, we must confess it. If we withhold our testimony to this grace, we will lose it. This light, hid under a bushel, will go out. God gives it to us that we may give light to all that are in the house, and in our church, community, and nation. Don't limit the power of testimony by unbelief. A torch loses no light and heat by lighting a thousand other torches.

Touch a piece of steel with a magnet, and it in turn becomes a magnet. It can then be used to turn ten thousand other pieces into magnets. But hang it up in idleness, and it gradually loses its power. So it is with us. Let the Holy Spirit touch us with cleansing power, and we become divine magnets, and in touching other souls we will quicken them and get added power and clearness of experience ourselves. But let us withhold our testimony, and we lose our power.

Testify, testify, testify—clearly, definitely, constantly, courageously, humbly. Testify to the Lord, and thank Him for the blessing. Testify to your companions. Testify to your own heart and to the devil. John said that the white-robed multitude in heaven overcame by the blood of the Lamb and the word of their testimony (Revelation 12:11). So testify, if you would overcome and keep the blessing.

*HTH, 6*

## Obstacles to Secret Prayer

*When you pray, go into your room and shut the door and pray to your Father who is in secret.* (Matthew 6:6)

A reluctance to secret prayer may arise from one or more of several causes:

1. From evil spirits. I imagine the devil does not care much about seeing the majority of cold-hearted people on their knees in public, who do it simply because it is proper and fashionable. But he hates to see one on his or her knees in secret, for that one means business and, persevering in faith, is bound to move God and all heaven. So the devils oppose that one.

2. From sluggishness of the body and mind, caused by sickness, loss of sleep, too much sleep, or overeating.

3. From a failure to respond quickly when led by the Spirit. If, when we feel we should pray, we hesitate longer than is necessary and continue reading or talking when we could just as well be praying, the spirit of prayer will be quenched.

We should cultivate gladness at the thought of getting alone with Jesus in prayer, as much as lovers anticipate each other's society. One daredevil, praying, believing man or woman can get the victory for a whole city or nation. Elijah did on Mount Carmel. Moses did for grumbling Israel. Daniel did in Babylon. But if a number of people can be led to pray in this way, the victory will be all the more sweeping.

*HH, 18*

## Knowing Jesus

*I want to know Christ—yes, to know the power of his resurrection and participation in his sufferings, becoming like him in his death.* (Philippians 3:10, NIV)

What an astonishing thing that we can know Jesus! The knowledge of Jesus Christ is of infinite value and will never pass away. It is profitable for this world and for that which is to come, and only by it can we come to the knowledge of ourselves.

How then shall we come to the knowledge of Jesus?

1. Renounce sin, and seek forgiveness, trusting in His atonement for acceptance with God, singing from our hearts, "the Blood, the Blood, is all my plea."[13] When we do this, we shall come into an initial knowledge of our Lord Jesus Christ.

2. Renounce self. People who seek this knowledge without sacrifice of self may flatter themselves that they know Him, but when the testing time comes, they will find their sad mistake. But to those who make and abide in this sacrifice, furnace fires and lions' dens and dungeon cells will disclose more fully the loveliness of His face, the certainty of His presence, the unfailing strength and comforts of His love.

3. Commune with Him. Sympathy, fellowship, friendship must be constantly cultivated. The heart must turn to Him, pour itself out before Him. It must draw its consolations, strength, courage, sufficiency—its life—from Him.

*HTH*, 10

## Sin's Startling Power

*Everyone who commits sin is the slave of sin.*
(John 8:34, NASB)

The most startling thing about sin is its power to enslave. Let a girl tell a lie, and she is henceforth the servant of falsehood unless freed by a higher power. Let the bank clerk misappropriate funds, let the young man surrender to lust, and henceforth he is a slave. The cords that hold them may be light and silken, and they may say they are free, but they deceive themselves.

We may choose our path in life; friends with whom we associate; habits we form, whether good or bad. But having chosen sin, we are then swept on swiftly and certainly down to hell, just as those who choose to board a ship are surely taken to the destined harbor, however much they may wish to go elsewhere. We choose, and then we are chosen. We grasp, and then we are grasped by a power stronger than ourselves. It is like taking hold of the poles of an electric battery; we grasp and then cannot let go.

Just so, the sinner is in the grasp of a greater power, to be surely crushed and ruined forever unless delivered by some outside power. What shall that sinner do? Is there hope? Is there a deliverer? Yes, thank God, there is. Jesus said, "If the Son sets you free, you will be free indeed" (John 8:36).

*HTH, 11*

## He Sets the Prisoner Free

*If the Son sets you free, you will be free indeed.* (John 8:36)

Some years ago near Boston, a young artist stopped me and said, "Brother Brengle, do you mean to say that Jesus can save a man from all sin?"

"Yes, sir," I replied, "that is exactly what I mean to say."

"Well, if He can," said he, "I want Him to save me, for I am the victim of a habit that masters me. I struggle and vow and make good resolutions, but fall again, and I want deliverance."

I pointed him to Jesus. We prayed, and the work was done. He remained in and around Boston for six months, and then went to California. Eleven years later, while in San Francisco, I heard a knock on my door. A young man entered, looked at me, and inquired, "Do you know me?"

I replied, "Yes, sir; you are the young man that Jesus saved from a bad habit about twelve years ago, near Boston."

"Yes," said he, "and He saves me still."

This freedom is altogether complete. The one whom Jesus makes free is loosed from the works of the devil— unhitched from them—as fully as was Lazarus from his grave clothes. It is a complete deliverance, a perfect liberty, a heavenly freedom.

*HTH,* 11

## Wrestlers with God

*You who call on the LORD, don't rest, and don't allow God to rest until he establishes Jerusalem, and makes it the praise of the earth.* (Isaiah 62:6-7, CEB)

Evangelist William Bramwell wrote on one occasion, "Almost every night there has been a shaking among the people. . . . I believe I should have seen many more, but I cannot yet find one pleading man. There are many good people; but I have found no wrestlers with God."[14]

That is what we want! In these days of organization, societies, committees, multiplied and diversified, soul-saving and ecclesiastical machinery, we lack wrestlers with God. Not those who merely say prayers, but those who pour out their hearts and "give the LORD no rest until he completes his work" (Isaiah 62:6-7, NLT).

One Sunday morning, snow was on the ground, and less than one hundred people were present at the meeting. But a wrestler with God was there, and oh, how he prayed! My heart melts within me yet as I think of it. He poured out his heart before God. In his manner and words, he was wondrously familiar with God, that sweet familiarity born of utter self-abasement and humility, which enables its possessor to come, with unabashed faith, face-to-face with God seeking great things, asking only for His honor and the glory of His Son. That morning twenty-four people knelt at the penitent-form seeking the Lord!

Oh, how the Lord wants wrestling, pleading souls.

*HTH, 12*

## Devote Yourselves to Prayer

*Devote yourselves to prayer with an alert mind and a thankful heart.* (Colossians 4:2, NLT)

Several years ago, two young Salvation Army officers began to pray; one of them prayed all Saturday night. Whereas it had previously been almost impossible to get anyone in their church to make a start for heaven, the next day they saw sixty-two people seeking God.

Another Salvation Army captain read an article on the prayers of soul-winners to her congregation, urging them to greater diligence in prayer. The spirit of prayer fell on them, and some of them would ask for the key to the chapel and spend half the night wrestling with God until His power fell on the people, and scores of sinners were converted, and the whole city was stirred.

A staff officer told me that he went into a town, and after two hours' wrestling with God, he got the assurance of a revival. In eighteen days, he saw 150 people seeking salvation, and fifty more seeking the blessing of a clean heart.

Indeed, there are many who are interested in the cause of Christ, and who are pleased to see it prosper. But there are few who bear the burden of the world upon their souls day and night. That is what we want! And it is what the Lord wants.

*HTH, 12*

## To Wreck and Ruin

*But Jonah rose to flee to Tarshish from the presence of the*
*LORD. He went down to Joppa and found a ship going to*
*Tarshish.* (Jonah 1:3)

Men and women who are running away from God often
meet favorable circumstances in their flight. The south
wind blows softly and, despite all warnings, they sail away
to storm-swept seas, to wreck and ruin.

"He . . . found a ship," we read of Jonah (Jonah 1:3).
*What good fortune!* he must have thought. Oh, the way-
ward souls who find ships waiting for them and, forgetting
God, set sail for Tarshish!

Absalom found the men of Israel ready to flock to him
in revolt against King David. He "found a ship." Judas
found the high priest and his party ready to pay cash for
the betrayal of Jesus. He "found a ship." These are egre-
gious examples. But we often find men and women illus-
trating in their lives the same principle.

Run away from the duty to which God in infinite wisdom and love calls you, and the devil will surely arrange to
have a ship ready to carry you to Tarshish. But he cannot
insure you against a storm, and he would not if he could.

Consider what happened to Jonah and how Absalom
and Judas met their end. Not that I would compare you
with them, but the smallest disobedience is a step toward
the steep and awful decline which leads to doom. Let it
not be so with you.

*RLP, 26*

## The Just for the Unjust

*Christ the just suffered for us the unjust, to bring us to God.* (1 Peter 3:18, *Phillips*)

A great teacher once had under his care a boy who flagrantly broke the rules again and again. One day he committed a particularly grave offense. The punishment was to be two or three sharp raps with a cane on his open palm.

The teacher was greatly perplexed. He loved the boy, and longed to bless and save him. He stood with an aching heart, when a happy inspiration came to him. He said, "I don't wish to punish you, but when law is broken somebody must suffer. It is always so. But instead of punishing you today, I will suffer for you."

The boy looked as if he were in a bath of fire. His heart began to melt. The teacher stretched forth his open hand and said, "Strike!" After long hesitation the boy nerved himself and struck one blow. And then his proud, rebellious heart broke. He burst into tears, and the teacher never had any more trouble with him.

That teacher had found a way to justify a disobedient child, and yet make wrongdoing look hateful in the eyes of every other child. This is the atonement—God's act of condescension and mercy—which bridges the gulf between sinful humanity and the holy God; between a willful and defiant child and a wounded and grieved and loving Father.

*GS, 1*

## The Inward Revelation

*No one can say, "Jesus is Lord," except by the Holy Spirit.*
(1 Corinthians 12:3, NIV)

The Holy Spirit must reveal Jesus to each heart. Oh, the joy and infinite peace and satisfaction of this spiritual manifestation! It is a fulfillment of Jesus' promise: "I will come to you. . . . You will know that I am in my Father, and you in me, and I in you. . . . I . . . will manifest myself to [you]" (John 14:18, 20-21).

I sat beside a student when Christ was manifested to him, and saw his face shining almost like the face of an angel.

I knelt beside a young lady in prayer, when she burst into tears and cried out, "O Jesus!" He had come, and she knew Him as Lord. With Christ in her heart, she went joyfully as a missionary, to live and labor and love, until one day He said, "It is enough, come up higher," and she went to heaven by way of Africa.

A great businessman found Jesus, and with deepest reverence, he said, "I was so mixed up with Jesus that for several days I hardly knew whether it was Jesus or I."

The inward revelation of Christ gave Paul great assurance and power. He said, "It pleased him to reveal his Son to me" (Galatians 1:15-16, NLT), and again, "It is no longer I who live, but Christ lives in me" (Galatians 2:20, NLT).

*GS, 1*

## The Spirit of Conquest

*Thanks be to God, who gives us the victory through our Lord Jesus Christ.* (1 Corinthians 15:57)

When Paul went forth to evangelize the Roman Empire, he was everywhere confronted and hunted with the same deadly hate and murderous opposition that he had once shown to the Jerusalem Christians, while every city he entered reeked with unmentionable vices and reveled in licentious idolatries. He had no completed Bible, no religious press, no missionary organization behind him to ensure his support, and the very name of Christ was unknown, while Caesar was honored as a god. The vested interests of the world and the age-long habits of humanity were all opposed to Paul. He had no other weapon than his personal testimony and the story of a crucified, resurrected Jewish peasant Carpenter, whom he heralded as the Son of God and the Savior of the world. Paul died, but he won souls.

Little faith sees the difficulties and often accepts defeat without a fight. Great faith sees God and fights bravely against all odds, and though the enemy apparently triumphs, wins moral and spiritual victory, as did Christ on Calvary and as did the martyrs who perished in flame. What could be more complete to doubting hearts and the eyes of unbelief than the defeat of Christ on the cross! And yet it was then that His victory over the enemy was supreme. The spirit of Jesus is the spirit of conquest.

*AP, 3*

## Disentangled Disciples

*They are not of the world, just as I am not of the world.*
(John 17:14)

The *Chicago Post*, in discussing a popular novel, refers to "the cry for light" by the book's hero:

> The authentic note of the human soul rings poignantly in that cry. . . . Can that cry be answered? Yes, but not by weak compromise . . . [and] not by abandoning the high demands of the cross for the pliant policy of "everything goes, and everything is all right." That sort of religion for a time may get glad hands; but it will never make glad hearts. Yes, there is light. . . . "The light of the knowledge of the glory of God in the face of Jesus Christ," as Paul called it. That is the light of the world.[15]

This is our great task—so to live and love and labor as to unveil the face of Jesus Christ, and let the world see the glory of God. And this we can only do as we keep ourselves disentangled from the world, as was our Master.

We read of Jesus that He was "holy, blameless, pure, set apart from sinners" (Hebrews 7:26, NIV). He mingled and ate with them, walked and talked with them, yet kept Himself separate. Only so could He draw everyone to Him and save them. And only so can His disciples to whom He has committed that great and unfinished work save them also.

*RLP, 9*

## Turn Your Eyes upon Jesus

*Behold, the Lamb of God, who takes away the sin of the world!* (John 1:29)

The office of the Holy Spirit is to illuminate mind and heart: "The Spirit . . . will bear witness about me" (John 15:26), said Jesus. "He will glorify me, for he will take what is mine and declare it to you" (John 16:14). "When the Spirit of truth comes, he will guide you into all the truth" (John 16:13).

The Holy Spirit is like a great searchlight that throws its rays upon some noble object. We are not to focus on the blinding light, but on the object revealed. We are not to focus upon the Spirit, but upon the Son, on whom the Spirit pours His glorious light.

I have never met a discouraged soul who was not continually telling me of feelings. Such people starve and destroy faith by dependence upon feelings instead of "looking to Jesus, the founder and perfecter of our faith" (Hebrews 12:2). They weep and cry for mercy, but they won't take it when it is extended to them. They have lost sight of the Son and seek deliverance where it can never be found.

Look to Jesus. Turn your eyes from yourself, your feelings, and your failures, and fix them on Jesus. Hear the Spirit whispering, "Behold, the Lamb of God, who takes away the sin of the world!" (John 1:29).

*RLP, 24*

## The Higher Law of Love

*Jesus answered, "My Kingdom is not an earthly kingdom.*
*If it were, my followers would fight."* (John 18:36, NLT)

The sons and daughters of God are a new order of being.
The Christian is a "new creation" (2 Corinthians 5:17). Just
as there are laws governing the life of the plant, and higher
laws of the bird and beast, so there are higher laws for
humanity, and still higher for the Christian.

Jesus said to Pilate, "My kingdom is not of this world.
If it were, my servants would fight" (John 18:36, NIV). The
unspiritual person is of this world, and he or she fights for
it with such weapons as this world furnishes, with fist and
sword, tongue and wit.

Christians are citizens of heaven, and are subject to its
law, which is universal, wholehearted love. They conquer
not by fighting, but by submitting. When an enemy takes
my coat, I overcome him, not by going to law, but by gen-
erously giving him my cloak also. When I am smitten on
one cheek, I win my foe by meekly turning the other. This
is the law of the new life from heaven, and only by recog-
nizing and obeying it can that new life be sustained and
passed on to others. This is the narrow way which leads to
life eternal, and few find it (Matthew 7:14), or, finding it,
are willing to walk in it.

*HGC, 19*

## Leprosy of the Heart

*Sin is lying in wait for you, ready to pounce; it's out to get you, you've got to master it.* (Genesis 4:7, *The Message*)

Is sin only a mild infirmity that will be outgrown and corrected by age, or is it a malignancy that will never correct itself? Is it a moral disease which, like measles, we need not seriously fear, or is it like leprosy or cancer? I once was met with the announcement that my boy had the measles. I was not alarmed, and he soon recovered. But later I visited a leper hospital, and saw hopeless invalids with their eyes and hands and feet eaten away by the awful disease.

The Bible says sin is an awful moral corruption, a malignant attitude of the will and the affections. Sin can appear innocent and fair to behold, but it is utterly false and cruel. Thus, I can understand how God, if He loves us and is truly interested in us, might make some great sacrifice, some divine interposition to save us.

If God does not hate sin, He is not holy; if He does not condemn sin, He is not righteous; if He is not prepared to punish sin, He is not just. But God is holy, righteous, and just. His great heart demands the utter condemnation of sin. Yet God is love, and His love calls for the salvation of the sinner.

*GS*, 1

## The Noblest and Freest Expression

*Sing and make music to the Lord with your hearts.*
(Ephesians 5:19, GW)

The joys, the faith, the hopes and aspirations, the deepest desires, the love and utter devotion, and the sweet trust of the Christian find noblest and freest expression in music and song. And yet it is probable that in no way do people more frequently and yet unconsciously deceive themselves (and actually lie to each other and to God) than in the public singing of songs and hymns.

Languidly, lustily, thoughtlessly in song they profess a faith they do not possess, a love and devotion their whole life falsifies, a joy their lack of radiance on the face and of light in the eye contradicts. They sing, "Oh, how I love Jesus!" while their hearts are far from Him, with no intention of doing the things that please Him. Or:

*Take my life, and let it be*
*Consecrated, Lord, to Thee*[16]

while they live selfishly.

It is a solemn thing to stand before God and sing such songs. We should think. A hush should be upon our spirits, for we are standing on holy ground, where mysteries are all about us, enshrouding us, while the angel of the Lord looks upon us through a pillar of cloud and fire.

*GS, 4*

## Can You, Will You?

*Sing psalms and hymns and spiritual songs to God with thankful hearts.* (Colossians 3:16, NLT)

Nearly fifty years ago, while preparing for ministry at the Salvation Army's training school, we were singing:

*My will be swallowed up in Thee;*
*Light in Thy light still may I see*
*In Thine unclouded face.*
*Called the full strength of trust to prove*[17]

and there my heart cried out, "Yes, Lord, let me prove the full strength of trust!" And then I was hushed into deep questioning and prayer, for a whisper within me asked, "Can you, will you, endure the tests, the trials, that alone can prove the full strength of trust? Will you bear patiently the trials I permit to come upon you, which alone can prove the full strength of your trust and train you for larger service and yet greater trials?"

My humbled heart dared not say, "I can," but only, "By Thy grace, I will." And my whole soul consented to any trial which the Lord in His wisdom and love might permit to come upon me. There God set His seal upon my consenting soul, for service, for suffering, for sacrifice.

*GS, 4*

## The Peaceful Fruit of Righteousness

*We know that for those who love God all things work together for good, for those who are called according to his purpose.* (Romans 8:28)

I happened to be present when a young wife and mother was weeping bitter tears of anguish. An older woman, who had herself once wept bitterly, put her arms around the younger and comforted her. I thought, *Ah, her painful trials worked for her good; left her enlarged in heart, enriched in experience, wise in sympathy, perfect in peace, with a spirit at rest in God.*

And I looked forward with joy in the hope that the younger woman, believing on Jesus, patiently submitting to chastenings and trials, would enter into an experience of God's love and faithfulness that would leave her spirit forever strengthened, sweetened, enriched, and fitted to minister to others. And so, after years, it proved to be.

Trials, afflictions, losses, and sorrows, borne with patience and courage and in faith, will surely develop in us spiritual graces and "the peaceful fruit of righteousness" (Hebrews 12:11) which are never found in those whose sky is never overcast, whose voyage is never troubled by storm and hurricane, whose soldiering is only on dress parade.

Holiness of heart does not insure us against painful trials, but it does prepare us for them. And patient endurance reveals the reality of our faith, the purity and integrity of our hearts, and the grace and faithfulness of our Lord.

*GS,* 4

## My Favorite Bible Verse

*How sweet are your words to my taste, sweeter than honey to my mouth!* (Psalm 119:103)

When I am asked for my favorite Bible verse, I smile. *It is not one text more than another, but* A WHOLE BIBLE that blesses me, assures me, warns and corrects and comforts me. A hundred promises whisper to me. I never know when one of the promises—perhaps one that I have not met for days or even months—may suddenly stand before me, beckon me, speak to me tenderly, comfortingly, authoritatively, austerely, as though God were speaking to me face to face.

The Bible teems with promises. They are on almost every page. But your eyes will not see them, your mind will not grasp them, your heart will receive no strength and consolation from them—if you have not faith. The one who goes through the Bible without faith is like people of long ago who walked over the diamond fields of Africa all unconscious of the immeasurable wealth beneath their feet.

My spiritual needs are manifold, and there seems to be a promise just suited to my every need, as a Yale key matches a Yale lock, as a glove fits the hand. I am like a man with a home full of sweet children, every one of whom is so dear to him that he cannot tell which he loves most.

*GS*, 8

## The Heavenly Vision

*I was not disobedient to the heavenly vision.* (Acts 26:19)

Several years ago a girl of eighteen entered a Salvation Army meeting for the first time. The people's faces enchained her eyes, and their testimonies went to her heart. She left the meeting convicted of sin. On her way home a heavenly vision spoke to her: "You ought to have gotten saved tonight."

"But there is the dance next Wednesday, and my lovely white dress and shoes. I will get saved after the dance."

"But you may die before Wednesday night, and lose your lovely dress and the dance—and your soul."

That was sufficient. She rushed upstairs, cut up her dress, and cast it into the fire. The next evening she went to the meeting, where she found Jesus almighty to save. She was not disobedient to the heavenly vision.

Sooner or later the heavenly vision comes to all. In the whisperings of conscience, strivings of the Spirit, calls of duty; in the crises of life, and in the entreaties of God's people. If people would turn aside and heed the vision as Moses did the burning bush, a voice would speak, and if they would obey, Jesus would turn them back from the pit, and satisfy every question and every longing of their hearts.

*HTH, 8*

## An Old Trick

*For with the heart one believes and is justified, and with the mouth one confesses and is saved.* (Romans 10:10)

The late Miss Frances E. Willard received the blessing and gave a burning testimony. She soon became a teacher in a region where there was much controversy regarding holiness. She was advised to keep still about sanctification. Years afterward she sorrowfully wrote, "I kept still until I soon found I had nothing in particular to keep still about. The experience left me."

That is an old trick of the devil, by which he has cheated many a soul out of this pearl of greatest price.

Paul says, "For with the heart one believes and is justified, and with the mouth one confesses and is saved" (Romans 10:10). The confession is as necessary as the believing, both in justification and in sanctification. If we do not testify to the blessed experience, we put our light under a bushel and it goes out.

Those who profess this blessing are often accused of boasting. But they are simply declaring that Jesus has done for them what He died to do—that is, to save them from sin. They do it in the spirit of one who, healed of a deadly disease, declares what the doctor has done.

As for me, I feel I am under a solemn obligation to let everybody know that Jesus is alive and that He can save to the uttermost.

*HTH, 9*

## A Union of Will

*I delight to do your will, O my God.* (Psalm 40:8)

Jesus said, "I have come down from heaven, not to do my own will but the will of him who sent me" (John 6:38). And so it is with those who are one with Jesus. There may, and doubtless will, be times when this will is hard, but even then the soul says with its Lord, "Not my will, but yours, be done" (Luke 22:42).

There can be no union with Jesus without this union of will, for the will is really all we can call our own. The mind may be reduced to idiocy. We may be robbed of our property. Health, and even life itself, may be taken away from us. But who can enter into the domain of our wills and rob us of that?

Not even God Himself would compel one's will. God wants to enter into a partnership, an infinitely tender and exalting fellowship, and yet we may resist and utterly thwart His loving thought and purpose. We can refuse to surrender. But surrender we must, if there is to be a union between us and God, for God's will, founded in infinite knowledge and wisdom and love, is unchangeable, and our highest good is in a hearty and affectionate surrender to it and a union with it.

*HTH, 13*

## A Union of Faith

*Trust God all the time.* (Psalm 62:8, NCV)

Union with Jesus is a union of faith—of mutual confidence and esteem. God can entrust faithful people with the honor of His name in the midst of a world of rebels. God can empower them and beautify them with His Spirit and adorn them with all heavenly graces, without any fear that they will take the glory of these things to themselves. God can heap upon them riches and honors without any fear that they will use such gifts for selfish ends or prostitute them to unholy purposes.

It is also a state in which we trust God. We have confidence in the faithfulness and love of God in adversity as well as in prosperity. We need not live in sunshine and sleep on roses in order to believe that God is for us. God can allow the thorns to prick us, and the storm clouds to roll all about, and yet we will stubbornly trust on.

God can be familiar with us when we are faithful. He can take all sorts of liberties with our property, reputation, position, friends, health, and life, and allow devils to test and taunt. But the soul that is unchangeably fixed in its estimate of God's holy character and everlasting love will still triumphantly trust on.

*HTH, 13*

## A Union of Suffering

*Rejoice insofar as you share Christ's sufferings, that you may also rejoice and be glad when his glory is revealed.*
(1 Peter 4:13)

Once, when I was passing through what seemed to me a perfect hell of spiritual temptation and sufferings, the Lord supported me with this text: "In all their affliction he was afflicted" (Isaiah 63:9). The prophet refers in these words to the afflictions of the children of Israel in Egypt and in the wilderness after their escape from the hard bondage of Pharaoh, and he says in all their sufferings Jesus suffered with them.

Let her child be racked with pain and scorched with fever and struggling to breathe, and the mother suffers more than the child; so let the people of God be sore tempted and tried, and Jesus agonizes with them. He is the world's great Sufferer. He once tasted death for everyone; He suffers still with everyone. There is no cry of anguish, nor heartache, nor pang of spiritual pain in all the world that does not reach His ear and stir all His mighty sympathies. But especially does He suffer and sympathize with His own believing children.

In turn, those who are one with Jesus suffer and sympathize with Him. They gladly say, with David, "The insults of those who insult you fall on me" (Psalm 69:9, NIV). Those who are one with Jesus rejoice to be "counted worthy to suffer dishonor for the name" (Acts 5:41).

*HTH, 13*

## A Union of Purpose

*May your will be done on earth as it is in heaven.*
(Matthew 6:10, GNT)

The soul's union with Jesus is a union of purpose. Most Christians serve God for reward: they do not want to go to hell, but to heaven. But there is a union with Jesus in which the soul is not so anxious to escape hell as it is to be free from sin, and in which heaven is not so desirable as holiness. Jesus' smile of approval is this soul's heaven.

The purpose of Jesus is to save the world and uphold the honor of God, and establish truth in the lives of men and women. For this, Jesus sacrificed every earthly prospect, and laid down His life. The soul that lives in union with Christ does the same. Such a one does not say, "If I were rich," but out of the abundance of his or her poverty pours into the lap of the world's need, and like the widow at Jerusalem's Temple gladly gives all to save the world.

The soul in union with Jesus does not struggle and resist the call to warn a wicked world of its peril. He or she does not say, "If only I were educated or gifted I would go," but with a heart flaming with love for Jesus and the world, cries out, "Here am I; send me" (Isaiah 6:8, KJV).

*HTH, 13*

## The Branch and the Vine

*I am the vine; you are the branches.* (John 15:5)

There is a union with Jesus as intimate as that of the branch and the vine. It is a union of nature, a commingling of spirit. How can one enter into this union?

1. Read God's promises until you see that it is possible. Especially read and ponder the fifteenth and seventeenth chapters of John's Gospel.

2. Read and ponder the commandments until you see that it is necessary. Without this union here, there will be no union in eternity.

3. Make the required sacrifice. The woman who will be a true wife must be prepared to give up all other lovers, forsake her home and family, and utterly identify herself, her prospects, her all, with the man she loves. The same is required of a true husband. And so must you be prepared to identify yourself utterly with Christ, to be hated, despised, rejected, crucified; but armed, empowered by the Holy Spirit, and crowned of God.

Does your heart consent to this? If so, make a perpetual covenant with your Lord just now. Do it with a true heart, in full assurance of faith, and God will seal you for His own. Do not waver or doubt. Do not cast away your confidence based on feelings, but stand by facts. Walk by faith, and God will soon prove His ownership in you.

*HTH, 13*

## Pain and Pleasure

*The LORD corrects those he loves, just as a father corrects a child in whom he delights.* (Proverbs 3:12, NLT)

We must be taught by both pain and pleasure. We must learn how to abound and how to suffer need. In this we shall often be plunged from the heights to the depths, and back again.

Today others look upon us and smile and shout "Hosanna!" but tomorrow they frown and gnash their teeth and cry out, "Crucify!" Today we have plenty and can feed the multitudes; tomorrow we ourselves are hungry and know not where to turn for bread. Today we pray and God answers while we are yet speaking; tomorrow we plead and weep and moan and the heavens seem shut, and the mocking tempter whispers, "Where is your God now?"

What means all this uncertainty? Ah, it means that God wants us for Himself. "Whom the Lord loves He chastens [disciplines]" (Hebrews 12:6, NKJV). It means that He sees in us something worth His while to educate, and He is educating us.

A friend of mine owned a gold mine. He promised the Lord every penny of profit. He made nothing, but lost a great sum. The Lord said to him, "I am educating you, and I can afford to spend millions to do so." My friend cried out, "O Lord, if Thou canst afford it, I can, for I want to be educated in Thy school!"

*HTH, 14*

## Self-Denial

*It is more blessed to give than to receive.* (Acts 20:35)

One day, while dining with John Wesley at the home of a rich man, a preacher said, "Oh, sir, what a sumptuous dinner! There is but little self-denial now among the Methodists." Wesley pointed to the table and quietly remarked, "My brother, there is a fine opportunity for self-denial."

Denial that is not self-imposed is not self-denial. We deny ourselves only when we voluntarily give up, for the Lord's dear sake, and the sake of the needy, that which we like and might lawfully keep.

Often I have heard, "If God did not mean me to enjoy these things, why did He supply them?" And these people thought they had crushed me with their logic.

But the answer is simple. God meant them to be stewards, but they considered themselves owners. God intended the greater blessing of giving (Acts 20:35), but instead they contented themselves with receiving. God meant them to pass on His bounty to the needy, but they dammed up and diverted the streams of God's mercy. They have not the Spirit of Jesus, Who, "though he was rich, yet for your sake he became poor, so that you by his poverty might become rich" (2 Corinthians 8:9).

Oh, there is a divine philosophy in self-denial that the worldly-wise never dream of!

*HTH, 15*

## Spiritual Power

*The word of God and prayer set it apart as holy.*
(1 Timothy 4:5, GW)

If we would have spiritual power, God should be sought constantly by meditation in His Word and by secret prayer.

A rather gifted officer appeared to be much impressed by my familiarity with the Bible, and remarked that he would give a fortune for an equal knowledge. He was taken back when I said he was quite mistaken as to the strength of his desire, for if he really wanted such knowledge, he could easily obtain it by spending the time he gave to the newspapers each day in prayerful study of God's Word.

The saintly John Fletcher said, "An over-eager attention to the doctrines of the Holy Spirit made me in some degree overlook the medium by which the Spirit works, I mean the word of truth, which is the wood by which that heavenly fire warms us. I rather expected lightning, than a steady fire by means of fuel."[18]

Prayer and meditation in the Word of God will keep the sanctified believer full of power, love, and faith—full of God. But neglect of these brings spiritual weakness, dryness, and fruitless toil. You will not reclaim the blessing by working yourself up into a frenzy of agony in prayer, but rather by quieting yourself and talking plainly to God about it, and then hearkening diligently to what God says in His Word and by His Spirit.

*HTH, 16*

## Fullness or Flabbiness

*Exercise daily in God—no spiritual flabbiness, please!*
*Workouts in the gymnasium are useful, but a disciplined*
*life in God is far more so, making you fit both today and*
*forever.* (1 Timothy 4:7-8, *The Message*)

People everywhere are crying and sighing for power and
the fullness of the Spirit, but neglecting the means by
which this power and fullness are secured.

Most people give about ten hours a day to their bodies
for eating, drinking, dressing, and sleeping, and maybe a
few minutes to their souls. We ought to give at least one
solid hour every day to restful, loving devotion with Jesus
over our open Bible, for the refreshing, developing, and
strengthening of our spiritual lives. If we would do this,
God would have an opportunity to teach, correct, inspire,
and comfort us, reveal His secrets to us, and make spiritual giants of us. If we will not do this, we shall surely be
spiritual weaklings all our days, however we may wish to
be strong.

The devil will rob us of this hour if we do not steadfastly fight for it. He will say, "Go and work," before we
have gained the spiritual food that strengthens us for work.
The devil's piety and eager interest in God's work is amazing when he sees us on our knees! It is then that he trans-
forms himself into an angel of light, and woe be to the soul
that is deceived by him!

*HTH*, 16

## When You Are Dead

*Trust in the LORD forever, for the LORD GOD is an everlasting rock.* (Isaiah 26:4)

We must die! We feel that we must live—must live for the sake of our children, for the people of God whom we love as our own souls, and for the perishing sinners about us. We are prone to magnify our own importance, to think no one's faith is so mighty, no one's labor is quite so fruitful, no one's love quite so unfailing, no one's presence quite so necessary as ours. But after we die, the blessed God will still live. His years fail not, and He will bless our sons and daughters, and carry on His work.

Some years ago I was talking with a young woman whom God marvelously blessed and used in His work. Each of us had lost both parents when we were quite young. They were godly parents, who had given us to the Lord, and then, when it seemed we most needed their counsel and discipline, they died. But God took us up and blessed us. As we talked about the past, we could see the hand of God through corrections and faithful Fatherly chastenings, shaping our whole lives, and bringing blessings out of what seemed the greatest calamities, until we were lost in wonder at His wisdom and goodness, and our mouths were filled with praise.

*HTH, 18*

## God Will Bless Your Isaacs

*After the death of Abraham, God blessed Isaac his son.*
(Genesis 25:11)

God may have blessed Isaac before the death of Abraham, but I am glad we are told that He blessed him afterward. God does not forget. He breaks no promises. He delights to show mercy and bestow blessings.

God said of Abraham, "For I know him, that he will command his children and his household after him, and they shall keep the way of the LORD" (Genesis 18:19, KJV). Do your part as well as you know how. Search the Bible to know what God will have you do, and do it.

Pray for wisdom. "If any of you lacks wisdom, you should ask God . . . and it will be given to you" (James 1:5, NIV). God will not rebuke you for your ignorance, if you want to be wise; therefore pray for wisdom.

Pray for patience. If you plant corn, it does not spring up the next morning. It lies in the ground for many days, and dies. But God will bless it, and cause it to bring forth fruit. And so will it be with your seed-sowing in the hearts of your children. If you are patient and have faith in God, you will continue to pray in hope, and to sow the Word of God (Luke 8:11). Though you may die, yet after you are dead, God will bless your Isaacs.

*HTH, 18*

# Fools for Christ

*We are fools for Christ's sake.* (1 Corinthians 4:10)

To the natural heart and the unsanctified mind the commands of God are foolishness. "Go from your country and your kindred and your father's house to the land that I will show you" (Genesis 12:1), said God to Abraham. How foolish to leave home to go to a land that he knew not! But Abraham obeyed and became heir of the world.

"I have appeared to you to appoint you as my servant and witness. . . . I am sending you to the Gentiles to open their eyes, so they may turn from darkness to light and from the power of Satan to God. Then they will receive forgiveness for their sins and be given a place among God's people" (Acts 26:16-18, NLT), said the Lord to Paul. Think of it! One lone man sent to the godless nations with the message that a crucified Jew was the Savior of the world. But God helped him to do more to bring the world to Himself than anyone else who ever lived.

Does your call to work for God seem foolish, unreasonable, impossible? "Have faith in God" (Mark 11:22). Obey like Abraham and Paul, and you will yet praise Him for the part He gave you in winning the world for God.

*HTH, 27*

## Don't Be Discouraged

*Do not be discouraged.* (Deuteronomy 31:8, NIV)

I was in the Mississippi Valley, a thousand miles from my home. I was weary, heartsick, homesick, exhausted, and lonely. I longed for the comfort of home, the fellowship of my wife, and the arms of the children about my neck. In this state of weariness, loneliness, and temptation, I went to the Lord in prayer, somewhat in the spirit of repining and whining, and it seemed as though the Lord spoke to me just a bit sharply: "Have I not commanded you? Be strong and courageous. Do not be frightened, and do not be dismayed, for the LORD your God is with you wherever you go" (Joshua 1:9).

I braced up and replied, "I will, I will, Lord." And strength and courage possessed me, and I went to my meeting feeling that I could chase a thousand, and that if I could find another fellow of the same mind and heart, we could put ten thousand to flight (Deuteronomy 32:30).

God loves each of us, however unworthy we may feel. And it is His will that we should have peace, unbroken and full; that we should be without fear; and that we should be strong—strong in faith, in spirit, "strong in the Lord and in his mighty power" (Ephesians 6:10, NIV), and strong through the glory and comfort of an indwelling God.

*RLP,* 15

# Don't Flinch

*Make sure there's no evil unbelief lying around that will trip you up and throw you off course, diverting you from the living God.* (Hebrews 3:12, *The Message*)

A Salvation Army captain told me how she came to faith in Jesus Christ. A few lines in a little book showed her that if she would ask God to save her and would "not flinch" in her faith, He would do it. So she prayed, and then waited for Jesus to come. She lived in a country full of spiritual darkness, and there was no one to teach her, and in her ignorance she thought Jesus would come in bodily presence. But He did not come.

So she wrote a note to a minister to come and pray with her. But something whispered to her that she was trusting the minister's prayer and not the Lord. So she tore the note up and, looking to God without flinching, she trusted. Suddenly Jesus came in Spirit, and her soul was flooded with light.

Many souls flinch and fail at the final test of faith. Just when all is on the altar and there is not one thing more to do, they give in to "an evil heart of unbelief" (Hebrews 3:12, KJV).

Flinching will prove as fatal to the revelation of Jesus as a movement will prove to your picture when in front of the photographer's camera. Be still in your heart and trust, look and wait, and Jesus will surely come.

*HTH, 20*

## Don't Be in Haste

*I waited patiently for the LORD; he inclined to me and heard my cry.* (Psalm 40:1)

Solomon built his Temple, placed everything in order, then prayed and waited, and the glory of God filled the Temple till the priests could not stand in His presence (1 Kings 8). Elijah placed his bull on the altar, poured water over it in faith, then prayed and waited till fire fell and consumed his sacrifice (1 Kings 18). The disciples prayed and waited on God for days; then suddenly the Holy Spirit fell on them in tongues of fire that filled the world with light (Acts 2).

If these men and women had failed to steadfastly look to God and believe, the world would never have heard of them.

A minister friend of mine lost the blessing of full salvation. I dealt faithfully with him. He called his people around the altar with him, but he failed to get the blessing. A wise friend explained his failure by saying, "He didn't stay on his knees long enough. He was in too big a hurry. He didn't give God time to deal with him." He failed to steadily watch and wait and trust.

The Lord God declared, "Whoever believes will not be in haste" (Isaiah 28:16). In watching and waiting, faith and patience are made perfect, and the Lord will come suddenly to the heart that has waited for Him.

*HTH, 20*

# Three Simple Conditions

*You are already clean because of the word which I have spoken to you.* (John 15:3, NKJV)

I met a sister with an intense hunger for full salvation. But for some reason our prayers did not prevail.

"Sister," said I, "there are three things you must believe. First, that God is able to sanctify you wholly. Second, that He is willing. Then there is but one other step to take: Will you believe that He does it? For 'Whatever you ask in prayer, believe that you have received it, and it will be yours'" (Mark 11:24).

"But won't I be lying to say that I believe, when I don't feel it?"

"No, feelings make no difference; your faith must precede all feeling. 'Faith comes by hearing, and hearing by the word of God' (Romans 10:17, NKJV). The word of God to you is this: 'You are already clean because of the word which I have spoken to you'" (John 15:3, NKJV).

She said, "I commit myself to God, and shall trust Him, till the witness of my acceptance comes." That night God woke her with a clear witness of the Spirit that she was entirely sanctified.

There must first be entire consecration, unwavering faith, and a frank confession of both. When these simple conditions are met and steadfastly maintained, against all contrary feelings, God will enter His holy temple, filling the soul with His presence, purity, and power.

*HTH, 21*

## One Thing

*This one thing I do.* (Philippians 3:13, KJV)

When they sought the man where he had last been seen, all they could find was a small streak of ashes.

One month earlier, a Salvation Army officer had visited a wealthy exporter, asking for a donation. The man replied, "If you can tell me one thing The Salvation Army does which has not as its ultimate object the winning of people to Christ, then I will give you a liberal donation. But you cannot do it; you march the streets, you carry banners, you conduct meetings, you open shelters and soup kitchens and rescue homes, you publish books and papers for just one object—to win people to Christ. I do not need your Christ. I am rich, but I will give you nothing." A month later came an earthquake and an all-consuming fire, and all that remained of the man was a poor little handful of ashes!

The proud man had grasped the central purpose of The Salvation Army, and the church. All should have this supreme object always in full view. Some serve tables, as did Stephen, Philip, and others; and some give themselves wholly to the ministry of the Word and prayer, as did Peter and the other apostles (Acts 6:1-7). But all have one object—winning souls and making them channels of His saving grace to others.

*AP, 8*

## What Flame Is to Fire

*The LORD their God is with them, and the shout of a king is among them.* (Numbers 23:21)

There is a secret spring of power and victory in shouting and praising God.

Yet many an honest, seeking soul goes mourning throughout life under the devil's spell. Frequently whole congregations will be under it. Their eyes are vacant or listless or restless. There is no attention, no expectation. A stifling stillness and the serenity of "death" settles upon them. But let a Spirit-surrendered believer bless the Lord, and the spell will be broken. Everyone there will come to their senses, wake up, remember where they are, and will begin to expect something to happen.

Shouting and praising God is to salvation what flame is to fire. When Joshua's armies shouted, the walls of Jericho fell flat (Joshua 6:20). When Jehoshaphat's people began to sing and praise, God's enemies were routed (2 Chronicles 20:22). When Paul and Silas, chained in the dungeon with bruised and bleeding backs, prayed and sang praises unto God, the Lord shook the foundations of the prison, loosed the prisoners, and converted the jailer and all his family (Acts 16:25-33).

Nothing can stand before Christians who have a genuine shout in their souls. Earth and hell flee before them, and all heaven throngs about them to help them fight their battles.

*HH, 27*

## Sanctification and Temptation

*If the Son sets you free, you will be free indeed.* (John 8:36)

"How can a person who is 'dead to sin' be tempted?" asked an earnest but unsanctified Christian of me some time ago. If the very tendencies and inclinations to sin be destroyed, what is there in the person to respond to a solicitation to evil?

This is a question everyone asks sooner or later, and when God showed me the answer, it threw great light on my pathway and helped me to defeat Satan in many a pitched battle.

The truly sanctified believer who is "dead to sin" does not have any inclinations remaining that respond to ordinary temptations. As Paul declares, "We wrestle not against flesh and blood"—against the sensual, fleshly, and worldly temptations which used to have such power over us—"but against principalities, against powers, against the rulers of the darkness of this world, against wicked spirits in heavenly places" (Ephesians 6:12, KJV, marginal reading).

Those who have "died to sin" have found such satisfaction, peace and joy, comfort, purity, and power in Christ that the power of temptation along any of the old lines is completely broken, and they now enjoy the liberty of the sons and daughters of God. They are as free as any archangel, for "if the Son sets you free, you are truly free" (John 8:36, NLT).

*HH, 4*

## Sanctified Warfare

*Fight the good fight of faith.* (1 Timothy 6:12, KJV)

While Christ has set the sanctified man or woman at liberty, and the fight against the old worldly passions and fleshly appetites is a thing of the past, there remains a continual warfare with Satan to keep this liberty. This warfare is what Paul calls "the good fight of faith" (1 Timothy 6:12).

The sanctified believer must fight to hold fast his or her faith in the Savior's blood, in the Spirit's sanctifying power. Although not seen by the world, this fight is as real as that of Waterloo or Gettysburg, and its far-reaching consequences for good or evil are infinitely greater.

By faith, we who are sanctified become heirs of God with Jesus Christ (Romans 8:17), and our faith makes this heavenly inheritance so real to us that the influence of unseen things far surpasses the influence of the things we see, hear, and handle. We say with Paul, and fully realize it in our hearts as we say it, that "the things that are seen are transient, but the things that are unseen are eternal" (2 Corinthians 4:18).

These things can only be held by faith; but so long as we thus hold them, Satan's power over us is utterly broken.

*HH, 4*

## The Accuser's Schemes

*Be sober-minded; be watchful. Your adversary the devil
prowls around like a roaring lion, seeking someone to
devour.* (1 Peter 5:8)

Satan knows that if he can get us to listen to his accusations
and lose faith in the cleansing blood of Jesus, he has us at
his mercy. Satan, "the accuser of [the] brothers and sisters"
(Revelation 12:10, NIV), will then turn right around and
declare that it is the Holy Spirit, instead of himself, condemning us! Here is the difference we want to notice: the
devil *accuses* us of sin; the Holy Spirit *convicts* us of sin. If
I break any of God's commandments, the Holy Spirit will
convict me at once. Satan will accuse me of having sinned
when I have not.

It is no use arguing with the devil. The Christian can
only look to the Savior and say, "Dear Lord, You know I
have done the best I could. If I have done anything wrong
or left anything undone, I trust Your blood to cleanse me."

If Satan is met this way at the beginning of his accusa-
tion, our faith will gain a victory, and we will rejoice in
the Savior's cleansing blood and the Spirit's keeping power.
But if we listen to the devil until our conscience and faith
are both wounded, it may take a long time for our faith
to regain the strength which will enable us to shout and
triumph over all the power of the enemy.

*HH, 4*

## Jesus' Prayer for You

*After Jesus said this, he looked toward heaven and prayed.*
(John 17:1, NIV)

The prayer known as "The Lord's Prayer" is rather the disciples' prayer. Jesus gave it to them to use, voicing their needs and desires.

The prayer of Jesus as our Great High Priest, the prayer which no doubt constitutes the substance of His ceaseless and eternal intercession for us, is recorded in John 17. That is peculiarly the Lord's Prayer.

If we wish to know His thought for us, the fullness of blessing He wishes to bestow upon us, we should ponder this prayer, make it a daily study, and cooperate with Him for its fulfillment.

Jesus first prays that the Father will glorify Him that He in turn may glorify the Father. He prays that His disciples may be kept from evil. He further prays, "Sanctify them" (v. 17). He prays for them to be one, as He and the Father are one. He concludes, "Father, I desire that they also, whom you have given me, may be with me where I am, to see my glory that you have given me" (v. 24).

O my soul, you who have wandered in darkness and grubbed in sin and have been plucked from the mire, you shall yet be lifted from the dunghill and seated with Him upon His throne, and shall behold the glory before which angels and archangels veil their faces and fall as dead!

*AP,* 16

## God Has Suffered

*Christ also suffered once for sins, the righteous for the unrighteous, that he might bring us to God.* (1 Peter 3:18)

An ancient king passed a law against a certain grave crime. The first to be found breaking that law was the king's own son.

How could the king save his son and justly uphold the law? The punishment decreed was that two eyes must be put out. Could they not be the eyes of a slave? If so, the king's subjects might fear him, but not reverence him. They would despise him, and the son would go on in his shameless career.

This is what the king did. He put out one of his son's eyes and one of his own. The people could only exclaim, "The king is merciful, and the king is just."

Will God act so? Will God suffer to save the sinner? Is there any other way by which God can justify the sinner, and yet Himself be just? Is there any other way by which God can display His hatred of sin and His pitying love of the sinner? Is there any other way by which God can break the sinner's proud and unbelieving heart and melt it into penitence and contrition? Oh, will God take my place, and in His love and pity die in my stead, to save me from my sin?

The Bible says that God will suffer, and that God has suffered.

*GS, 1*

## Such a Great Salvation

*How shall we escape if we neglect such a great salvation?*
(Hebrews 2:3)

The Sufferer hanging on the cross was God, suffering for us—God, the blessed Son. The Bible says that Jesus is God. Jesus says so, John says so, Paul says so. The church in all its creeds says so. The wisest Christian teachers say so. The saints and martyrs, who have perished by flame and wild beast's fang, cry out with Thomas, "My Lord and my God!" (John 20:28). Think of Him pouring out His life, an innocent Sufferer for sinners, for you and me! "God was in Christ, reconciling the world unto himself" (2 Corinthians 5:19, KJV). "God made him who had no sin to be sin for us, so that in him we might become the righteousness of God" (2 Corinthians 5:21, NIV).

It was "through the eternal Spirit" that Christ "offered himself without blemish to God" (Hebrews 9:14), in our stead and on our behalf. Truly does Paul say, "Without question, this is the great mystery of our faith: Christ was revealed in a human body and vindicated by the Spirit" (1 Timothy 3:16, NLT).

And truly does the writer to the Hebrews describe our salvation as "such a great salvation" (Hebrews 2:3).

*GS, 1*

## The Same Power

*God's power is very great for us who believe. That power is the same as the great strength God used to raise Christ from the dead.* (Ephesians 1:19-20, NCV)

Paul tells us that the same power which raised Christ from the dead is in us who believe (Ephesians 1:19-20). He says of Jesus, "When he ascended on high he made captivity itself a captive; he gave gifts to his people" (Ephesians 4:8, NRSV).

In ancient times victorious generals carried captive the captains and kings they conquered, and distributed gifts to their own people from the spoils of the enemy. So Jesus, having triumphed over all the power of the enemy, distributes gifts of love, joy, faith, patience, and wisdom to His people that shall enable them also to prevail over all the power of the enemy.

The practical, everyday teaching of Scripture to me is this: that since Jesus rose from the dead and ascended on high, He puts at my disposal the same power to do His will that His heavenly Father gave to Him. Jesus "was crucified in weakness, but lives by the power of God" (2 Corinthians 13:4), and when He rose from the dead, He broke every fetter forged by Satan, sin, and hell, and opened a way by which every human soul may go free and enter into union with God through the indwelling Holy Spirit, and have the power of God working mightily and triumphantly in him or her.

*HTH, 22*

## Revelation and the Bible

*The Law of the Lord is a lamp, and its teachings shine brightly.* (Proverbs 6:23, CEV)

We do not discover God. God reveals Himself to us. God seeks us before we seek God. God reveals His wisdom and power through nature, His holiness through conscience, His hatred of sin through judgment, His redeeming love through faith.

We see God's power in starry heavens, storm-swept seas, flaming volcanoes, and silent forces lifting mighty forests from tiny seeds. We see His wisdom in the marvelous adaptations of nature: of the eye to light and color, the ear to sound, the nose to odors, the tongue to flavors, and the skin to heat and cold. We see His redeeming love in Christ, in His works of pity and mercy, and most clearly in His atoning death on the cross.

But all this manifold unveiling and revelation of Himself God sums up in His Word. "The LORD revealed himself to Samuel at Shiloh through the LORD's own word," we read (1 Samuel 3:21, CEB). He declares His power, His wisdom and knowledge, His holiness and righteousness, His redeeming purpose and plan, in His Word. And the Holy Spirit applies the words of Scripture to our hearts with life-giving energy: "When you walk, they will guide you; when you sleep, they will watch over you; when you awake, they will speak to you" (Proverbs 6:22, NIV).

*AP, 12*

## The Final Stone

*The Holy Spirit proved that Jesus is the powerful Son of God, because he was raised from death.* (Romans 1:4, CEV)

The Resurrection was God's complete attestation and vindication of Jesus as the Christ. Even John the Baptist had once doubted, and asked, "Are you the one who is to come, or should we look for another?" (Matthew 11:3, CEB). But the Resurrection was God's complete answer, and swept away forever every ground of doubt. As Paul declares, the lowly, suffering, crucified Jesus was "declared to be the Son of God in power according to the Spirit of holiness by his resurrection from the dead" (Romans 1:4).

Jesus Christ is the revelation of God. The Father's heart of love, of pity, of sympathetic understanding, of infinite yearning was made known in Jesus. In Him, too, was seen the Father's hatred of sin, His holiness, His spotless purity, His exact and unswerving justice, and His detestation of all unrighteousness.

Jesus came into the world to reveal the Father and to do the will of the Father. He also came to save lost humanity from our sins and from ourselves. He came to bring us into reunion with God. He came to make us holy, happy, dutiful, unafraid children of the Father once more. And the Resurrection was the final stone in the everlasting foundation on which this work was to be built.

*RLP, 1*

## Fruits of the Resurrection

*All things are yours . . . and you are Christ's, and Christ is God's.* (1 Corinthians 3:21, 23)

As it was for Jesus' first followers, so is it for us. The foundation of their, and our, faith was not fully laid by His life and ministry; it was made complete by His resurrection from the dead.

Having been baptized with the Holy Spirit, those early disciples thenceforth received life and power from Christ; and as the vine produces fruit through the branches, so the fruit of Christ's life and Spirit was formed in them. In Him was sacrificial, deathless love, and this love was reproduced in them. Joy, the very joy of Jesus, was perfected in them; He bequeathed His joy to them (John 15:11). What a treasure! He left them His peace (John 14:27), the peace of an assured and endless life over which death has no power. Patience was perfected in them; eternity was in their hearts. The gentleness, goodness, faith, and meekness of their Lord—all these were reproduced in them, and made manifest in word and deed. It was Christ living His life in them.

Can this Resurrection life and power be yours and mine? Yes, it is for all. It is for you and me. All is ours, since we are Christ's and Christ is God's.

*RLP, 1*

## Two Tombs

*I am the resurrection and the life. Those who believe in me, even though they die, will live.* (John 11:25, NRSV)

After the death of John the Baptist, his disciples buried him, then went and told Jesus, and from that time we hear no more of them. The power that united them failed in the death of John, and they fell apart and were soon lost in the crowd.

When Jesus died and was buried, the same disintegrating forces affected His disciples. Amazed, disappointed, heartbroken, they said, "We had hoped that he was the one to redeem Israel" (Luke 24:21), and they started for their homes.

But a wonderful thing happened. The scattering, discomfited disciples were rallied by the strange story that His grave was empty, and that Jesus Himself had appeared to certain of their company. From that hour we find the power that bound them together strengthening until, on the Day of Pentecost, the Holy Spirit welded them into a divine oneness such as was never known before, and the prayer of Jesus was answered, that they might be one, even as He and the Father are one.

How different are the graves of John and Jesus! That of John is still shrouded in darkness, but that of Jesus is aflame with light. It is the first rift in the surrounding gloom through which we get foregleams of the full glory yet to be revealed.

*RLP, 2*

## The Crowning Evidence

*It is no longer I who live, but Christ who lives in me.*
(Galatians 2:20)

When my friend in New York sails for Liverpool, how do I know that he has arrived safely? I know it by the cablegram or letter he sends back to me. How do I know that Jesus is not dead, but risen and ascended to the right hand of the Father where all power in heaven and earth is His? I know it by the Holy Spirit whom He has sent to me, filling my whole soul with light and love, and making me to know my risen Lord better than I knew my mother. This is the crowning evidence which He gives to them that obey Him.

The other evidences are historical and general, and are to be sifted, considered, weighed, as is the evidence of any historical fact. The evidence given in the blessing of the Holy Spirit is personal and living, confirming the faith of him or her who receives it.

The external historical evidences are for the natural mind. They are given once and for all, and never repeated. The inward spiritual evidence is for the spiritual mind and is God's new, ever-recurring, ever-living, and eternal answer to the soul that from the heart sings, "Thee to know is all my cry."[19]

*RLP, 2*

## Filled with Resurrection Power

*You have loosed my bonds.* (Psalm 116:16)

A brilliant young minister opened his heart and told me what an awful struggle he was having with fleshly temptations. He had been reconciled to God by the death of Jesus, but he had not been saved to the uttermost by His life. After having the way of holiness explained to him, he yielded himself to Jesus, received Him by faith, and found himself filled with resurrection power.

Some weeks later he wrote, "I have burned the last bridge behind me, and am all under the blood. Oh, what weeks these have been since I saw you, such as I never believed could be realized this side of heaven."

A revival broke out in his church, and nearly all the leading members got sanctified, while many wayward souls were saved. A year later there was a second revival, with scores of people flocking to the Lord.

Many years have now passed, and the fire still burns in that minister's heart. He received the very same life and Spirit that the disciples received in the upper room on the Day of Pentecost, and it is for you, too. Jesus' life and power is your portion. Rise up in glad faith before Him and claim it now.

*RLP, 2*

## Witness to the Resurrection

*And with great power the apostles gave witness to the
resurrection of the Lord Jesus.* (Acts 4:33, NKJV)

Several years ago, I knelt with a young woman who wanted
to be holy. While we were praying, she burst into tears and
cried out, "O Jesus!"

She had never seen Jesus, never heard His voice, and
had no more idea of such a revelation of Jesus to her soul
than one born blind has of a rainbow. But she knew Him!
She had no more need that someone should tell her this
was Jesus than you have need of the light of a candle to
see the sun come up. The sun brings its own light, and so
did Jesus.

She knew Him, she loved Him, she rejoiced in Him
with "joy inexpressible and full of glory" (1 Peter 1:8,
NASB). This young woman became a witness for Jesus—a
witness that He is not dead but living, and as such a witness to His resurrection.

Such witnesses are needed in every age. They are needed
today as much as in the days of the apostles. People's hearts
are just as wicked, their pride as stubborn, their selfishness as universal, and their unbelief as obstinate as at any
time in the world's history, and it takes just as powerful
evidence to subdue their hearts and beget living faith in
them as it ever did.

*HH, 19*

# The Need for Living Witness

*You will be my witnesses.* (Acts 1:8)

The faith that saves is the faith that brings the life and power of God into the soul. It is a faith that purifies the heart, sets the Lord always before the eyes, and fills the soul with humble, holy, patient love toward God and others.

To beget this faith is needed not only the Bible with its historical evidences, but also a living witness; one who has "tasted the good word of God, and the powers of the world to come" (Hebrews 6:5, KJV); one who can witness to the Resurrection, because he or she knows the Lord, who is "the resurrection and the life" (John 11:25).

I remember a little girl in Boston, whose quiet, earnest testimony for Jesus drew people to our meetings. One day she said to me, "As I was in my room getting ready for the meeting, Jesus was with me. I felt He was there, and I knew Him."

This is the Holy Spirit's chief work—to reveal Jesus to the spiritual consciousness of each individual believer, and by so doing to purify the heart, to destroy all evil dispositions, and to implant in the soul of the believer the very dispositions of Jesus Himself.

*HH, 19*

## Another Helper

*"It is to your advantage that I go away, for if I do not go away, the Helper will not come to you."* (John 16:7)

On that last eventful evening in the upper room, the disciples were troubled, for what could Jesus' death and departure mean but the destruction of all their hopes, of all their cherished plans? Jesus was the Seed of David, the promised Messiah. He was their Leader, their Teacher, their Defense. How could their poor hearts be otherwise than troubled?

But then He gave them a strange, wonderful, reassuring promise: "I will ask the Father, and he will give you another Helper, to be with you forever, even the Spirit of truth" (John 14:16-17).

Jesus had been external to them. Sometimes asleep when they felt they sorely needed Him. Sometimes on the mountains, while they were in the valley. Sometimes surrounded by vast crowds, and they had to wait till He was alone to seek explanations of His teachings. But no human being, nor untoward circumstance, nor physical necessity could ever separate them from this other Helper. Jesus promised, "He dwells with you and will be in you" (John 14:17). At every point of need, there would He be as an ever-present and all-wise, almighty Helper. He would meet their need with His sufficiency, their weakness with His strength, their foolishness with His wisdom, and their blindness and shortsightedness with His perfect, all-embracing vision. Hallelujah! What a Comforter! *HGC, 1*

## The Witness of the Spirit

*The Spirit himself bears witness with our spirit that we are children of God.* (Romans 8:16)

How shall I know that I am accepted of God—that I am saved or sanctified? The Bible cannot tell me this; it tells me what to do, but it does not tell me when I have done it. My religious teachers and friends cannot tell me, for they cannot read my heart, nor the mind of God toward me. My own dark, deceitful, erring heart is not a safe witness.

How, then, shall I know? Only by the witness of the Holy Spirit. God must make me to know it; and this He does when, despairing of my own works of righteousness, I cast my poor soul fully and in faith upon Jesus. "For you did not receive a spirit of slavery to fall back into fear," said Paul, "but you received the Spirit of adoption, by whom we cry out, '*Abba!* Father!' The Spirit Himself testifies together with our spirit that we are God's children" (Romans 8:15-16, HCSB). Unless He Himself assures me, I shall never know that He accepts me, but must continue in uncertainty all my days.

*Come, Holy Ghost, Thyself impress*
*   On my expanding heart:*
*And show that in the Father's grace*
*   I share a filial part.*[20]

HGC, 4

## Secondary Witnesses

*Because we are his children, God has sent the Spirit of his Son into our hearts.* (Galatians 4:6, NLT)

When the Holy Spirit witnesses to me that I am saved and adopted into God's family, then other evidences begin to abound also.

1. My own spirit witnesses that I am a new creature. I know that old things have passed away, and all things have become new. My very thoughts and desires have been changed. Love and joy and peace reign within me. My heart no longer condemns me. Pride, selfishness, lust, and temper no longer control my thoughts nor lead captive my will. I infer without doubt that this is the work of God in me.

2. My conscience bears witness that I am honest and true in all my purposes and intentions, that I am without guile, that my eye is single to the glory of God, and that with all simplicity and sincerity of heart I serve Him. And this sincerity of heart is His blessed work in my soul, and is a fruit of salvation.

3. The Bible becomes a witness to my salvation. In it are accurately portrayed the true characteristics of the children of God, and as I study it prayerfully and find these characteristics in my heart and life, I again infer that I am God's child.

*HGC, 4*

## Jesus the Workingman

*He had to be one of us, so that he could serve God as our merciful and faithful high priest and sacrifice himself for the forgiveness of our sins.* (Hebrews 2:17, CEV)

The artists portray Jesus with a face of almost feminine softness, and would picture Him to us as a delicate man, with hair parted in the middle and with patrician hands and tapering fingers. But the Bible rather pictures Him as a man of toil with calloused hands who earned His bread by the sweat of His brow. Indeed, He was "made in every respect like us, his brothers and sisters" (Hebrews 2:17, NLT).

Jesus was a workingman, and as such understands working men and women. He knows their weakness, He has been pinched with their poverty, He can sympathize with them in their long hours of toil. He understands. But while He suffered and toiled and was tempted and tried as we are, He was nonetheless pure, holy, loving, patient, kind, and true, even to the point of dying for us that we might escape from our sins and become like Him.

We may not erect a Brooklyn Bridge or build a St. Peter's Basilica, but we can do our little task well and in the spirit of Jesus. We can be kind and patient, faithful and true. The carpenter who builds houses, the clerk who toils over the ledger, the farmer who plows the fields and feeds cattle, all can become partakers of His Spirit.

*HTH, 17*

# The Acts of the Holy Spirit

*We have received not the spirit of the world, but the Spirit who is from God, that we might understand the things freely given us by God.* (1 Corinthians 2:12)

The personality of the Holy Spirit is as clearly revealed in Acts as is the personality of Jesus Christ in the Gospels. In truth, the Acts of the Apostles are in a large measure the acts of the Holy Spirit, as the disciples were under the direct leadership of the Spirit after Pentecost.

We read of the church at Antioch, "While they were worshiping the Lord and fasting, the Holy Spirit said, 'Set apart for me Barnabas and Saul for the work to which I have called them.' Then after fasting and praying they laid their hands on them and sent them off. So, being sent out by the Holy Spirit, they went" (Acts 13:2-4).

Later, Paul and his companions "were forbidden by the Holy Spirit to preach the word in Asia," and when they would have gone into Bithynia, "the Spirit did not permit them" (Acts 16:6-7, NKJV).

Again, when the messengers of Cornelius were seeking Peter, "The Spirit said to him, 'Behold, three men are looking for you. Rise and go down and accompany them without hesitation, for I have sent them'" (Acts 10:19-20).

Oh, the rapture mingled with reverential, holy fear, to be indwelt and led by the Holy Spirit!

*HGC, 1*

## Suffering and Rejoicing

*They left the presence of the council, rejoicing that they were counted worthy to suffer dishonor for the name.*
(Acts 5:41)

Doubtless all suffering is a result of sin, but not necessarily the sin of the sufferer. Jesus was the sinless One, but He was also the Chief of sufferers. Paul's great and lifelong sufferings came upon him, not because of his sins, but rather because he had forsaken sin, and was following Jesus and seeking the salvation of others. In this path there is no escape from suffering, though there are hidden and inexpressible consolations. "In the world you will have tribulation," said Jesus (John 16:33). "All who desire to live a godly life in Christ Jesus will be persecuted," wrote Paul (2 Timothy 3:12).

Sooner or later, suffering in some form comes to each of us. And nothing more clearly distinguishes the person filled with the Spirit from one who is not than the way each *receives* suffering. One person responds with doubts and fears, murmurs and complaints, and to other miseries adds those of a rebellious heart and discontented mind. The Spirit-filled person, with triumphant faith and shining face and strong heart, glories in tribulation and counts it all joy. One sees the enemy's armed host, and unmixed distress and danger; the other sees the angel of the Lord, with abundant help and safety (2 Kings 6:15-17).

*HGC, 20*

# The Strongest Argument

*You are witnesses of these things.* (Luke 24:48)

A lecturer on the evidences of Christianity would meet skeptics in public debate, each supported by colleagues who were confirmed in their opinions. It was heady, a rivalry of wits, an intellectual fisticuffs—all to no profit. There was no changing of sides, no converts were made.

One day one of the most formidable skeptic debaters was stricken with a fatal illness. His friends had no words of comfort, and left him to himself. Then a sweet, humble Salvation Army sister stepped in and nursed the dying man. She could not and did not argue, but revealed to him a redeemed, Christlike life. Love was in her face, tenderness in her touch, grace on her lips; peace and joy in Jesus radiated from her. Soon, where knowledge and argument had failed, a humble, inspired life prevailed. He was converted and died in the faith.

A skeptic challenged a man of God to debate. "I accept on this condition," replied the man of God, "that I bring one hundred believers to testify what faith in Christ has done for them, and you bring one hundred to testify what atheism has done for them." The challenger withdrew the challenge.

Meek and lowly, but glad and bold witnesses, who witness by lip and life and shining look, are the strongest argument for the faith they live.

*AP, 15*

## Fruit unto Perfection

*"Whoever believes in me, as the Scripture has said, 'Out of his heart will flow rivers of living water.'"* (John 7:38)

The soul in whom the Spirit of God dwells will possess a wisdom that is from above. That soul's conduct will be pure, "peace-loving, considerate, submissive, full of mercy and good fruit" (James 3:17, NIV). Such a life is compelling, and will win souls.

A hard-headed businessman saw a poor widow with her brood of children going to the house of God Sunday after Sunday, and one day it convicted him and turned him in repentance and faith to the Savior. Her "patience in well-doing" (Romans 2:7), a fruit of the Spirit, was more effective than any word she could have spoken.

Through us are to flow all the streams and rivers of God's grace. He is the Vine; we are the branches. Through us His beauty is to be made manifest, the beauty of holiness; and in us His fruit is to be found.

This fruit of the Spirit often works more silently, deeply, effectively than our preaching; and only the sanctified blessing can produce this fruit unto perfection in our lives. The Christian who bears this fruit—full, rich, and ripe—is reproducing the life of Jesus upon earth. Out of such a person, most often unconsciously, flow influence and power that are like "rivers of living water" (John 7:38) in desert lands.

*GS, 2; AP, 3 and 16*

## Overcoming the Devil

*Resist the devil, and he will flee from you.* (James 4:7)

What shall the sanctified person do to overcome the devil?

Listen to what Peter says: "Be sober-minded; be watchful. Your adversary the devil prowls around like a roaring lion, seeking someone to devour. Resist him, firm in your faith" (1 Peter 5:8-9).

Hear James: "Resist the devil, and he will flee from you" (James 4:7).

Listen to Paul: "Fight the good fight of faith" (1 Timothy 6:12, KJV). "The righteous shall live by faith" (Romans 1:17). "Above all, taking the shield of faith with which you will be able to quench all the fiery darts of the wicked one" (Ephesians 6:16, NKJV).

And John: "This is the victory that has overcome the world—our faith" (1 John 5:4). "And they overcame him" (the devil, the Accuser) "by the blood of the Lamb, and by the word of their testimony; and they loved not their lives unto the death" (Revelation 12:11, KJV). They obeyed God at all costs, and denied themselves to the uttermost.

The author of Hebrews attaches the same importance to testimony in saying, "Let us hold fast the confession of our hope without wavering" (Hebrews 10:23).

"So brothers and sisters, be careful that none of you has an evil, unbelieving heart that will turn you away from the living God" (Hebrews 3:12, NCV).

*HH, 4*

## Evil-Speaking

*Speak evil of no one.* (Titus 3:2)

"Speak evil of no one." This is a command of God. It should be meditated upon and obeyed, lest in speaking evil:

*We wrong that person.* You consider it wrong for anyone to speak evil of you. Why? When you have answered that question, you have given yourself a reason to speak no evil.

*We wrong those to whom we speak.* It fills their minds with unholy, unjust prejudice. It tempts them to think and speak evil.

*We wrong our own souls.* It destroys all generous and kindly thoughts in us, and quenches love. It opens our hearts for the devil to enter. It prevents us from praying for the person, which would be infinitely better, and which is especially needed if he or she is wrong in any way.

*We grieve the Holy Spirit.* The Spirit leads us to love others—even our enemies. But evil-speaking destroys love. The Spirit leads us to pray for others, but evil-speaking quenches the spirit of prayer as water quenches fire.

*We wrong Jesus.* He died for that person. Even if that person is a hypocrite or rebel, yet Jesus loves and spares such a one. Jesus identifies Himself with that person, and in the Judgment will face us with the wrong as done to Himself unless we hastily and heartily repent.

*HTH, 23*

## Honoring Others

*Be humble and give more honor to others than to
yourselves.* (Philippians 2:3, NCV)

If someone is bad or faulty in any way, consider that he
or she may have secret trials and temptations: business
troubles and cares, family trials, very faulty early training. Not that these things will excuse anyone in the Day of
Judgment, but they should lead you and me to pity rather
than to abuse by speaking evil. Think instead about your
own evils. This will be infinitely more profitable in making
a better man or woman of you.

One of the chief dangers to ourselves in evil speaking
is that we come to underestimate others, and to esteem
ourselves more highly than we ought. We look at our own
virtues and other people's faults, when we ought to look
long at their virtues and our own faults. We must obey
the command, "Be humble and give more honor to others
than to yourselves" (Philippians 2:3, NCV).

Get a clean heart, full of the Holy Spirit, and you cannot
speak evil of anyone. With a heart flaming with love, you
will pray for the wrongdoer. If you see evil in anyone, you
will try to correct him or her in love, just as you would go
to a blind person walking toward a precipice, and try to
turn him or her from certain death.

*HTH, 23*

## How to Read the Bible

*They received the word with all eagerness, examining the Scriptures daily.* (Acts 17:11)

A few suggestions as to how to read and study the Bible:

1. Read it as a young lover reads a letter from his beloved—meditating on it, going over it again and again, delighting in it—that is the way to read the Bible.

2. Read it with a ready mind, as the disciples in Berea did (Acts 17:11). Search the Scriptures. Go to them daily. Once this habit is formed, your delight in God's Word will become inexpressible.

3. Read and study not to get a mass of knowledge, but a flame of love in the heart. "Knowledge puffs up while love builds up" (1 Corinthians 8:1, NIV).

4. Read it not that you may know, but that you may *do*. "Meditate on it . . . so that you may be careful to *do* everything written in it" (Joshua 1:8, NIV, emphasis added).

5. Pray for understanding. You will love and understand the Word only as Jesus reveals it to you, as "he opened [the disciples'] minds to understand the Scriptures" on the road to Emmaus (Luke 24:45).

6. Finally, do not be discouraged if progress seems slow at first. Like learning to play an instrument, at first it appears impossible, but some glad day you will be doing the impossible with ease. Keep at it!

*HTH, 24*

## Jesus in the Company

*Supposing him to be in the group they went a day's journey.* (Luke 2:44)

When Jesus was a boy, He tarried behind in Jerusalem after the Passover feast, but His parents did not know it. Their mistake was in taking it for granted that Jesus was in their company. But when they sought Him, He was not there. Just so, people frequently suppose Jesus is in the company, and yet He may not be in their midst at all.

I remember arriving at a camp meeting where no one had come to faith in Jesus. At the appointed hour, the people, who had been laughing and joking and visiting, would come strolling in. Then the meeting would begin with a rush and a bang, and songs and prayers and testimonies and a Bible reading would follow, and the meeting would end again without souls.

At last a prayer meeting was called. And when Jesus was told that He was expected and that He must come, and that we would not let Him go except He blessed us, He came. Then there was a shout of a King in the camp (Numbers 23:21), and dead souls were raised to life!

Oh, that we may always make sure that He is with us, and not take it for granted, else we find we have been going on a fool's errand without Him!

*HTH, 25*

## If You Would Be Useful

*Get Mark and bring him with you, for he is very useful to me for ministry.* (2 Timothy 4:11)

Does the devil ever tempt you to feel that you are of no use and can do nothing? Every genuine Christian wants to be useful, fruit-bearing, and a soul-winner. This desire is characteristic of the new nature. When you first came to faith, you tried to so live your life before your friends that they would be brought to Jesus. But now that you are farther along, do you ever feel that you are useless, that your words are powerless to lead people to Jesus?

I would say, do what you can. "Angels can do no more." Use what talents you have, and God will surely increase them. Cultivate your talents. Begin and keep at it. That is the way to become mighty in prayer, to become acquainted with the Bible, to learn to speak or sing or fish for souls.

God has a work for you to do, and no one else can do it. Do not sit down in the discouragement of unbelief and think because you have not the talents of some gifted person you therefore can do nothing. That is dishonoring to God, pleasing to the devil, and will surely result in a great loss to your soul.

Believe God, and go on with your work.

*HTH, 26*

## The Basal Work of the Blessing

*John baptized with water, but you will be baptized with the Holy Spirit.* (Acts 1:5)

A minister of the gospel wrote to a preacher of entire sanctification, saying, "I like your teaching on the blessing of the Holy Ghost. I need it, and am seeking it. But I do not care much for entire sanctification or heart-cleansing. Pray that I may be filled with the Holy Ghost."

The brother immediately replied, "I am so glad you believe in the blessing of the Holy Ghost, and are so earnestly seeking it. I join my prayer with yours. But let me say to you, if you get the gift of the Holy Ghost, you will have to take entire sanctification with it."

Thank God, he humbled himself and permitted the Lord to sanctify him.

Many have looked at the promise of power, the energy of Peter's preaching on the Day of Pentecost, and the marvelous results which followed, and have erroneously concluded that the blessing is for work and service only.

It does bring power—the power of God. And it does fit for service—the proclamation of salvation and peace to a lost world. But not that alone, nor primarily. The primary, the basal work of the blessing of the Holy Spirit, is that of cleansing. The incoming of the Holy Spirit means the outgoing of all sin.

*HGC, 5*

# The Spirit and the Bible

*"He will teach you all things and bring to your remembrance all that I have said to you."* (John 14:26)

The Holy Spirit will not call attention to Himself, but will point to Jesus (John 15:26; 16:13-14). Nor does He come to reveal any new truth, but rather to make us understand the old. "He will teach you all things and bring to your remembrance all that I have said to you" (John 14:26). He will make your Bible a new book to you. He will teach you how to apply it to everyday life, so that you will be safely guided by it.

The reason people get mixed up over the Bible is because they do not have the Holy Spirit. A young Christian full of the Holy Spirit can tell more about the Bible than all the theological professors in the world who are not filled with the Holy Spirit.

The Holy Spirit will make your entire Bible "sweeter also than honey and drippings of the honeycomb" (Psalm 19:10). He will make you tremble at the warnings of God's Word (Isaiah 66:2), exult in His promises, and take delight in the commandments. You will say with Jesus, "No one can live only on food. People need every word that God has spoken" (Matthew 4:4, CEV). You will understand what Jesus meant when He said, "The words that I have spoken to you are spirit and life" (John 6:63).

*HH, 5*

## Highs and Lows

*Testing of your faith produces endurance. Endure until your testing is over. Then you will be mature and complete.* (James 1:3-4, GW)

While you walk in humble obedience and childlike faith, the Comforter will abide with you, and the "low-water mark" of your experience will be perfect peace. I will not dare to say what the high-water mark may be! You need not fear that the experience will wear out or grow tame. God is infinite, and your little mind and heart cannot exhaust the wonders of His wisdom and goodness and grace and glory in one short lifetime.

Do not think, however, when the tide flows out to "low-water mark" that the Comforter has left you. I remember well how, after I had received the Holy Spirit, I walked for weeks under a weight of divine joy and glory that was almost too much to bear. Then there would be alternate days of joy and peace. And on the days when there was no special experience, the devil would suggest that I had in some way grieved the Holy Spirit. But God taught me that I must "hold fast the profession of [my] faith without wavering" (Hebrews 10:23, KJV). So I say to you, do not think He has left you because you are not overflowing with emotion. Hold fast your faith. He is with you, and will not leave you.

*HH, 5*

## The Time Is Now

*I will not let you go unless you bless me.* (Genesis 32:26)

A friend claimed the blessing of a clean heart, and testified to it at the breakfast table the next morning. He said he had been led to study the Bible, and to observe the lives of those who professed the blessing, and he had come to the conclusion that he could not serve God acceptably without holiness of heart.

The difficulty was to come to the point where he would take it by faith. He said he had expected to get it sometime, he had hoped for it, he had looked forward to the time when he should be pure; but he saw that it must be claimed now, and right there began his fight of faith. He took hold of one end of the promise, and the devil got hold of the other end, and they pulled and fought for the victory.

This time, the man would not cast away his confidence, but came "boldly unto the throne of grace" (Hebrews 4:16, KJV). The devil was conquered by faith, and the brother walked off with the blessing of a clean heart.

*HH, 6*

## Breaking Satan's Stronghold

*Be sober-minded; be watchful. Your adversary the devil prowls around like a roaring lion, seeking someone to devour.* (1 Peter 5:8)

The last thing a soul has to give up, when seeking salvation or sanctification, is "an evil, unbelieving heart" (Hebrews 3:12). This is Satan's stronghold. He does not care much if people give up outward sin. A respectable sinner will suit his purpose quite as well as the most disreputable. Nor does he care very much if people indulge a hope of salvation or of purity if he can get them to stop there. But let a poor soul say, "I must have the blessing now," and the devil will use all his wits to deceive the soul and switch it onto some sidetrack or rock it to sleep with a promise of victory at some future time.

This is where the devil really begins. Many people who say they are fighting the devil do not know what fighting the devil means. It is a fight of faith, in which the soul takes hold of the promise of God and declares it to be true in spite of the devil's lies, in spite of all circumstances and feelings to the contrary. Such a soul will soon get out of the fog and twilight of doubt into the broad day of perfect assurance that Jesus saves and sanctifies, and shall sense God's everlasting love and favor.

*HH, 6*

## A Heart like His

*"This is my command: Love each other."* (John 15:17, NIV)

*"Give me a heart like Thine,"* [21] we sang with all our might, one morning when I was a cadet in the Salvation Army training school. A fellow cadet came to me with a serious look and asked, "Do we really mean it, that we can have a heart like His?" I told him that I was certain we could. Indeed, we are to be like Jesus. "As he is so also are we in this world" (1 John 4:17).

Jesus had a loving heart. There was no hatred with His love, no venom, no spite, no selfishness. He loved His enemies and prayed for His murderers. It was not a fickle love, but a changeless, eternal love. "I have loved you with an everlasting love" (Jeremiah 31:3), God says.

It is just this kind of love He wants us to have. He says, "A new commandment I give to you, that you love one another: just as I have loved you" (John 13:34). That is tremendous, to command me to love my brothers and sisters even as Jesus loves me. But that is what He says, and to do that I must have a heart like the heart of Jesus.

*HH, 7*

## A Humble Heart

*Clothe yourselves, all of you, with humility.* (1 Peter 5:5)

Jesus had a humble heart. Paul tells us that He "made himself nothing by taking the very nature of a servant" (Philippians 2:7, NIV).

Though He was the Lord of life and glory, yet He stooped to become a human being and live among the lowly, hardworking, common people. He cleaved to them. Just before His death, He took the menial place of a slave, and washed His disciples' feet, and then said, "I have given you an example, that you also should do just as I have done to you" (John 13:15).

How that has helped me! My second day at the Salvation Army training school, they sent me to black half a cart-load of dirty boots. The devil came at me, and reminded me that I had graduated from a university, had attended a leading theological school, had been pastor of a metro-politan church, had just left evangelistic work in which I saw hundreds seeking the Savior, and that now I was only blacking boots for a lot of ignorant lads. But I reminded my old enemy of the example of my Lord, and he left me, and that little cellar was changed into one of heaven's ante-rooms, and my Lord visited me there.

If you would have a heart like that of Jesus, it will be one filled with humility.

*HH, 7*

## A Meek and Gentle Heart

*Blessed are the meek.* (Matthew 5:5)

Jesus had a meek and gentle heart. Peter tells us that "when he was reviled, he did not revile in return; when he suffered, he did not threaten" (1 Peter 2:23). He did not strike back when He was injured; He did not try to justify Himself, but committed His cause to His heavenly Father (Isaiah 53:7).

That was the very perfection of meekness, that not only would He not strike back when He was lied about, but suffered the most cruel and shameful wrongs.

It is just this kind of heart He wants us to have. "Do not resist an evildoer. But if anyone strikes you on the right cheek, turn the other also" (Matthew 5:39, NRSV).

I know an African American brother, over six feet tall, with a full chest and brawny arms, who was recently put off a streetcar in the most indecent and brutal manner, where he had as much right to be as the conductor. Someone asked, "Why don't you fight him, George?"

"I couldn't fight him, for God has taken all the fight out of me," replied George. "When you put your knife in the fire and draw the temper out of it, it won't cut," he added, and fairly shouted for joy.

*HH, 7*

## Wait on God

*They that wait upon the Lord shall renew their strength.*
(Isaiah 40:31, KJV)

If I could deliver a single three-word exhortation to all Christians, I would say, "Wait on God!"

Wherever I go, people are falling away by the thousands, until my heart aches over the great army of discouraged souls, the way in which the Holy Spirit has been grieved, and the way in which Jesus has been treated.

These people would give ten thousand different reasons for their falling away when, after all, there is but one: they did not wait on God. If they had waited on Him when the fierce assault was made that overthrew their faith and bankrupted their love, they would have renewed their strength and mounted over all obstacles as though on eagles' wings. They would have run through their enemies and not been weary. They would have walked in the midst of trouble and not fainted.

Waiting on God means more than an occasional prayer of thirty seconds. It may mean one prayer that gets hold of God and comes away with the blessing, or it may mean a dozen prayers that persist and will not be put off, until God arises on behalf of the pleading soul.

The secret of all failures, and of all true success, lies in the soul's private walk with God. Whoever courageously waits on God is bound to succeed.

*HH, 8*

## Where Spiritual Failure Starts

*When you pray, go into your room and shut the door and pray to your Father who is in secret. And your Father who sees in secret will reward you.* (Matthew 6:6)

I went to a cold and discouraged corps [Salvation Army church], but there I found one sister with a wondrous glory in her face, and glad, sweet praises in her mouth. She had looked at others falling and noted the decline of vital piety among that company, until she felt disheartened and her feet almost slipped. But she went humbly to God and prayed and waited, until He drew near and showed her the awful precipice on which she herself was standing—showed her that her one business was to walk before Him with a perfect heart, and to cleave to Him, though the whole corps lost faith. Then she renewed her covenant, until an unutterable joy came to her heart, and God filled her with the glory of His presence.

The next day she fairly trembled to think of the awful danger she had been in, and declared that that time of waiting on God in the silence of the night saved her, and now her heart was filled with the full assurance of hope not only for herself, but also for the corps. Oh, for ten thousand more like her!

Know, then, that all failure has its beginning in private, in neglecting to wait on God until filled with wisdom, clothed with power, and all on fire with love.

*HH, 8*

## The Leakage of Spiritual Power

*Keep your heart with all vigilance, for from it flow the springs of life.* (Proverbs 4:23)

I knew a Salvation Army officer who let all his spiritual power leak out, until he was as dry as an old bone. All the way to the hall he was talking about things that had no bearing upon the coming church meeting—nothing wrong or trifling, but this turned his mind from God and the souls he was so soon to face. The result was that instead of going before the people clothed with power, he went stripped of power.

In the meeting, his prayer was good, but there was no power in it. It was words, words, words! The Bible reading and talk were good. He said many true and excellent things, but there was no power in them. Altogether the meeting was a dull affair.

Now, the officer had a good experience and was one of the brightest I know. But instead of communing with God in his heart until his soul was ablaze with faith and hope and love and holy expectation, he had wasted his power in useless talk.

Christians must keep the way always open between their hearts and God. They must keep a constant watch over their mouths and their hearts. God will bless such people and honor them, and show them how to get at the hearts of those who do not yet know Him.

*HH, 9*

## Ways of Letting Power Leak

*Delight yourself in the LORD, and he will give you the desires of your heart.* (Psalm 37:4)

There are many ways of letting spiritual power leak away. I knew a Christian who came to church early, and instead of tuning his soul, spent the time playing soft, dreamy music on his violin. Though faithfully, lovingly warned, he continued that practice till he lost his faith.

Others tell funny stories and play the clown to make things lively. And things *are* lively, but not with divine life. Those who are filled with the power of the Spirit will certainly make others laugh at times. They may say tremendously funny things. But they will not be doing it just to have a good time. It will come naturally, and it will be done in the fear of God, and not in a spirit of lightness and jesting.

There is no substitute for the Holy Spirit. He is life. He is power. And if He is sought in earnest, faithful prayer, He will come, and when He comes the smallest church meeting will be mighty in its results.

How happy are those who find God to be their delight (Psalm 37:4)—who give themselves up to loving, serving, trusting God with all their hearts.

*HH, 9*

## Whom God Wants

*If you keep yourself pure, you will be a special utensil for honorable use.* (2 Timothy 2:21, NLT)

A Christian merchant expressed a great and important truth: "People are crying to God to use them, but He cannot. They are not given up to Him. Plenty of people seek work in my store, but they are not suitable. When I need someone, I have to advertise, and sometimes spend days trying to find someone who will fit the opening, and then I have to test that worker to know whether he or she will suit me."

The fact is, God is using everyone He can, and using them to the full extent of their fitness for His service. So, instead of praying so much to be used, people should search themselves to know whether they are usable. It is only those who are "holy and pleasing to their Master, and . . . able to do all kinds of good deeds" (2 Timothy 2:21, CEV) that He can bless with great usefulness.

Like the merchant, God has to pass by hundreds before He finds the right individuals. Oh, how God wants to use you! But first see to it that your heart is "perfect toward him" (2 Chronicles 16:9, KJV). Then you may be sure that God will show Himself strong on your behalf.

*HH, 10*

## God's Coworkers

*We are God's coworkers.* (1 Corinthians 3:9, GW)

When God searches for a man or woman to work in His vineyard, He does not ask, "Has he great natural abilities? Is she thoroughly educated? Is he eloquent in prayer? Can she talk much?"

Rather, He asks, "Is his heart perfect toward Me? Does she love much? Is he willing to walk by faith, and not by sight? Will she be weary and faint when I correct her and try to fit her for greater usefulness? Or will she, like Job, cry out, 'Though He slay me, yet will I trust in Him' (Job 13:15, NKJV)? Does he search My Word, and 'meditate on it day and night,' in order to do 'everything written in it' (Joshua 1:8, NIV)? Does she wait on Me for My counsel and seek in everything to be led by My Spirit? Or is she stubborn and self-willed, like the horse and the mule, which have to be held in with bit and bridle (Psalm 32:9), so that I cannot guide her 'with My eye' (Psalm 32:8, NKJV)? Is he a people-pleaser and a time-server, or is he willing to wait for his reward, and does he seek for 'the honor that cometh from God only' (John 5:44, WBT)?"

When God finds such a person, He will use him or her.

*HH, 10*

## Don't Feel Useless

*Be strong, and let your heart take courage, all you who wait for the LORD!* (Psalm 31:24)

Paul was whipped, stoned, and shut up in prison, yet he declared with unshaken faith, "I am suffering, bound with chains as a criminal. But the word of God is not bound!" (2 Timothy 2:9). Neither devils nor humans could put shackles on God's Word, but it pierced right through the prison walls, and flew across oceans and continents and down through the years, everywhere bringing light and comfort and salvation to dark, troubled, sinful hearts. Though more than eighteen centuries have passed since they cut off Paul's head, yet his usefulness increases and his mighty words and works are today bearing such fruit as passes the comprehension of an archangel.

Poor, troubled soul, cheer up! You think you are useless, but be of good courage! Trust God!

Paul saw dark days. He wrote to Timothy, "You are aware that all who are in Asia turned away from me" (2 Timothy 1:15). Study his life in the Acts and the Epistles, and see what conflicts and discouragements he had, and take courage!

See to it that you are "filled with the Spirit" (Ephesians 5:18), and you will be surprised, at the reckoning day, to behold the vastness of your reward as compared with the littleness of your sacrifices and your work.

*HH, 10*

## Take Care of Your Soul

*The LORD is good to those who wait for him.*
(Lamentations 3:25)

I was once asked, "Cannot one take too much care of one's own soul? I see everywhere so much suffering and injustice that I am perplexed at God's way of ruling the world, and it seems to me that Christians ought to help others, instead of looking out for their own souls." We see all around us sorrow and suffering which we cannot help. Our perplexity at the sight is the Lord's prompting for us to take the very uttermost care of our own souls, lest we stumble and fall through doubt and discouragement.

By "the care of your soul," I do not mean that you should coddle and pity yourself, nor work yourself up into some pleasant feeling. I mean that you should pray and pray and pray, and seek the presence and teaching of the Holy Spirit, until your soul is filled with light and strength, that you may have unquestioning faith in the wisdom and love of God, that you may have unwearied patience in learning His will (Hebrews 6:12), and that your love may be equal to the great need you see all about you.

You cannot help people if you go to them robbed of your strength through doubts and fears and perplexities. So, wait on God till He strengthens your heart.

*HH, 11*

# Keep Watch over Yourself

*Keep a close watch on yourself and on the teaching. Persist in this, for by so doing you will save both yourself and your hearers.* (1 Timothy 4:16)

Paul said, "Keep watch [1] over yourselves and [2] over all the flock which the Holy Spirit has placed in your care" (Acts 20:28, GNT). And again, "[1] Watch yourself and [2] watch your teaching. Keep on doing these things, because if you do, you will save both yourself and those who hear you" (1 Timothy 4:16, GNT).

Paul did not mean to promote selfishness by telling us to first take heed to ourselves. But he did mean to teach that, unless we are full of faith and hope and love in our own souls, we shall be unable to help others.

One morning, after a half-night of prayer, I got up early to be sure of an hour with God and my Bible, and God blessed me till I wept. An officer who was with me was much moved, and then confessed, "I do not often find God in prayer—I have not time."

Take time. Miss breakfast if necessary, but take time to wait on God, and when God has come and blessed you, then go to the miserable ones about you and pour upon them the wealth of joy, love, and peace God has given you. But do not go until you know you are going in His power.

*HH, 11*

## Gideon's Band (1)

*Whoever is fearful and trembling, let him return home.*
(Judges 7:3)

One hundred and twenty thousand Midianites had come against Israel, and thirty-two thousand Israelites rose up to fight for their families, their homes, their liberty, their lives. But God saw that if one Israelite whipped nearly four Midianites, he would be so puffed up with pride and conceit that he would forget God, and say, "My own hand has saved me" (Judges 7:2).

The Lord also knew that there were a lot of weak-kneed followers among them, with cowardly hearts, who would like an excuse to run away. So He told Gideon to say, "Whoever is fearful and trembling, let him return home and hurry away." The sooner fearful folks leave us, the better.

Twenty-two thousand left, but the Lord made a still further test. Gideon "brought the people down to the water. And the LORD said to Gideon, 'Every one who laps the water with his tongue, as a dog laps, you shall set by himself. Likewise, every one who kneels down to drink.' . . . And the LORD said to Gideon, 'With the 300 men who lapped I will save you and give the Midianites into your hand'" (Judges 7:5, 7). That was one to four hundred. No chance of self-conceit there! They won the victory, but God got the glory.

*HH, 12*

## Gideon's Band (2)

*God said to Gideon: "I'll use the three hundred men who lapped at the stream to save you and give Midian into your hands."* (Judges 7:7, *The Message*)

Gideon's three hundred meant business. They were not only unafraid, but they were not self-indulgent. They knew how to fight, but even more important, they knew how to deny themselves. They were, no doubt, quite as thirsty as the others, but they did not throw down their arms and fall down on their faces to drink in the presence of the enemy. They stood up, kept their eyes open, kept one hand on shield and bow, while with the other they brought water to their thirsty lips.

Moses and Elijah and Jesus fasted and prayed for forty days, and immediately after, mighty works were done.

And so, all mighty men and women of God have learned to deny themselves and keep their bodies under discipline, and God has set their souls on fire, helped them to win victory against all odds, and bless the whole world.

We should not deny ourselves food and drink to the injury of our bodies. But one night of watching and fasting and praying can starve no one. And those who are willing to forget their bodies occasionally for a short time, in the interest of their own souls and the souls of others, will reap amazing blessings.

*HH*, 12

## Gideon's Band (3)

*And they cried out, "A sword for the LORD and for Gideon!"* (Judges 7:20)

Gideon's band of three hundred got ahead of their enemies by getting up early (Judges 7:19).

John Fletcher used to mourn if he knew of a laborer getting out to his daily toil before he himself was up praising God and fighting the devil. He said, "What! Does that man's earthly master deserve more ready service than my heavenly Master?"

We read that Jesus arose early and went out alone to pray. Joshua got up early in the morning to set battle in array against Jericho and Ai.

John Wesley went to bed at ten o'clock sharp—unless he had an all-night of prayer—and got up promptly at four. Six hours of sleep was all he wanted, although he traveled thousands of miles each year, in winter and summer, on horseback and in carriages, and preached hundreds of sermons.

A Salvation Army captain wrote me the other day that he had begun to do his praying in the morning when his mind was fresh and before the cares of the day had got the start of him. Four hundred devils cannot stand before the man or woman who makes it a rule of life to get up early to praise the Lord and plead for God's blessing on his or her own soul and on the world. They will flee away.

*HH*, 12

## Is Death a Mystery?

*The righteous are taken away from calamity, and they enter into peace.* (Isaiah 57:1-2, NRSV)

The beauties of a landscape and the glories of the vaulted heavens are not made known to us through the sense of hearing. The harmony of a song is not made known to us by the sense of sight. If we would know the flavor of some fruit, we must not seek to discover it by the sense of touch, but by taste.

A man blind from his birth said he thought the sun must look like the sound of a bass drum! We smile wisely at this, forgetting that we probably miss the mark quite as far in matters more important.

To every faculty and sense but one, death is an awful and unfathomable mystery. We look into the coffin where lies our precious dead and peer into the yawning grave with our poor little reason and understanding, and it is all heartbreaking amazement, desolation, mystery.

But faith is the faculty with which we must approach this problem, and to faith there is no mystery in death. To faith, death simply means that the appointed task in this world's harvest field is done, and the dear one has gone home.

Faith accepts death as God's appointment. This is a fact to be believed, not to be reasoned over; and if we simply believe it, the sting of death is drawn.

*RLP, 3*

## Sorrow and Comfort

*"Let not your hearts be troubled. Believe in God; believe also in me."* (John 14:1)

The sorrow of bereavement may be inexpressibly bitter, but faith finds its firm footing on God's Word. It grasps the promises and fixes its eyes upon His unchangeable wisdom and love, and emerges from the flood and storm chastened, but strengthened—still sorrowing, but triumphant and serene.

To our sainted dead, the coffin is not a narrow and locked prison, but an easy couch of sleep. The grave is not a bottomless abyss, but an open door through which the dear one has passed into the presence of the King, into the unveiled vision of Jesus—a door of escape from the limitations and tears and temptations and travails of time into the ageless blessedness of eternity where "God shall wipe away all tears from their eyes; and there shall be no more death, neither sorrow, nor crying, neither shall there be any more pain" (Revelation 21:4, KJV).

Philosophy may enable us to endure the agony following the death of our loved ones, but only faith nourished by the promises and examples of God's Word can enable us to triumph in that hour. And we shall be wise if we fill our minds and hearts now with those precious truths God has revealed, so that when the storm overtakes us, as it someday surely will, we shall be prepared.

*RLP, 3*

## Eternity Is Here

*Truly, truly, I say to you, whoever hears my word and believes him who sent me has eternal life. He does not come into judgment, but has passed from death to life.*
(John 5:24)

I read a fine exhortation by a brother who urged us to get ready because eternity is coming. Eternity is not coming. Eternity is here. We call that period in which we live in our bodies "time," and we say we shall lay off the body and enter into "eternity." That is like a deep-sea diver saying, "Were it not for my diving bell I should be in the ocean." He is in the ocean now, only its power to affect him is limited. If he got out of his bell, the ocean would swallow him up. So eternity will swallow us up and work our everlasting undoing unless we learn to live the eternal life while in the body. John Wesley said that those who live a truly religious life are now living in eternity.

We are now becoming what we shall ever be—lovers of God and the things of God, or haters of God and the things of God—either learning the sweet and heavenly art of loving, trusting, and obeying God, or else by unbelief, disobedience, and selfishness, forming ourselves into vessels of wrath and dishonor.

O my soul, when you love and trust and obey, you have the life that is everlasting! Death cannot touch you, and when others say you are dead, you will be reveling in fullness of life.

*RLP, 5*

MAY 30

## Electricity and Magnetism

*When the day of Pentecost arrived . . . they were all filled with the Holy Spirit.* (Acts 2:1, 4)

The Day of Pentecost was the inaugural day of the church, the dawn of the dispensation of the Holy Spirit, and the beginning of the days of power.

In the morning of that day, there were only a few Christians in the world. They had no Bibles, church buildings, colleges, religious books, or papers. But before night they had enrolled three thousand new followers and had filled Jerusalem with amazement.

What was the secret? Power. God the Holy Spirit had come.

The Holy Spirit kindles a fire of love in the hearts of those who are freely and fully presented to Him. He lights the flame of truth in their minds. He endues them with power.

If you ask how the Holy Spirit can dwell within us and work through us without destroying our personality, I cannot tell. How can electricity fill and transform a dead wire into a live one? How can a magnetic current fill a piece of steel, and transform it into a mighty force which by its touch can raise tons of iron?

What electricity and magnetism do, the Holy Spirit does in the spirits of those who follow Jesus and trust Him intelligently. He dwells in them and inspires them, till they are all alive with the very life of God.

*HGC, 6*

## More Power to You

*You formerly walked according to the course of this world, according to the prince of the power of the air. . . . Among them we too all formerly lived in the lusts of our flesh.*
(Ephesians 2:2-3, NASB)

The transformation and power wrought in men and women by the Holy Spirit are amazing beyond measure. He gives:

1. Power over the world. People who have not the Holy Spirit sell themselves for worldly things. But men and women who are filled with the Holy Spirit are free. They can turn from these things without a pang, or they can take them and use them as servants for the glory of God and the good of humanity.
2. Power over the flesh. I knew an old man, a drunkard for over fifty years, delivered instantly through sanctification. I knew a young man, the slave of a vicious habit of the flesh, set free at once by the fiery work of the Spirit. Electrical current cannot transform the dead wire into a live one more quickly than the Holy Spirit can flood a soul with light and love, destroy the carnal mind, and fill a soul with power over all sin.
3. Power over the devil. The soul filled with the Spirit outwits the devil and, clad in the whole armor of God, overcomes the old enemy.

This blessing is power for service or sacrifice, according to God's will. Have you this power? It is for you.

*HGC, 6*

## The Guidance of the Spirit

*The LORD will guide you continually.* (Isaiah 58:11)

It is the work of the Holy Spirit to guide the people of God through the uncertainties and dangers and duties of this life. When He led the children of Israel out of Egypt, He guided them through the wilderness in a pillar of cloud by day and of fire by night. And this was but a type of His perpetual spiritual guidance of His people.

We need to be guided always by Him. Innumerable influences threaten to deflect us from the safe and certain course. We start out in the morning, and we know not what person we may meet, what paragraph we may read, what word may be spoken, what message we may receive, what subtle temptation may assail or allure us, what immediate decisions we may have to make during the day, that may turn us almost imperceptibly, but nonetheless surely, from the right way. We need the guidance of the Holy Spirit.

And God's Word assures us that we may have it. "The LORD will guide you continually" (Isaiah 58:11). Not occasionally, not spasmodically, but "continually." The psalmist says, "This is God, our God forever and ever. He will guide us forever" (Psalm 48:14). Jesus said of the Holy Spirit, "When the Spirit of truth comes, he will guide you into all the truth" (John 16:13).

*HGC, 8*

# How God Guides Us

*You guide me with your counsel.* (Psalm 73:24)

How does God guide us?

1. By faith. Paul says, "We walk by faith, not by sight" (2 Corinthians 5:7). God never leads us in such a way as to do away with the necessity of faith.

2. By "sanctified common sense." The Spirit enlightens our understanding and directs our judgment by sound reason and sense.

3. By enlightening our study. The Bible says, "I will instruct you and teach you in the way you should go; I will counsel you with my eye upon you" (Psalm 32:8). The guidance of the Holy Spirit will require us to listen attentively, study diligently, and patiently learn the lessons He would teach us.

4. By revealing the deep, sanctifying truths of the Bible, especially the character and Spirit of Jesus.

5. By the circumstances and surroundings of our daily lives.

6. By the counsel of others, especially wise men and women of God.

7. By deep inward conviction, which increases as we wait upon Him in prayer and readiness to obey. It is by this sovereign conviction that people are called to devote their time, talents, money, and lives to God's work.

*HGC, 8*

## Why Some Fail

*"You will seek me and find me, when you seek me with all your heart."* (Jeremiah 29:13)

Why do some people seek for guidance and not find it? It is because:

1. They do not diligently study God's Word. They neglect the cultivation of their minds and hearts in the school of Christ.

2. They do not humbly accept their everyday circumstances as a part of God's present plan for them, in which He would train them for greater things.

3. They are not humble and teachable, and are unwilling to receive instruction from other Christians.

4. They do not wait on God, and listen and heed the inner leadings of the Holy Spirit.

5. They are filled with fear and unbelief, like that which caused the Israelites to turn back from conquering Canaan.

6. They do not take everything promptly to God in prayer. Slowness to pray, and laziness in prayer, rob God's children of the glad assurance of His guidance.

7. They are impatient and hasty. Some of God's plans unfold slowly. Wait on Him; in due time He will make His way plain.

*HGC, 8*

## Run to the Battle

*David ran quickly toward the battle line.* (1 Samuel 17:48)

The devil haunts us with fears of tomorrow to weaken faith and turn our eyes from our Lord. Trials may come—they *will* come—but our Lord will be there with abundant grace when they do come if, looking unto Him, we go forward in His strength. We are not alone, and we must not fear, though the temptation to fear may be present.

"I will give your flesh to the birds of the air and to the beasts of the field," said battle-hardened, mocking Goliath.

"You come to me with a sword and with a spear and with a javelin," David answered, "but I come to you in the name of the LORD of hosts, the God of the armies of Israel, whom you have defied. This day the LORD will deliver you into my hand" (1 Samuel 17:44-46). The Lord was David's shield. "I have set the LORD always before me" (Psalm 16:8), he wrote long years after, and Goliath could not reach him without first encountering the Lord.

That is the way to face fears and spiritual enemies and doubts and temptations. Face them "in the name of the LORD of hosts." Run to meet them, but put no confidence in yourself, only as you are "strong in the Lord and in the power of His might" (Ephesians 6:10, NKJV).

*AP, 13*

## A Soul-Thrilling Fact

*Whatever you ask in prayer, believe that you have received it, and it will be yours.* (Mark 11:24)

The Holy Spirit helps us to understand the things we may pray for, and the sanctified heart wants only what is lawful. This is mystery to people who are under the dominion of selfishness and the darkness of unbelief, but it is a soul-thrilling fact to those who are filled with the Holy Spirit.

"What do you want me to do for you?" asked Jesus of the blind man (Luke 18:41). He had respect for the will of the blind man, and granted his request, seeing he had faith. And He still has respect for the will of His people—the will that has been subdued by consecration and faith into loving union with His will.

Adoniram Judson heard an account of the conversion, through his writings, of a number of Jews in Constantinople. Judson had prayed for years that he might be used in some way to bless the Jews, and now, after many years and from far away, the evidence of answer had come. Judson said he had never prayed a prayer for the glory of God and the good of people but that, sooner or later, God had worked to answer his prayer.

Oh, the faithfulness of God! He means it when He makes promises and exhorts and urges and commands us to pray.

*HGC, 15*

## The Spirit-Stirred Memory

*The Holy Spirit will teach you in that very hour what you ought to say.* (Luke 12:12)

The Holy Spirit inspires men and women who receive Him to use the Scriptures to awaken, convict, and save others.

Charles Finney was invited to a certain place to preach. On his way there this text, spoken by Lot in Sodom, came to mind: "Up, get you out of this place; for the LORD will destroy this city" (Genesis 19:14, KJV). Finney preached the text and applied it to his hearers. While he spoke, they began to look exceedingly angry; then, as he earnestly exhorted them to give up their sins and seek the Lord, they fell from their seats and cried to God for mercy. A great revival followed.

To Finney's amazement, he learned afterwards that the place was called Sodom because of its extreme wickedness, and the man who had invited him to preach was called Lot because he was the only God-fearing man there.

Such inspiration is not uncommon with those who are filled with the Holy Spirit. The Spirit makes the Word alive. He brings it to the remembrance of those in whom He abides, and He applies it to the hearts of their hearers, lighting up the soul as with a sun until sin is seen in all its hideousness, or cutting as a sharp sword, piercing the heart with resistless conviction.

*HGC, 17*

## Faithless Anxiety

*Be on guard so that you will not be carried away by the errors of these wicked people and lose your own secure footing.* (2 Peter 3:17, NLT)

Nothing is more likely to disjoint our relationship with God and precipitate trouble than faithless anxiety about the future and our loved ones.

The children of Israel had seen God's unfailing faithfulness, but they could not trust Him to bring them into Canaan! They said, "Our wives and our little ones will become a prey. Would it not be better for us to go back to Egypt?" (Numbers 14:3). And this fearfulness proved their undoing. Job said, "What I fear comes upon me, and what I dread befalls me" (Job 3:25, NASB). And so it always does.

A husband and wife felt called to become Salvation Army officers, but they refused, saying, "We must educate our children." They lost their faith, and left the Army. After some time, their daughter surrendered her life to Jesus Christ, and wanted to join The Salvation Army. But her parents said, "No, it will give you no social opportunities." Then the girl herself lost faith, and at sixteen, betrayed and soon to become a mother, was threatening to take her own life to hide her shame.

The parents feared to obey lest their children should lose educational and social opportunities. But in their unbelief, the things they feared came upon them. Let it not be so with you. Trust God for your future and that of your loved ones.                                    *RLP, 18*

# The Guest of the Soul

*The fellowship of the Holy Spirit be with you.*
(2 Corinthians 13:14)

A friend said recently, "I like the term, 'Holy Ghost,' for the word *ghost* in the Old Saxon was the same as the word for *guest*." It may certainly be said that the Holy Ghost is the Holy Guest. He visits every heart, seeking admittance. He may come to the soul unbidden, but He will not come *in* unbidden. He may be turned away, but He comes. He is in the world like Noah's dove, looking for an abiding place. He comes as a Guest, but as an abiding one, if received. He forces Himself upon no one.

He comes in love. He comes on a mission of infinite goodwill, of mercy and peace and joy. He is the Advocate of the Father and of the Son to us humans. He represents and executes the redemptive plans and purposes of the triune God. As my old teacher, Daniel Steele, wrote, "He is the Executive of the Godhead."

When the Holy Ghost becomes the Holy Guest in the yielded, welcoming heart, He dwells there ungrieved and with delight. He rejoices over that soul, while the soul has sweet, ennobling, purifying fellowship with its Lord. He illuminates that soul. He purifies, sanctifies, empowers, instructs, comforts, protects, adjusts it to all circumstances and crosses, and fits it for effective service.

*GS*, 3

## When the Holy Guest Abides Within

*Consider the Apostle and High Priest of our confession,*
*Christ Jesus, who was faithful to Him who appointed Him.*
(Hebrews 3:1-2, NKJV)

Some time ago, a high-ranking Salvation Army officer received transfer orders to proceed to England for a new appointment.

To go from sunny Australia to foggy London in mid-winter was not pleasant. To leave a field and work and people he loved for work where all would be new and strange was not what he expected or would have chosen. But he told me that the text "Christ did not please himself" (Romans 15:3) kept whispering in his heart, and so with perfect and glad resignation, and in great peace, he and his wife were on their way.

As he told me this, his face was as serene as a summer's eve, and my own heart sensed the divine calm that possessed him. It was the indwelling Holy Guest who whispered to his heart and made him so ready for service and so peaceful in sacrifice.

When the Holy Guest abides within, the soul does not shun the way of the Cross, nor seek great things. It is content to serve in lowly as in lofty ways. To wash a poor disciple's feet is as great a joy as to command an army, to follow as to lead, to serve as to rule—when the Holy Guest abides within the soul.

*GS, 3*

## Power for Living

*"I am going to send you what my Father has promised;
but stay in the city until you have been clothed with power
from on high."* (Luke 24:49, NIV)

"Sanctification through the Holy Spirit is for power for
service!" so many people say. And so it is. It does reinforce
and empower the soul. Those who are given over to the
Spirit are "endued with power from on high" (Luke 24:49,
KJV). A holy and divine Presence abides within and fits
them for the service of their Lord.

But what we *are* is more important than what we *do*.
Goodness is better than greatness. We may do much and
earn a great name, and still end in hell; but the person who
loves God and others, though unknown beyond a small
circle, is on the way to heaven, and is well known there.

The blessing of the Holy Spirit is to bring us into union
with Christ, into loving fellowship with the heavenly
Father, as well as to equip us for such service or sacrifice as
falls to our lot. We all need the blessing of Pentecost if we
are to live worthy lives that shall glorify God, from which
will flow influences that often are more effective than the
busy activity we call service.

*GS, 2*

## To Destroy the Devil's Works

*The Son of God came to destroy the works of the devil.*
(1 John 3:8, NLT)

The Son of God came into this world to accomplish a two-fold purpose: "to take away sins" and "to destroy the works of the devil" (1 John 3:5, 8). The first work is justification and regeneration, which are done for us. The second is entire sanctification, which is a work done in us.

When you come to God with a penitent heart and put your trust in Jesus, you are freed from your sins. Guilt vanishes. The power of evil is broken. The burden rolls away. But behind and below your own sins are the "works of the devil," which must also be destroyed before the work of grace in your soul can be complete.

God teaches very plainly how this is done. "Put off your old self" (Ephesians 4:22). "Put out of your life every evil thing and every kind of wrong" (James 1:21, NCV). The Bible says we are to get rid of something that hinders our spiritual life. This work is not to be a slow, evolutionary process, but an instantaneous work wrought by the Holy Spirit. And the one thing needful on our part is an obedient faith that laughs at impossibilities, and cries, "It shall be done."[22]

*HTH, 1*

## Ask, and It Will Be Given

*Ask, and it will be given to you.* (Luke 11:9)

God wants to put the dynamite of the Holy Spirit into every converted soul, and forever do away with that troublesome sinful nature, so that truly, "Old things are passed away; behold, all things are become new" (2 Corinthians 5:17, KJV).

Any child of God can have this. You must give yourself wholly to God in faith. "Ask, and it will be given to you; seek, and you will find. . . . If you then, who are evil, know how to give good gifts to your children, how much more will the heavenly Father give the Holy Spirit to those who ask him!" (Luke 11:9, 13).

Seek Him with all your heart, and you shall indeed find Him, for God says so, and He is waiting to give Himself to you.

A dear young fellow felt his need of a clean heart, knelt by his bed, read Acts chapter 2, and then told the Lord that he would not rise till he was sanctified. He had not prayed long before the Lord filled him with glory.

You can have it, if you will go to the Lord in the Spirit and with faith. And the Lord will do for you "far more abundantly than all that [you] ask or think, according to the power at work within [you]" (Ephesians 3:20).

*HH, 2*

## The Promise of the Father

*He ordered them not to depart from Jerusalem, but to wait for the promise of the Father.* (Acts 1:4)

Before He ascended to the Father, Jesus promised His disciples, "You will be baptized with the Holy Spirit not many days from now" (Acts 1:5). On the Day of Pentecost came the ample fulfillment. They were all filled with the Holy Spirit.

The blessing of the Spirit is not given to everybody. Jesus spoke of Him as One "whom the world cannot receive, because it neither sees him nor knows him" (John 14:17). Jesus did not say, "*may* not receive," but "*cannot* receive." He is given only to those who can receive, to those who see and know. A person who has eyes closed to the light, a heart turned from true knowledge, cannot receive. And yet such people are responsible for their own deprivation because their blindness is due to their own action. Such people cannot receive the Holy Spirit because they have turned away from the Savior and the truth that alone could fit them to receive Him.

The blessing of the Holy Spirit is for those who have become sons and daughters of God through penitent, obedient faith. It is that which, received and wisely used, will fit us for the final and full reward, but which, rejected or neglected, will leave us eternal paupers among those who weep and gnash their teeth in outer darkness.

*GS, 2*

## The Blessing of Pentecost

*When the day of Pentecost arrived, they were all together in one place. . . . And they were all filled with the Holy Spirit.* (Acts 2:1, 4)

Jesus promised, "I will ask the Father, and he will give you another Helper, to be with you forever" (John 14:16). And so He did.

1. This blessing is for our comfort. Where the Spirit is, there Jesus is. When He is come we are no longer orphans, lonely and bereft. Though unseen, He is present with us, and our hearts are strangely warmed and comforted.

2. It is for our instruction. The Holy Spirit is the great, silent, inward Teacher, speaking to the ears of the soul, instructing in the hours of prayer and communion.

3. It is for our guidance. There are many attractive and alluring byways, but only the one true way, and we need the Comforter to guide us in that way (John 16:13) and teach us the truth.

4. It is for power. We are naturally weak. We fall before temptation. We faint with fear. But when the Helper comes, He strengthens us and lifts us up.

We should watch and pray and wait, daily and hourly and momentarily, for that inner strengthening by the Spirit, that we may be strong to work, to fight, to resist, serve, sacrifice, suffer, dare, and bear up and press on joyfully, growing neither weary nor fainthearted.

*GS*, 2

## The Noble Guest

*"In that day you will know that I am in My Father, and you in Me, and I in you."* (John 14:20, NASB)

When a noble guest comes into my home, that guest imparts to me something of his or her own nobility. Low things sink lower, base things seem baser, and in such a guest's ennobling presence, things that are true, honorable, just, pure, and lovely (Philippians 4:8) are the worthwhile matters. And if this be so when a mere human comes in, how much more when God the Holy Spirit comes in!

Some people lay great stress upon the second coming of Christ as an incentive to fine and holy living. I would not minimize this. But Jesus said, "In that day"—when the Comforter has come—"you will know that I am in My Father, and you in Me, and I in you" (John 14:20, NASB). When the Holy Guest abides within, the Father and the Son are there too. And what finer incentive to holy living can one have than this indwelling presence of Father, Son, and Holy Spirit, as Guest of the Soul?

And having thus glimpsed the mind of Christ, the soul yields itself eagerly to the Holy Guest to be conformed to that mind. That is its great business. To be like Him, to live in His favor, in fellowship and friendship with Him, is its life, its great and solemn joy.

*GS, 3*

## The Spirit's Work of Conviction

*When he comes, he will convict the world concerning sin and righteousness and judgment.* (John 16:8)

When the Holy Spirit comes into a human heart, He convicts of sin. We cease to be self-complacent. Our moral and spiritual nakedness is exposed. Our eyes are opened, and we see how self-deceived we have been—how unChristlike in our dispositions, corrupt in our desires, selfish in our ambitions, puffed up in our vainglory, slow to believe, quick to excuse ourselves and justify our own ways, how far from God we have wandered.

The Holy Spirit also convicts of righteousness. We no longer justify ourselves and condemn God. Our mouths are stopped. We see that God is true and righteous altogether, and in the presence of His holiness and righteousness, all our righteousness is seen to be as filthy rags (Isaiah 64:6, KJV). We can only cry, as did the leper, "Lord, if you will, you can make me clean" (Luke 5:12).

Finally, the Holy Spirit convicts of judgment—both now, accompanying our every act, word, thought, intent, and motive, as our shadow accompanies our body, and at the final judgment to come. He convicts of judgment unto life or of judgment unto banishment, if we are found outside of Christ, disapproved of God.

*GS*, 3

## The Mystic Universe in My Backyard

*All your works praise you, LORD.* (Psalm 145:10, NIV)

I am discovering a universe in my backyard. A clump of yellow and blue iris; a flowering shrub that has never bloomed for eight years; a rambler rose bush, now preparing to burst into a blaze of pink flame; a crab apple tree; and a few square yards of green grass sprawling around iris and shrub and tree.

Just outside the border of my backyard stands a big oak tree, and on another side a maple, and they cast cool shadows when the sun is hottest. Some distance away are a few other glorious oaks. They are not so large as their forefathers, but I think of them as the heirs of all the ages, and as I look at their broad-reaching limbs and into their deep-green foliage, they suggest the solemn, whispering, primeval forest that once clothed this continent.

An ocean of fresh air, fifty miles deep, laves me in its waves that beat upon every shore and isle, every mountain and plain. Sunbeams ninety million miles long unerringly find me with their life-giving rays. If health and strength can be found in the wilderness of plain or forest, or on mountain or sea, I believe it can be found among the teeming wonders, the mystic universes, and in the ocean of air and sunshine I find in my backyard.

*AP, 19*

## Heavenly Fruit in Harsh Climate

*The fruit of the Spirit is love, joy, peace, patience,*
*kindness, goodness, faithfulness, gentleness, self-control.*
(Galatians 5:22-23)

Many years ago one of my campaigns coincided with the annual meeting of the Methodist Conference. Many Methodist preachers attended our open-air meetings, and some came to our hall. I was invited to come to their meeting and give my testimony. After speaking for some time, I was going to sit down, but they begged me to speak on. Then the presiding elder came in. Seeing me in the pulpit, he peremptorily ordered me to sit down. The preachers protested, while my peace flowed like a river. I assured him I would be through in a moment, and I hurried out to my holiness meeting.

Several preachers said, "We have not believed in the blessing, but that Salvationist has it, else instead of keeping calm, he would have taken offense." They came to our holiness meeting and knelt at the mercy seat for the blessing. One of them received the cleansing and became a witness to the blessing and a flaming evangelist in that region.

I am not by nature calm and peaceful. Quite the contrary. It was supernatural. "The fruit of the Spirit is love, joy, peace, patience, kindness, goodness, faithfulness, gentleness, self-control" (Galatians 5:22-23). The blessing is given to cleanse and empower the soul and produce this heavenly fruit in earth's harsh climate.

*GS, 2*

## What We Need Evermore

*We are witnesses to these things, and so is the Holy Spirit, whom God has given to those who obey him.* (Acts 5:32)

The Holy Spirit does not concentrate our attention upon His own Person and work, but upon Jesus and His work and sacrifice for us. He does not glorify Himself. He points us to Jesus, to glorify Him who humbled Himself unto the shameful and agonizing death of the cross, to make us to see Him in all His beauty, to knit our hearts to Him in faith and love, conform us to His image, and fit us for His work.

What we need evermore, in every place, at all times—in prosperity and adversity, in comfort and distress, in victory and defeat, in deliverance and temptation, in life and in death—what we need and shall ever need, is to see Jesus and to walk in His footsteps, "*who committed no sin, nor was deceit found in His mouth*"; who, when He was reviled, did not revile in return; when He suffered, He did not threaten, but committed *Himself* to Him who judges righteously" (1 Peter 2:22-23, NKJV).

And the Holy Guest delights to help us do so. To those, and those only, who obey Jesus is this Holy Guest given (Acts 5:32). And He is given that He may abide as Comforter, Counselor, Helper, and Friend.

*GS, 3*

# The Chained Ambassador

*I am an ambassador in chains.* (Ephesians 6:20)

My soul was stirred recently by Paul's appeal for the prayers of the church, in which he declares himself "an ambassador in chains" (Ephesians 6:20).

An ambassador represents one government to another. The dignity and authority of a country are behind him or her, and any injury or indignity to the ambassador is an injury and indignity to that country.

Now Paul was an ambassador of heaven, representing Jesus Christ. But instead of being respected and honored, he was thrust into prison and chained between two ignorant, and probably brutal, Roman soldiers.

What stirs me are his quenchless zeal and the work he did in the circumstances. Most Christians would have considered their work done, or at least broken off. But Paul, from his prison and chains, sent forth letters that have blessed the world, and will bless it to the end of time. He also taught us that there is a ministry of prayer, as well as of more active work. We live in an age of restless work and rush and excitement, and we need to learn this lesson.

Let no one called of God imagine that this lesson of the chained ambassador is for those who are free to go. It is not. It is only for those who are in chains.

*HH, 13*

## The Content Ambassador

*I have learned to be content whatever the circumstances.*
(Philippians 4:11, NIV)

Paul was the most active of all the apostles—"in labours more abundant" (2 Corinthians 11:23, KJV). But as he was set to be the chief exponent of the doctrines of the gospel, so he was set to be the chief exponent of its saving and sanctifying power under trying conditions.

It is difficult—if not impossible—to conceive of a trial to which Paul was not subjected, from being worshiped as a god to being whipped and stoned. But he declared that none of these things moved him. He had learned in whatsoever state he was to be content (Philippians 4:11). He did not murmur, but kept on his way, trusting in the love of Jesus, and through faith in Him, becoming more than conqueror.

It will be well for us all to learn the lessons of Paul's imprisonment. Doubly important that those who are sick or recovering learn them. We get impatient, are tempted to murmur and repine, and imagine we can do nothing. But God may possibly use us more widely in prayer and praise, if we will believe and rejoice and watch and pray in the Holy Spirit, than at the head of a battalion of soldiers. We should watch unto prayer for those who are at work and for those in need of salvation.

*HH, 13*

## The Unsung Ambassador

*Godliness with contentment is great gain.* (1 Timothy 6:6)

If you are hopelessly sick, you are chained. If you are shut in by family cares and claims, you are chained. But remember Paul's chains, and take courage.

If we really long to see God's glory and souls saved rather than to have a good time, why should we not be content to lie on a sickbed, or stand by a loom and pray, as well as to stand on a platform and preach?

The platform man or woman sees the work and its fruit. Yet the certainty that the prayer warrior is being used by God may be as great as or greater than that of one who sees with the eye. Many a revival has had its secret source in the closet of some poor washerwoman or blacksmith who prayed in the Holy Spirit. The person on the platform gets glory on earth, but it may be that the neglected, chained ambassador will march by the King's side, while the preacher comes on behind.

God did not choose to loose Paul. Yet Paul did not grumble, or fall into despair. He prayed and rejoiced and believed. He wrote to the struggling churches and the weak converts he had left behind, wept over them, and prayed for them night and day. In so doing, he moved God to bless multitudes of whom he never even dreamed.

*HH, 13*

## The Convalescing Ambassador

*Pray for us, too, that God may open a door for our message, so that we may proclaim the mystery of Christ, for which I am in chains.* (Colossians 4:3, NIV)

For eighteen months I was laid aside with an injury. God put His chain on me, and I had to learn the lessons of passive ministry—prayer and praise and patience—or lose faith altogether. But I did not lose faith. He helped me to nestle down into His will. I watched reports of the salvation war, studied the needs of some parts of the world, and prayed on until I knew God heard and answered. And my heart was made as glad as though I had been in the thick of the fight.

During that time, my heart ached and burned for God to send salvation to a certain country. I poured out my heart to God, and I knew He heard and would yet do great things there. Shortly after this, I learned of dreadful persecutions and the banishment of many earnest Christians to this country, and while I was greatly grieved at their sufferings, yet I thanked God that He was taking the light of His glorious salvation into that loveless, needy land.

"God does not see as humans see" (1 Samuel 16:7, GW). He looks at the heart and marks for future glory and boundless reward all those who cry and sigh for His honor and the salvation of others.

*HH,* 13

## Don't Argue

*The Lord's servant must not be quarrelsome.*
(2 Timothy 2:24)

Some years ago, in Boston, I attended an "all night of prayer." Of all the many excellent things said that night, only one burned itself into my memory, never to be forgotten. Just before the meeting closed, Commissioner James Dowdle said, "Remember, if you want to retain a clean heart, don't argue!"

There were twenty years of practical holiness behind that advice, and it fell on my ears like the voice of God.

In writing to young Timothy, Paul sought to fully instruct him in the truth so that, on the one hand, Timothy might escape all the snares of the devil and walk in holy triumph; and on the other hand, he might be "thoroughly equipped" (2 Timothy 3:17, NIV) to instruct and train others. "Remind them of these things, and charge them before God not to quarrel about words, which does no good, but only ruins the hearers" (2 Timothy 2:14). Again, he says, "Have nothing to do with stupid and senseless controversies; you know that they breed quarrels. And the Lord's servant must not be quarrelsome but kindly to everyone, an apt teacher, patient, correcting opponents with gentleness" (2 Timothy 2:23-25, NRSV).

It takes fire to kindle fire, and it takes love to kindle love. Cold logic will not make anyone love Jesus.

*HH, 15*

## The Bond of Peace

*Keep the unity of the Spirit in the bond of peace.*
(Ephesians 4:3, KJV)

Among the luxurious and licentious nobility of France, the Marquis de Renty attained a purity of faith, a simplicity of life and character, and a cloudless communion with God that proved a blessing, in his own age and to succeeding generations.

In reading his life a few years ago, I was struck with his humility, his sympathy for the poor, his fervor in prayer and praise, and his constant hungering and thirsting after all the fullness of God. But what impressed me as much as, or more than, all the rest was the way he avoided all argument. Whenever matters of business or religion were discussed, he thought carefully, then expressed his views and the reasons upon which he based them, clearly, fully, and quietly. However heated the discussion, he declined to be drawn into it. His quiet, peaceful manner, added to his clear statements, gave great force to his counsels.

In this the Marquis seems to me to have been closely patterned after "the meekness and gentleness of Christ" (2 Corinthians 10:1), and his example has encouraged me to follow a like course, and so "keep the unity of the Spirit in the bond of peace" (Ephesians 4:3, KJV), when otherwise I would have been led into wranglings and disputes which would have clouded my soul and destroyed my peace.

*HH, 15*

## When Others Oppose You

*Be kind to everyone.* (2 Timothy 2:24, NLT)

All through the Gospels, I fail to find Jesus engaged in argument, and His example is of infinite importance to us.

By nature we are proud and vain, ready to stoutly resist those who oppose either us or our principles. Our object at once is to subdue them—whether by force of argument or of arms. We are impatient of contradiction and hasty to judge others' motives and condemn all who disagree with us. And then we are apt to call our haste and impatience "zeal for the truth" when, in fact, it is often a hotheaded, unkind zeal for our own way of thinking.

But let us who have become "partakers of the divine nature" (2 Peter 1:4) see to it that this root of the carnal nature is destroyed. When others oppose us, let us not revile nor condemn, but lovingly instruct them—not with an air of superiority, but with meekness, solemnly remembering that "a servant of the Lord must not quarrel but be gentle to all, able to teach, patient" (2 Timothy 2:24, NKJV).

I am often strongly tempted to strive for the last word. But God blesses me most when I commit the matter into His hands, and by so doing I most often win my adversary.

*HH,* 15

## The Truth That Saves the Soul

*The kingdom of heaven is like treasure hidden in a field.*
(Matthew 13:44)

The truth that saves the soul is not picked up as we would pick up pebbles along the beach, but only after diligent search and much digging. "If you call out for insight and raise your voice for understanding, if you seek it like silver and search for it as for hidden treasures, then you will understand the fear of the LORD and find the knowledge of God" (Proverbs 2:3-5). Those who seek the truth will need much prayer, self-examination, and self-denial. They must listen diligently for God's voice. They must watch lest they fall into sin and forgetfulness, and must meditate in the truth of God day and night.

Men and women who are walking embodiments of the truth have not become so without effort. They have longed for it more than for their necessary food. They have sacrificed all for it. When they have fallen, they have risen again, and when defeated, they have not yielded to discouragement, but with more watchfulness and greater earnestness have renewed their efforts. Wealth, ease, reputation, pleasure, everything the world holds has been counted as dung and dross, and just at that point where truth took precedence over all creation, they found it— the truth that saves the soul, that satisfies the heart, that brings fellowship with God and joy unutterable and perfect peace.

*HH, 16*

## Surpassing Greatness

*I consider everything a loss compared to the*
*surpassing greatness of knowing Christ Jesus my Lord.*
(Philippians 3:8, NIV 1984)

This is an age of specialists. One learned professor will give fourteen hours a day for forty years to studying fishes, another to birds, another to bugs, and yet another to old bones. Another, more ambitious, devotes her life to the study of history, the rise and fall of nations, and yet another to astronomy, the origin and history of worlds. But to know Jesus Christ is infinitely better, for He it was that made the worlds, and "without him nothing was made that has been made" (John 1:3, NIV). To know Jesus Christ is the first and best of all knowledge.

Indeed, in the knowledge of Jesus is hidden the germ of all knowledge, for in Him "are hidden all the treasures of wisdom and knowledge" (Colossians 2:3). Am I eager for learning and knowledge? Let me then constantly seek to know Him, and in due time, in this world or in the next, I shall know all that is of value for me to know.

O Jesus, Savior, how I bless You that You sought me and revealed Yourself to me, and made me to know You, and ravished my heart and humbled my pride with the joy and love and glory that that best of all knowledge brings!

*HTH, 10*

## Letting the Truth Slip

*Do not turn away from the words of my mouth.*
(Proverbs 4:5)

Just as it costs effort to find the truth, so it requires watching to keep it. "Riches have wings,"[23] and, if unguarded, flee away. So with truth. It will slip away if not earnestly heeded. "Buy the truth and do not sell it" (Proverbs 23:23, NIV). It usually slips away little by little. It is lost as leaking water is lost—not all at once, but by degrees.

Here is a man who was once full of the truth. He loved his enemies and prayed for them. But he neglected that truth, and it slipped away, and instead of love for his enemies have come bitterness and sharpness. Another once believed that "women who profess to worship God" should "dress modestly, with decency and propriety" (1 Timothy 2:9-10, NIV). But little by little, she let the truth of God slip. Now, instead of neat, respectable apparel, she is decked out in gaudy and costly attire, but she has lost the "imperishable beauty of a gentle and quiet spirit, which in God's sight is very precious" (1 Peter 3:4).

But what shall these people do? Let them repent, and do their first works over again (Revelation 2:5). Let them dig for truth again as people dig for gold, and they will find it again. God "rewards those who seek him" (Hebrews 11:6).

*HH, 16*

## Hold the Truth Fast

*Teach me your way, O Lord, that I may walk in your truth.* (Psalm 86:11)

It is hard, slow work to dig for truth as for gold. But it is sure work. "Seek, and you will find" (Luke 11:9). And your soul's eternal destiny depends upon it. Then how shall a person avoid slipping?

1. "Observe and seek out all the commandments of the Lord your God" (1 Chronicles 28:8).

2. "Meditate on it day and night." For what? "That you may be careful to do" *some* of the things "written in it"? No! "All that is written in it" (Joshua 1:8). If you want to hold the truth fast and not let it slip, you must read and reread the Bible. You must constantly refresh your mind with its truths, just as the diligent student refreshes his mind by reviewing his textbooks, as the lawyer studies her law books.

3. "Do not quench the Spirit" (1 Thessalonians 5:19). Jesus calls the Holy Spirit "the Spirit of truth" (John 14:17; 15:26; 16:13). Therefore, if you do not wish the truth to slip, ask Him to abide with you. Delight yourself in Him. Live in Him. Yield yourself to Him. Consider Him your Friend, your Guide, your Teacher, your Comforter. "Do not grieve the Holy Spirit of God, by whom you were sealed for the day of redemption" (Ephesians 4:30).

*HH, 16*

## God's Recipe for Holy People

*Your words became to me a joy and the delight of my heart.* (Jeremiah 15:16)

A young rabbi asked his old uncle if he might not study Greek philosophy. The old rabbi quoted Joshua 1:8: "This Book of the Law shall not depart from your mouth, but you shall meditate on it day and night." Then he said, "Find an hour that is neither day nor night; in that hour you may study Greek philosophy."

The "blessed one" David speaks of is not only one who "does not walk in step with the wicked or stand in the way that sinners take or sit in the company of mockers, but"—notice—one "whose delight is in the law of the LORD, and who meditates on his law day and night" (Psalm 1:1-2, NIV).

The Bible is God's recipe book for making holy people. You must follow the recipe exactly if you want to be like Christ. The Bible is God's guidebook to show the way to heaven. You must follow its directions if you are ever to get there. The Bible is God's medical book, to diagnose soul-sickness. You must diligently consider its methods of cure if you want soul-health.

Jesus said, "One does not live by bread alone, but by every word that comes from the mouth of God" (Matthew 4:4, NRSV). And again He said, "The words that I have spoken to you are spirit and life" (John 6:63).

*HH, 16*

## Obstacles to Restoration

*I will forgive them for all the times they turned away from me and sinned. I will cleanse them.* (Ezekiel 37:23, GW)

When a person falls into sin, the difficulty in the way of restoration is in that person, not in the Lord. It is difficult for us to trust one whom we have wronged, doubly so when that one has been a tender, loving friend. See the case of Joseph's brethren. They grievously wronged him by selling him into Egypt, and when they were in his power, they were filled with fear. But he assured them of his goodwill (Genesis 45:5), and finally won their confidence by his kindness. This confidence was apparently perfect until the death of Jacob, their father, and then all their old fears revived. But once again Joseph reassured them (Genesis 50:19-20).

If you have fallen into sin, see your situation in this simple story. By your sin you have done violence to your own sense of justice, and now it is next to impossible for you to trust your grievously wronged Brother, Jesus. And yet His tender heart is breaking over your distrust. Your first step is to renew your consecration to the Lord, confessing your sins. Then your second and only step is to cry out with Job, "Though he slay me, yet will I trust in him" (Job 13:15, KJV), and this ground you must steadfastly hold, till the witness comes of your acceptance.

*HH, 17*

## Don't Seek the Old Experience

*Return to the LORD your God, for he is gracious and merciful.* (Joel 2:13)

Many people, in returning to God, refuse to believe because they do not have that same old experience they had when they were first saved. God says, "I will lead the blind in a way that they do not know, in paths that they have not known I will guide them" (Isaiah 42:16). In seeking the old experience, you refuse to acknowledge that you are blind and insist upon going in familiar paths. In other words, you want to walk by sight and not by faith.

You must yield yourself to the Holy Spirit, and He will surely lead you into the Promised Land. Seek simply to be right with God. Do whatever He tells you to do. Trust Him, love Him, and He Himself will come to you, for Jesus "became to us . . . sanctification" (1 Corinthians 1:30). It is not a blessing you need, but the Blesser.

A sister who had wandered for ten years was reclaimed and filled with the Holy Spirit. She said, "Put your all on the altar, and leave it there; do not take it back, and God's fire will surely come and consume the offering."

Do it, do it! God will surely come if you can wait; and you can wait, if you mean business for eternity.

*HH, 17*

## No Higher Service

*Righteousness exalts a nation, but sin is a disgrace to any people.* (Proverbs 14:34, HCSB)

It is righteousness that exalts a nation, and the spirit of Christ that ensures peace and goodwill on earth. Ten righteous people could have saved Sodom, but for lack of them the city was destroyed. Righteous men, just women, people of loving-kindness and goodwill, whose hearts are pure, are more surely the bulwarks of nations than battleships and trained armies.

I honor the police officer and soldier who maintain law and order and uphold the rights of all to life and liberty and the lawful pursuits of happiness. But how immeasurably increased would be their task if God's ministers and heralds of the gospel were to cease saving souls and training them in truth and righteousness! C. H. Spurgeon is reported to have said, "Take The Salvation Army out of London and you will have to increase its police force by seven thousand."

We must "hold fast our confession" (Hebrews 4:14). We serve our country and all humankind by doing so. An evil man, a false woman, a person of uncontrolled passion and appetite is a menace to all, especially in a time of crisis. We can find no higher service than that of saving men and women from all sin and getting them filled with the Holy Spirit and the fire of truth and love.

*RLP, 17*

## Persevering, Prevailing Knee-Work

*Pray in the Spirit on all occasions with all kinds of prayers and requests.* (Ephesians 6:18, NIV)

All great soul-winners have been people of much and mighty prayer, and all great revivals have been preceded and carried out by persevering, prevailing knee-work in the closet.

Before Jesus began His ministry, He spent forty days and nights in secret prayer and fasting (Matthew 4:1-4). Pentecost was preceded by ten days of prayer and heart-searching. On that day three thousand were converted, and the disciples continued in prayer until, on another day, five thousand were converted (Acts 2:4-6, 37-41; 4:4). Paul prayed without ceasing. Day and night his prayers and pleadings and intercessions went up to God (Acts 16:25; Philippians 1:3-11; Colossians 1:3, 9-11).

Luther used to pray three hours a day, and he broke the spell of ages and set captive nations free. John Knox spent nights in prayer, crying to God, "Give me Scotland, or I die!" And God gave him Scotland. Over and over again, John Wesley, in his journals—which, for lively interest, are next to the Acts of the Apostles—tells us of half, and whole, nights of prayer, in which God drew near and blessed people beyond expectation. The night before Jonathan Edwards preached the wonderful sermon that started the revival which convulsed New England, he and some others spent the night in prayer.

Oh, my Lord, raise up some praying people!

*HH, 18*

## Prayer Is the Key

*The earnest prayer of a righteous person has great power.*
(James 5:16, NLT)

When I went to England, I determined, if possible, to find out the secret of Bramwell Booth's mighty holiness meetings. "For one thing," said an officer, "Mr. Bramwell used to conduct young men's meetings and ask each saved young fellow to spend five minutes alone with God every day, wherever they could get it, praying for those Friday night meetings. One who was employed in a large warehouse had to squeeze himself into a great wicker packing-case to get a chance to pray for five minutes."

God has not changed. He waits to do the will of praying men and women.

Charles Finney tells of a church in which there was a continuous revival for thirteen years. When the revival stopped, everybody feared and questioned why, till one day a tearful man arose and told how for thirteen years he had prayed every Saturday night till after midnight for God to glorify Himself and save the people. But two weeks before, he had stopped this praying, and then the revival stopped. If God will answer prayer like that, what a tremendous responsibility rests on us all to pray! Let us come boldly to the throne of grace and ask largely, that our joy may be full (Hebrews 4:16; John 16:24)!

*HH, 18*

## Conformity to the Divine Nature

*God disciplines us for our own good so that we can become holy like him.* (Hebrews 12:10, GW)

Holiness does not consist in perfection of intellect or perfection of conduct, but in complete deliverance from the sinful nature. Righteousness is conformity to the divine law, but holiness is conformity to the divine nature. Three things testify to this experience:

1. The Scriptures, which tell us that God chastens us "for our good, that we may share his holiness" (Hebrews 12:10). He has "granted to us his precious and very great promises, so that through them you may become partakers of the divine nature, having escaped from the corruption that is in the world because of sinful desire" (2 Peter 1:4).

2. The testimony of holy men and women, who declare that God has brought them into this glorious experience.

3. The hunger and thirst of our own regenerate hearts. If these desires—to be like God and to have His love and holiness so fill our hearts as to cast out every sinful thought—are begotten in us by the Spirit of God, then they may be considered proof that holiness is possible.

It is the gift of God and the heritage of every soul that is born again, an inheritance into which we can enter at once by hearty consecration and childlike faith.

*HTH, 3*

## A Clean Heart

*Create in me a clean heart, O God.* (Psalm 51:10)

A man more than eighty years old once said, "I believe in holiness, but I believe we grow into it gradually."

He was asked if, after sixty years of Christian experience, he felt any nearer to a clean heart than when he first believed. He honestly confessed that he did not. He was asked next if he thought sixty years long enough to prove the growth theory, if it were true. He thought it was, and so was asked to come forward and seek the blessing at once.

He did not win through that night. But the next night he had scarcely knelt five minutes before he stood up, tears running down his cheeks, his face glowing with heaven's light, and cried, "As far as the east is from the west, so far has He removed my transgressions from me" (Psalm 103:12, NKJV).

When we are converted, our sins are forgiven. We receive the witness of adoption into God's own family. But before we go very far, we find the fruit of the Spirit all mixed up with the works of the flesh. This will be done away with when we get a clean heart, and it will take a second work of grace, preceded by wholehearted consecration and unwavering faith, to get it.

*HH, 2*

## Resistance and Surrender

*I was not disobedient to the heavenly vision.* (Acts 26:19)

For five years, I resisted the Lord's call to preach. The job looked small to me and beneath the dignity of a full-orbed man. But at last I surrendered, and one day, when in an agony of desire for purity of heart and the blessing of the Holy Spirit, God graciously sanctified me. A great passion for the saving and the sanctifying of others burned within me.

About that time a multimillionaire had built a fine church in my native state, and one day I received a call to the pastorate there. I was elated. I felt that God Himself had opened a great door of opportunity and usefulness.

While still considering this call, I traveled to a holiness convention. There, God laid His hand upon me, and I knew that I was not to accept the call to that church. I found that that which I had least esteemed, had most despised, was the work to which God called me. On my knees I talked it over with the Lord as I would with an earthly friend, and by faith into evangelistic work I plunged. It has not been an easy job. But He has called me to share His cross, to endure hardness as a good soldier, and to attend strictly to the work He has given me to do.

*AP, 8*

## A Present Help in Trouble

*God is our refuge and strength, a very present help in trouble.* (Psalm 46:1)

In all the little vexatious trials and delays of our everyday, plodding life, if we trust and keep on rejoicing right through all that bothers us, we will find God at work for us, for He is a "present help in trouble" (Psalm 46:1)—all trouble—to those who keep their minds stayed on Him.

The Lord once allowed me to pass through a series of little troubles just calculated to annoy me to the uttermost. But while I was waiting on Him in prayer, He showed me that if I had more confidence in Him in my difficulties, I would keep on rejoicing, and so get blessings out of my trials, as Samson got honey out of the carcass of the lion he slew. Bless His holy name! I did rejoice, and one trial after the other vanished away, and only the sweetness of my Lord's presence and blessing remained.

Does not God do all this to hide pride from us, to humble us, and make us see that our character before Him is of more consequence than our service to Him, to teach us to walk by faith and not by sight, and to encourage us to trust and be at peace?

*HH, 21*

JULY 11

## Load and Fire

*I commend you to God and to the word of his grace, which is able to build you up and to give you the inheritance among all those who are sanctified.* (Acts 20:32)

One day, a few months after I got the blessing of holiness, I felt most gloomy. I knew beyond doubt that I had a clean heart, but somehow I felt I couldn't properly teach others how to get it.

That morning I met a certain brother who gets more people sanctified than anyone I know, and I asked him, "How shall I teach holiness?" His reply was, "Load and fire, load and fire."

Light broke in on me at once. I saw that it was my business to pray and study my Bible and talk with those who had the blessing, until I got myself so loaded that it would almost talk itself, and then fire away as best I could, and that it was God's business to make the people receive the truth and become holy.

That was on Saturday. The next day, I went to my people loaded with truth, backed by love and faith, and I fired as hard and straight as I knew how, and twenty people sought holiness. I had never seen anything like that before in my life, but I have seen it many times since. From then till now I have attended strictly to my part of the business, and trusted God to do His part.

*HH, 22*

## The Devil's Lies

*Our God is a consuming fire.* (Hebrews 12:29)

Satan will tell you that your disposition is so peculiar, your circumstances so disagreeable, that you cannot hope to be holy. That is a lie. Don't believe it.

Your disposition may be peculiar, but God will take all the sin out of it. Where it is impatient and jealous, envious and lustful, it will be good and patient, loving and generous, humble and chaste. A quick-tempered girl got sanctified and became gentle like Jesus. A proud, ambitious young fellow got a clean heart and was made humble and self-sacrificing.

Holiness will also make you master of your circumstances instead of their servant. The other day, I wanted a hole in the hard rubber cap of my fountain pen, so I heated a pin and burned the hole right through. Holiness will make you hot enough to burn through your circumstances. "Our God is a consuming fire" (Hebrews 12:29), and holiness is God in you.

Satan may tell you that you have failed so often that God will not give you the blessing. Peter failed often, even cursed and swore that he did not know Jesus. But within a few weeks of that time Peter got the blessing, and we find him winning three thousand souls in a single day.

To get the blessing, you must resist the devil, and believe that it is for you.

*WH, 3*

## The Word Is Near You

*"The word is near you, in your mouth and in your heart"*
*(that is, the word of faith that we proclaim).* (Romans 10:8)

The Lord has led me to continually emphasize three points regarding holiness.

First, we cannot make ourselves holy. No amount of good works can take out the roots of pride, lust, hatred, strife, and the like, and in their stead put perfect love, peace, faith, and self-control. Truly, millions who have labored to purify themselves, only to fail, can testify, "It is 'not a result of works, so that no one may boast'" (Ephesians 2:9).

Second, the blessing is received by faith. A poor woman wanted some grapes from the king's garden for her sick boy. She met the king's daughter and offered to buy the grapes. The daughter said, "My father is a king; he does not sell his grapes." Then she led the poor woman to the king and told him her story, and he gave her as many as she wanted. Our God is King of kings. He will not sell His holiness and grace, but He will give them to all who ask in faith.

Third, the blessing is to be received by faith NOW. The person who expects to get it by works will always have something more to do before he or she can claim the blessing. But the humble soul, who expects to get it by faith, sees that it is a gift and trusts and receives it at once.

*HH, 22*

## Another Chance for You

*I know the thoughts that I think toward you,*
*saith the LORD, thoughts of peace, and not of evil.*
(Jeremiah 29:11, KJV)

I remember a time, years ago but after I was sanctified, when I failed my Lord. It was not a sin of commission, but one of omission. I felt God had given me a chance that I had let slip by, and that I never could be the mighty man of faith and obedience I might have been had I been true. Satan taunted me and accused me till life became an intolerable burden.

But God drew me up out of that horrible pit with these words: "Hold it for certain that all such thoughts as create disquiet proceed not from God, who is the Prince of Peace, but proceed either from the devil, or from self-love, or from the good opinion we hold of ourselves."[24]

Quick as thought, I saw it. God's thoughts are "thoughts of peace, and not of evil" (Jeremiah 29:11, KJV). Then I saw that the devil was deceiving me, and instantly I was free. This can be your experience.

Do not seek to do some great thing, but study your Bible, pray, talk often and much with God, asking Him to open your understanding, and you will have another chance of showing your love for Him and of blessing others.

*HH, 23*

## Birds of Prey

*When birds of prey came down on the carcasses, Abram drove them away.* (Genesis 15:11)

We read in Genesis 15 that Abraham offered a sacrifice to God. While he was waiting for the witness of God's acceptance, birds of prey came to snatch away the sacrifice. But Abraham drove them away until evening, and then the fire of God consumed the offering.

Just so, if you would be sanctified, you must make an unreserved offering of yourself. This act must be real, not imaginary—a real transfer of self, with all hopes, plans, property, cares, joys, reputation, "in an everlasting covenant that will never be forgotten" (Jeremiah 50:5). Then you must, like Abraham, patiently, expectantly wait for God to witness that you are accepted.

Now, during this waiting, the devil will send his birds of prey to snatch away the offering. "You ought to feel different if you have consecrated yourself." Remember, that is the devil's bird of prey—drive it away. "Maybe your consecration is not complete; go over it again and be sure." Drive it away. "But you do not have the deep and powerful emotions that others claim." Drive it away.

I tell you, everything contrary to present faith is a bird of prey, and you must resolutely drive it away. Quit reasoning with the devil! "Demolish arguments and every pretension that sets itself up against the knowledge of God" (2 Corinthians 10:5, NIV), and trust.

*HH, 24*

## Act Out Your Faith

*See if I don't open up heaven itself to you and*
*pour out blessings beyond your wildest dreams.*
(Malachi 3:10, *The Message*)

The very same Jesus who saved you can purge your heart
of all unholy conditions by the work of the Holy Spirit, as
fire purges gold of dross. Give yourself up fully to God,
ask for it, believe for it, and if it does not come at once,
patiently and expectantly wait for it.

Act out your faith, regardless of your feelings, and a
heaven of love, joy, peace, and patience will soon fill your
poor heart. Your business is to wait on God, and then to
trust and obey. It is His business to cleanse you, to fill you
with the Spirit and with joy.

Claim the promise. Feed on the Word of God. Wait
on Him in believing, expectant prayer. Hold on this way,
resisting the devil, firm in your faith, encouraging your
own heart with the promises of God, and God will say,
"This soul has come to stay." He will open the windows of
heaven and pour out a blessing so great, "there shall not
be room enough to receive it" (Malachi 3:10, KJV). Then
down into your heart will come the Comforter, and up
from the deepest center of your soul will spring the arte-
sian well of living waters of holy love and praise.

*HTH, 3*

## Get Off the Fence

*I have told the glad news of deliverance in the great congregation; behold, I have not restrained my lips, as you know, O LORD.* (Psalm 40:9)

A lady said to me, "I have always hesitated to say, 'The Lord sanctifies me wholly.' I now see that I secretly desired a bridge behind me, so that I might escape back from my position. If I profess sanctification, I must be careful lest I bring myself into disrepute. But if I do not profess it, I can do questionable things and then shield myself by saying, 'I do not profess to be perfect.'"

Be careful not to become a religious fence-rider, for all who are astride the fence are really on the devil's side. "Whoever is not with me is against me" (Matthew 12:30). Get over on God's side, by a definite profession of your faith.

The devil will say, "You had better not say anything about this, till you find out whether you will be able to keep it." Drive that thought away quickly. You are not to "keep the blessing" at all; you are to boldly assert your faith in the Blesser, and He will keep you.

You must assert that you believe God to be honest, and He has promised that "whatever you ask in prayer, believe that you have received it, and it will be yours" (Mark 11:24). Count God faithful.

*HH, 24*

## Try Again and Again

*Keep on seeking, and you will find.* (Luke 11:9, NLT)

Wesley declared that he was persuaded, from his observations, that people usually lose the blessing several times before they learn the secret of keeping it. So if you have lost the blessing, and are tormented by the old enemy of souls—the devil—with the thought that you can never get and keep it, let me urge you to try again and again.

You prove your real desire and purpose to be holy, not by giving up in the presence of defeat, but by rising from ten thousand falls, and going at it again with renewed faith and consecration. If you do this, you shall surely win the prize, and be able to keep it in the end.

The promise is: "Seek, and you will find." "But how long shall I seek?" Seek till you find! "But suppose I lose it?" Seek again till you find it. God will surprise you someday by pouring out such a fullness of His Spirit upon you that all your uncertainty will vanish forever, and you will never fall again.

Look up and trust Jesus, and keep on seeking, remembering that God's delays are not denials. Jesus is your Joshua to lead you into the Promised Land, and He can cast down all your foes before you.

*HH, 25*

## Use All Diligence

*For this very cause [add] on your part all diligence.*
(2 Peter 1:5, asv)

One day, I followed an old divinity school chum onto the train to say good-bye, perhaps forever. He looked up and said, "Sam, give me a text that will do for a life motto."

Instantly I lifted my heart to God for light. Now, if you want to keep the blessing, you must constantly lift your heart to God for light, not only in the crises of life, but in all its details. By practice, you can get into such a habit of this that it will become as natural for you as breathing, and as important to your spiritual life as breathing is to your natural life. Keep within whispering distance of God always. That morning on the train, the first chapter of 2 Peter came immediately to my mind—not simply as a motto, but as a plain rule laid down by the Holy Spirit.

The apostle speaks of being made "partakers of the divine nature, having escaped from the corruption that is in the world because of sinful desire" (2 Peter 1:4). That is holiness, to escape our hearts' corruption and receive the divine nature. And in verse 5 the apostle urges "all diligence" (asv). Then you may not only keep the blessing and never fall, but also prove fruitful in the knowledge of God.

*HH, 25*

# Encourage Yourself in the Lord

*David encouraged himself in the LORD.* (1 Samuel 30:6, KJV)

The devil is an old hand at overthrowing souls, but remember that Jesus is God from everlasting to everlasting, and He has put all wisdom and power at our disposal. Are you downhearted and afraid? Pluck up courage, and learn from the example of King David, who had a good deal more trouble than we do.

David had to flee from Saul and dwell in Philistia. Then the Philistines went to war against Saul, and David went too. But they feared David might turn against them in the hour of battle, so they sent him home. There David and his men found that some enemies had burned their village, and had carried off their goods, their wives, and their little ones. The men were mad with grief and determined to stone David. Certainly there was reason for fear. But "David encouraged himself in the LORD" (KJV). Read the story for yourself, and see how wonderfully God helped him reclaim everything (1 Samuel 30).

As for me, I am determined to be of good courage. God has been better to me than all my fears, and He has proved stronger than all my foes, and enabled me, by His power and infinite love and goodness, to walk in holiness before Him for many years.

*HH, 25*

## You Will Need Courage

*Fear not, for I am with you.* (Genesis 26:24)

You must have courage to keep the blessing of holiness. The devil will roar like a lion. The world will frown upon you, and maybe club you, and possibly kill you. Your friends will pity you, or curse you, and at times your own flesh may cry out against you. Then you will need courage.

They told me I would land in a bog of fanaticism or in the poorhouse. They said I would utterly ruin my health, and become an invalid, a torment to myself and a burden to my friends. The very bishop whose book on holiness had stirred my soul, after I got the blessing, urged me to say very little about it, as it would cause much division and trouble. (I afterward learned that he had lost the blessing.) The devil sorely tempted me, and even stirred up a man to nearly knock my brains out.

I found it took courage to keep this "pearl of great price." And God says, "Have I not commanded you? Be strong and courageous" (Joshua 1:9). And He adds, as a sufficient reason why we should not fear, "for I am with you" (Genesis 26:24). If He is with me, why should I be afraid? And why should you?

*HH, 25*

## The God Who Answers by Fire

*The God who answers by fire, he is God.* (1 Kings 18:24)

Once we have yielded ourselves to God—our very inmost selves, our minds and wills, our tongues, our hands and feet, our reputations, our doubts and fears, our disposition to pity ourselves and repine when He tests our consecration—when we have really done this and taken our hands off, as Elijah placed his bullock on the altar and took his hands off, then we must wait on God and cry to Him with a humble, yet bold, persistent faith till He blesses us with the Holy Spirit and fire. He promised it, and He will do it, but we must expect it, pray for it, and if it delays, wait for it.

One man fell on his knees, saying, "Lord, I will not get up from here till You baptize me with the Holy Spirit!" God saw He had a man on His hands who meant business, and He there and then anointed him with the Holy Spirit.

Two Salvation Army officers whom I know found that "the vision tarried," so they spent all their spare time for three weeks crying to God to fill them with the Spirit. They did not get discouraged; they held on to God with a desperate faith. And they got their heart's desire. "All Heaven is free plunder to faith," says a friend of mine.

*HH, 26*

## God Loves to Be Compelled

*Be it done for you as you desire.* (Matthew 15:28)

God *loves* to be compelled. God *will* be compelled by persistent prayer and faith. I imagine God is often grieved and disappointed and angry with us, as the prophet was with the king who struck the ground three times rather than five or six (2 Kings 13:18-19), because we ask so little.

The woman who came to Jesus to have the devil cast out of her daughter puts most Christians to shame. She would not be turned away. At first, Jesus answered her not a word, and so He often treats us today. We pray and get no answer. God is silent. Then Jesus rebuffed her. That would have been enough to make blaspheming skeptics of most modern folks. Not so with her. Her desperate faith grew sublime. At last, Jesus declared, "It is not right to take the children's bread and throw it to the dogs."

Then the woman's faith compelled Him, for she said, "Yes, Lord, yet even the dogs eat the crumbs that fall from their masters' table."

She was willing to receive the dogs' portion. Oh, how her faith triumphed, and Jesus, amazed, said, "Great is your faith! Be it done for you as you desire" (Matthew 15:21-28). Jesus meant to bless her all the time, if her faith would hold out. And so He means to bless you.

*HH, 26*

## Pleasure-Seekers and Misery-Hunters

*For the kingdom of God is not a matter of eating and drinking but of righteousness and peace and joy in the Holy Spirit.* (Romans 14:17)

There are two classes of people who profess to consecrate themselves to God but are consecrated to something else entirely.

Pleasure-seekers see that sanctified people are happy, and thinking it is due to what they have given and done, begin to give and to do, never dreaming of the infinite Treasure these sanctified ones have received. The secret of him who wrote, "'The LORD is my portion,' says my soul" (Lamentations 3:24) is hidden from them. So they never find God. They are seeking happiness, not holiness.

Misery-hunters are always seeking something hard to do. Like Baal's priests, they cut themselves—not their bodies, but their minds and souls. They give their goods to feed the poor, they give their bodies to be burned, and yet it profits them nothing (1 Corinthians 13:3). Their religion does not consist in "righteousness and peace and joy in the Holy Spirit" (Romans 14:17), but rather of grit and resolution and misery.

What both classes of people need is a faith that sanctifies (Acts 26:18), that receives all God has to give, and that joyfully gives all back to God—a way that keeps the soul both from Laodicean sloth and ease and from hard, cold Pharisaical bondage, an abounding spiritual life which walks by faith and trusts Jesus to fulfill all the precious promises of His love. *HH, 26*

## Where There Is Victory

*The LORD their God is with them, and the shout of a king is among them.* (Numbers 23:21)

Shouting is the highest expression of faith made perfect. When a sinner comes to God in hearty repentance and surrender and looks to Jesus for salvation, the first expression of that faith will be one of confidence and praise. No doubt, there are many who claim justification who never praise God. But either they are deceived, or their faith is weak and mixed with doubt and fear. When it is perfect, praise will be spontaneous.

And when this saved soul recognizes the absolute claim of God upon every power of his or her being, and comes to God to be made holy, the final expression of the faith that resolutely and perfectly grasps the blessing will be praise.

And when this saved and sanctified soul goes forth to war "against principalities, against powers, against the rulers of the darkness of this age, against spiritual hosts of wickedness in the heavenly places" (Ephesians 6:12, NKJV), in order to rescue the slaves of sin and hell, after weeping and agonizing in prayer to God for an outpouring of the Spirit, in which faith and patience for others are made perfect and victorious, prayer will be transformed into praise, weeping into shouting, and apparent defeat into overwhelming victory!

*HH, 27*

## We Have a Right to Rejoice

*Shout unto God with the voice of triumph.* (Psalm 47:1, KJV)

Many people, in fierce temptation and hellish darkness, have poured out their hearts in prayer and then sunk back in despair. If only they had closed that prayer with thanks, and dared in the name of God to shout, it would have filled hell with confusion, and won a victory.

Many a prayer meeting has failed at the shouting point. Songs were sung, testimonies were given, the Bible was read and explained, sinners were entreated, prayers were poured forth to God, but no one wrestled through to the point where they could and would intelligently praise God for victory, and the battle was lost for want of a shout.

From the moment we are born of God, we have a right to rejoice, and we ought to do it. It is our highest privilege and our most solemn duty. Weeping and fasting and watching and praying and self-denying and cross-bearing and conflict with hell will cease. But praise to God, and hallelujahs "to him who loves us and has freed us from our sins by his blood, and has made us to be a kingdom and priests to serve his God and Father" (Revelation 1:5-6, NIV), shall ring through heaven eternally.

*HH, 27*

## Stir Yourself Up

*Today we have seen that God can speak to us humans.*
(Deuteronomy 5:24, NLT)

God has powerfully spoken to me through the words of Scripture. The first words I remember coming to me with irresistible divine force came when I was seeking the blessing of a clean heart. Although I was hungering and thirsting for the blessing, yet at times a kind of spiritual stupor would come over me and threaten to devour all my holy longings. I was in great distress. To stop seeking, I saw, meant infinite, eternal loss. Yet to continue seemed quite out of the question with such a paralysis of desire and feeling. But one day I read, "There is none who calls on your name, or attempts to take hold of you" (Isaiah 64:7, NRSV).

God spoke to me as unmistakably as He spoke to Moses from the burning bush. I said, "By the grace of God, if nobody else does, I will stir myself up to seek Him, feelings or no feelings."

That was ten years ago, but from then till now, regardless of my feelings, I have sought God. I have not waited to be stirred up, but when necessary I have fasted and prayed and stirred myself up. And whether I have felt any immediate quickening or not, I have laid hold of Him, I have sought Him, and I have found Him.

*HH, 28*

## The Abiding and the Transitory

*I know a man in Christ who . . . was caught up into paradise—whether in the body or out of the body I do not know, God knows—and he heard things that cannot be told.* (2 Corinthians 12:2-4)

There are two experiences mentioned by Paul in 2 Corinthians 12:2-4. One is abiding—the blessed but common, everyday life of the Christian. The other is transitory.

"In Christ" is the abiding experience. We are to live in Christ. Daily, hourly we are to choose Him as our Master, look unto Him, trust Him, obey Him. We draw from Him every gift and grace needed for our soul's life. The supply of all our need is in Him. Our sap, our life, our leaf, and our fruit are from Him. Cut off from Him we wither, we die, but in Him we flourish and have life evermore.

"Caught up into paradise" is the transitory experience. It passes in an hour and may, possibly, never in this life be repeated, any more than was the burning bush experience of Moses, or the "still small voice" experience of Elijah, or the Jabbok experience of Jacob.

The man or woman who has had such an experience will be changed. But let no humble, earnest soul be discouraged because he or she does not constantly live in such rapturous fellowship. These glimpses of heaven, these rapt moments of fellowship are given to confirm faith and fit the soul for the fight and labor that lie ahead.

*LS, 2*

JULY 29

## The Revelation of God's Children

*The creation waits in eager expectation for the children of God to be revealed.* (Romans 8:19, NIV)

I knew a blacksmith who had been a hard, brutal drunkard, but was now "in Christ." One day a farmer brought his mare to have her shod, and with her he brought straps and tackle, for she was so fearful or so savage that no one could shoe her otherwise. But the blacksmith said, "Let me get acquainted with her." He stroked her gently and spoke softly, while she rubbed her soft nose against him, smelled his garments, and got acquainted with him.

The blacksmith was a new creature to her—a kind she had never met, especially in a blacksmith's shop. Everything about him seemed to say, "Fear not." From that day forth he shod that mare without strap or tackle, while she stood in perfect quiet and unconcern. That poor horse had waited all her lifetime to see one of the children of God, and when she saw him she was not afraid.

And the whole earth is waiting for the unveiling, "the revelation of God's sons and daughters" (Romans 8:19, CEB)—waiting for those who live in Christ and in whom Christ lives. When the world is filled with such people, then, and only then, will strikes and wars, bitter rivalries and insane hatreds, and disgusting and hellish evils cease, and the promise and purpose of Christ's coming be fulfilled.

*LS, 2*

# Holy Counting

*I count everything as loss because of the surpassing worth of knowing Christ Jesus my Lord.* (Philippians 3:8)

A young Paul was on the way to Damascus, "breathing threats and murder against the disciples of the Lord" (Acts 9:1), when Jesus met him and won his heart. Paul made an unconditional surrender, and long years afterwards he wrote, "Whatever gain I had, I counted as loss for the sake of Christ" (Philippians 3:7).

Youthful steps shape all future life. Those who do not consecrate themselves in youth are not likely to do so at all. Youth is generous, hopeful, daring, and unentangled. Youth is not held back by prudence and caution. Youth sees visions and is prepared to make sacrifices to realize the vision—to transform it into something tangible.

But age brings cares and infirmities, weariness and insomnia, deferred hopes and unfulfilled ambitions. Age is prudent, cautious, and often timid. With age comes the temptation to slow down, draw back, or hold back part of the price (Acts 5:2).

No doubt Paul was so tempted. But he declared, "I counted . . . and I count." He had counted the cost in the past, and he continued to count. "I counted . . . [and] I count everything as loss because of the surpassing worth of knowing Christ Jesus my Lord" (Philippians 3:7-8). He had put his hand to the plow, and he never looked back.

*LS, 4*

JULY 31

## Uttermost Consecration

*Let your heart therefore be wholly true to the LORD our God.* (1 Kings 8:61)

The human soul can never be satisfied short of full consecration. We may be gratified with base matters, but we can
be satisfied only by the highest. As Augustine said, "Thou,
O God, hast made us for Thyself, and we are restless till
we rest in Thee."[25]

Only an uttermost and sustained consecration can satisfy the imperious claims of Jesus—claims not of an arbi-
trary will, but of infinite love. He does not *compel* us to
follow Him; He *invites* us to do so, with the understanding
that if we choose to follow, we must gird ourselves for lifelong service and uttermost devotion and sacrifice.

And it is only by an utter and sustained consecration
that we can meet the needs of the world about us. "You
are the salt of the earth," said Jesus (Matthew 5:13). But if
our consecration fails, we lose our savor, our saltiness, and
society falls into rottenness. Who can estimate the harm
that is done to Christianity by halfhearted Christians?
The world looks on at selfish, ignoble lives spent by those
who claim to know Christ, and says, "We see nothing in
it. These people are just like ourselves." Salt saves from
corruption, and true Christians alone save society from
utter corruption.

*LS, 4*

# The Manifold Character of God

*God is kind, but he's not soft. In kindness he takes us firmly by the hand and leads us into a radical life-change.*
(Romans 2:4, *The Message*)

Of all the innumerable books written, the Bible is the only one that gives us an authoritative representation of God.

The book of nature reveals to us the goodness and the severity of God. Fire will not only bake our food and bless us, but it will also burn us. Water will not only quench our thirst and refresh us, but if we trifle with it, it will drown us. If we recognize God's ways of working in nature, and take heed and obey, we shall find nature's laws most kind and helpful. If we neglect or refuse to obey, we shall find them most terrible and destructive.

But if we want to know God in all the richness of His character, and all the fullness of His self-revelation, we must study the Bible and compare Scripture with Scripture. The Bible shows us that no one word, not even the sweet word "mercy," will sum up the rich and manifold character of God. The Bible says, "God is love" (1 John 4:8), but it also says, "Our God is a consuming fire" (Hebrews 12:29). The Bible tells us of God's unutterable love leading Him to seek sinners in mercy, but His righteousness requires of the sinner penitence, faith, separation from evil, and obedience to His will.

*LS, 6*

## Confessing Other People's Sins

*If we confess our sins, he who is faithful and just will forgive us our sins and cleanse us from all unrighteousness.*
(1 John 1:9, NRSV)

"Have you eaten of the tree of which I commanded you not to eat?" asked the Lord of Adam (Genesis 3:11). And Adam replied, "'The woman whom you gave to be with me, she gave me fruit of the tree, and I ate.' Then the LORD God said to the woman, 'What is this that you have done?' The woman said, 'The serpent deceived me, and I ate'" (Genesis 3:12-13). They confessed the sins of others and ignored their own, and the curse fell upon them instead of a blessing.

Nothing more surely makes manifest a person's hardness of heart than hiding behind others' faults, and nothing will more surely confirm that person in blindness and sin. It is a deadly kind of hypocrisy. It can meet only with God's displeasure.

Let me beg you to take your eyes off other people and fix them upon yourself and upon Jesus. When we cease to blame others, and look only at our own sin, and confess our wrongdoing with a broken and contrite heart, then we can receive pardon and enter into peace.

*LS, 7*

## The Dangers of Middle Age (1)

*Be careful that none of you fails to respond to the grace which God gives.* (Hebrews 12:15, *Phillips*)

We read and hear much about the dangers of youth, but little about the dangers of the middle-aged! And yet they, too, are very many and very deadly.

A man, considerably past fifty years of age, stopped me on the street and told me of his sins and temptations. He had been a follower of Jesus, but had fallen. He was becoming more and more entangled in a network of evil, and was sinking deeper and deeper in the quicksands of his iniquity—and his sins were of the flesh!

The middle-aged are not safe from the awful corruption of the flesh. So let both the young and also the mature followers of Christ take heed lest they fall. Let them watch for and guard themselves against the beginnings of sin—the unclean thought, the lascivious look, the impure imagination. Let them hate "even the garment stained by the flesh" (Jude 1:23). Let them beware of selling their place among God's people, the happiness of their home, the smile and favor of God, and their hope of heaven. Let them "see to it that no one comes short of the grace of God . . . that there be no immoral or godless person like Esau, who sold his own birthright for a single meal" (Hebrews 12:15-16, NASB).

*LS, 8*

## The Dangers of Middle Age (2)

*If you think you are standing, watch out that you do not fall.* (1 Corinthians 10:12, NRSV)

The more constant spiritual danger of the middle-aged is the loss of the freshness of their early experience, when they were "holy to the LORD" and ran after Jesus "in the wilderness" (Jeremiah 2:2-3).

There is nothing so delightful as the constant renewal of spiritual youth amid the increasing cares and burdens and disappointments of age. And there is nothing so sad as the gradual loss of fervor, heart devotion, triumphing hope, and glowing love of spiritual youth.

Multitudes lose the bloom and blessedness of their early experience and become like Ephraim, of whom the prophet said, "Strangers devour his strength, and he knows it not; gray hairs are sprinkled upon him, and he knows it not" (Hosea 7:9). This loss may steal upon us like a creeping paralysis if we do not watch and pray.

The Salvation Army's founder had a morning-like freshness, perennial youth, and unfailing faith in God and in others—despite all the shameful failures and desertions which pierced him with many sorrows. Comradeship with Jesus is the secret of victory over every obstacle and every foe. In fellowship with Him, the flesh loses its subtle power, the charms of the world are discovered to be but painted mockery, and while life is a warfare, it is also a victory.

*LS, 8*

## When Others Fail and Fall

*Consider him who endured from sinners such hostility against himself, so that you may not grow weary or fainthearted.* (Hebrews 12:3)

I shall never forget the chill that gripped American Christians some years ago, when a mighty evangelist, the author of books of great spiritual insight and power, fell into sin and shame. It was heartbreaking for his influence to be ruined, his reputation gone, his family put to shame, God's cause mocked, and for a soul whom he should have shepherded to be dragged to the mouth of hell to gratify his passing pleasure.

We are continually tempted to lean upon others rather than upon God and His Word. And when others fail and fall, we feel as though the foundations were swept away. But instead of looking at those who have fallen, why not look at those who have stood? Instead of losing heart and faith because of those who have thrown down the sword and fled the field, should we not shout for joy and emulate those who were faithful unto death, who came up out of great tribulation with robes washed in the blood of the Lamb (Revelation 7:14)? Why not triumph with Joseph in his victory rather than sneer and thus suffer defeat with David in his fall? Why not consider Jesus, "who endured from sinners such hostility against himself"? If we do, we shall not "grow weary or fainthearted" (Hebrews 12:3).

*LS, 8*

## Holiness in Action

*Love the Lord your God with all your heart and with all your soul and with all your mind and with all your strength.* (Mark 12:30)

As I reflected on the Salvation Army's founder, William Booth, standing before the thronging multitudes by night and before his own people by day, pleading for righteousness, for holiness, for God, toiling with flaming passion to accomplish his purpose, the great commandment began to unfold to me in fuller, richer meaning than ever before. I said to myself, "There is a man who loves God with all his heart." Then, as I considered how his whole life was being poured without stint into God's service, I said, "There is a man who loves God with all his soul." Again, when I noted how diligently he labored to make plain the great thoughts of God to even the feeblest intellect, I said, "There is a man who loves God with all his mind." And when I saw him old and worn, burdened with the weight of many years, still toiling, praying, singing, exhorting, into the late hours of the night that Jesus might triumph and sinners be won, I said, "There is a man who loves God with all his strength."

Afflicted, oftentimes wounded and heartsore, burdened with care, he still seemed to me to fulfill each part of that great fourfold commandment. And that was holiness in action.

*LS, 9*

## The All-Conquering Life

*He will baptize you with the Holy Spirit and fire.*
(Matthew 3:11)

A Salvation Army officer who had lost the blessing of holiness left one of my officers' meetings with her heart breaking after God. She prayed nearly all that night. She spent the next day reading the Bible and *Helps to Holiness*, and crying to God for the blessing. Saturday she went about her duties, but with a yearning cry in her heart for the blessing. Sunday morning came, and she was again wrestling with God, when suddenly the great deep of her soul was broken up and she was flooded with light and love and peace and joy. The Holy Spirit had come. She went to the meeting that morning and told her experience. The Spirit fell on her soldiers and they, too, sought and found. And His Presence became an abiding Presence with that officer, and she went on to sweeping victory.

Our Lord still baptizes with the Holy Spirit and fire. He wants to give us an experience that shall manifest a heavenly and all-conquering life.

Then shall we be like the blessed one who trusts in the Lord, and who is as a tree planted by the waters, spreading out its roots by the river, and thriving forevermore (Jeremiah 17:7-8).

*LS, 9*

## Where Some Heard Thunder

*Then a voice came from heaven.* (John 12:28)

Even the Scriptures fail to fully reveal God unless with penitence and faith we have been born from above and sanctified by the Holy Spirit. The Book is in large measure sealed to unspiritual minds.

When Jesus prayed, "Father, glorify your name," a voice came from heaven, saying, "I have glorified it, and I will glorify it again." People interpreted the voice according to their spiritual condition and relationship. Some said it had thundered—a material interpretation, with no spiritual significance. Others said an angel had spoken—a spiritualistic interpretation (John 12:28-29). Only Jesus heard the voice of the Father.

One person will see in the Old Testament nothing but myths, folklore, bits of biography, exaggerated stories of wars among semi-savage tribes, and songs of a people slowly emerging from barbarism into civilization. Another will read it and discover God down among His wayward creatures, revealing Himself to them in dreams, judgments, deliverances, and through His prophets, until at last the full revelation came in Christ.

Well may we pray David's prayer: "Open my eyes, that I may behold wondrous things out of your law" (Psalm 119:18). And well may we covet the experience of the disciples: "Then he opened their minds to understand the Scriptures" (Luke 24:45).

*AP, 12*

## Covet Wisdom

*The wisdom from above is first pure, then peaceable, gentle, open to reason, full of mercy and good fruits, impartial and sincere.* (James 3:17)

God gives wisdom to those who seek Him, and there are several marks by which to know this heavenly wisdom (James 3:17):

"Pure." The truly wise person will flee from all impurity in thought, word, and act. Filthy habits of every kind are broken and put away by this heavenly wisdom. "Peaceable." The one who has wisdom from God does not meddle with strife, but seeks peace and runs after it (1 Peter 3:11). "Gentle." Those who live in the spirit of this world are often rough and boorish, but the one who is wise from above will possess gentleness alongside lionlike strength and determination. "Open to reason." Though sinned against seventy times seven in a day, yet the heavenly-wise person stands ready to forgive (Matthew 18:21-35). His or her heart is an exhaustless fountain of goodwill. "Full of mercy and good fruits." Like the heavenly Father, the wise man or woman is "rich in mercy" (Ephesians 2:4). "Impartial." The wise person rises above party and class prejudice and is a lover of all. "Sincere." There is no guile in the wise person's heart, no white lies on the tongue, no double-dealing whatsoever.

Blessed be God for such wisdom, which He waits to bestow upon all those who covet it and who ask for it in faith. Covet wisdom.

*LS, 11*

## Pray to the Lord of the Harvest

*The harvest is plentiful, but the laborers are few; therefore pray earnestly to the Lord of the harvest to send out laborers into his harvest.* (Matthew 9:37-38)

When young Adoniram Judson went to Burma, he found a land covered with agelong growths of superstition. For years he plowed and sowed the gospel in hope. After seven years with no converts, a friend wrote and asked him what the prospects were. Judson replied, "The prospects are as bright as the promises of God."[26] Already the fields had whitened unto harvest, and shortly after he had written to his friend, he was reaping what he had sown—thirty thousand souls were won to Jesus.

It is not often that someone sows in tears and reaps in joy as Judson did. The plowers and sowers often toil in hope, and yet must wait for others to reap. At the present time the world seems to be one vast ripened or ripening harvest field, waiting for earnest and skilled reapers. Our harvest is at hand. The great crowds of the unsaved need our faithful ministry speedily.

We must determine to reach them. We should give ourselves to God and do His work. If we cannot go ourselves, we may send generous help. Did not Jesus command us to pray the Lord of the harvest to send forth laborers? And shall we not fulfill so simple and yet so urgent a command, praying and pleading His promises till He rain righteousness upon the earth?

*LS*, 14

## Encourage One Another

*Encourage each other and give each other strength.*
(1 Thessalonians 5:11, NCV)

Caleb and Joshua returned from their scouting mission full of courage and exhorted the people to go up at once and take Canaan. But their ten fellow spies gave an evil report, and the people said, "Our brothers have made our hearts melt" (Deuteronomy 1:28). So, disheartened and afraid, they turned back and wandered for forty years, till all of that unbelieving generation perished, except Joshua and Caleb.

Thus we learn the importance of encouraging rather than discouraging one another. How shall we do this? (1) By keeping in such close communion with God that our inward peace and the joy in our hearts bubble out in hearty, helpful testimony wherever we meet a brother or sister. (2) By talking more about our victories than our defeats and praising God for what He has done and what He has promised to do. (3) By dwelling more upon the good than the bad in other people. (4) By being aware of the burdens upon our leaders, and not being too quick to criticize, but more ready to pray for them.

The glorious work of encouraging others is for all. The weakest of us can at least say with loving zeal, "Be strong and courageous. Do not be frightened, and do not be dismayed, for the LORD your God is with you wherever you go" (Joshua 1:9).

*LS*, 15

## From Nobody to Somebody

*A woman who had been subject to bleeding for twelve years came up behind him and touched the edge of his cloak.* (Matthew 9:20, NIV)

She was a nobody. Everybody was tired of the sight of her, but into the throng she came with her bloodless face and tired eyes and threadbare clothes. The crowd jostled her, trampled upon her feet, and blocked her way, but she was inspired by a new hope. If she could only reach Jesus and touch but the hem of His garment . . . Edging her way through the crowd, she at last stretched forth a wasted, bony hand to touch His robe, and something happened! Instantly she was well!

And something had happened to Jesus! He said, "Who touched me?" That one timid touch was different from the crush of the crowd. Jesus said, "Somebody touched me, for I felt the power went out from me" (Luke 8:46, *Phillips*).

The nobody had suddenly become somebody. Others may have sneered at her, but she pressed on as best she could till she touched Jesus, and that touch gave her all her heart's desire and rewarded all her effort.

People who go to Jesus do not always find it easy. Others get in the way—sometimes they stoutly oppose; sometimes they sneer and ridicule. But those who press on and on will find Him, reach Him, touch Him, and get all their heart's desire.

*LS*, 16

## Growing Old Gladly

*Even when I am old and gray, do not forsake me, my God, till I declare your power to the next generation, your mighty acts to all who are to come.* (Psalm 71:18, NIV)

I feel sorry for folks who don't like to grow old and are ashamed of their age. I revel in my years. They enrich me. Some lessons that I have learned, or partially learned, I here pass on:

(1) Have faith in God—in His providence, His superintending care, and His unfailing love. (2) Accept the bitter with the sweet and rejoice in both. The bitter may be better for us than the sweet. If you fall into many trials, count it all joy, "knowing that the testing of your faith produces patience. But let patience have its perfect work, that you may be perfect and complete, lacking nothing" (James 1:3-4, NKJV). (3) Keep a heart full of love toward everybody. Don't carry around hard thoughts and feelings. (4) Don't waste time and fritter away faith by living in the past, mourning over long-ago failures. Commit them to God and look upward and onward (Philippians 3:13-14). (5) Give heed to failing bodily strength. We must remember that our bodies are temples of the Holy Spirit; hence, they need sufficient nourishing food and restful sleep and must be neither pampered nor mistreated.

A great man once said, "The frosts of seventy winters are upon my head, but the springtime of eternal youth is in my heart."[27]

*LS*, 18

## Red-Hot Religion

*Be on fire in the Spirit as you serve the Lord!*
(Romans 12:11, CEB)

One of the problems of science is to produce a physical light that is cold. The problem we face is to produce a spiritual light that is hot.

Red-hot men and women are those who have hungered and thirsted for God, and have found Him. They have burst into flame. Holy fire kindles in every soul that lives with Him.

Red-hot men and women believe God. They burn because they believe. They seek His will and listen for His voice and follow where He leads.

Red-hot men and women get alone with God as Jesus did in His all-nights of prayer. They pray in secret and seek out kindred spirits to pray with them.

They love God, His people, His house, His service. They love righteousness and holiness, and they hate every sin. They guard the gateway of eye and ear and every sense, lest sin get into their hearts.

Red-hot men and women do not entangle themselves with the affairs of this life. They do not mix with people of the world except to do them good and, if possible, win them to Christ.

Oh, let us be burning and shining lights, and then great shall be our reward, and great shall be our peace and joy.

*RLP,* 13

## Burning and Shining Lights

*Shine . . . like stars in the sky.* (Philippians 2:15, NIV)

Jesus said of John the Baptist, "He was a burning and a shining light" (John 5:35, KJV). He shone until all the region was startled and awakened by the light and multitudes confessed their sins. King Herod himself and his adulterous wife were so scorched that Herod shut John up in prison and had his head cut off, as though the loss of his head could quench the fire that shone and burned in John's heart and life.

Those who most mightily move others to righteousness are burning and shining lights. Stephen burned into the guilty souls of priests and rulers until their wrath knew no bounds, and they sent him to heaven in a shower of stones. The apostles burned their way into idolatrous, pagan civilizations reeking with unmentionable lusts (Romans 1:22-32) until the world was transformed. William and Catherine Booth, the founders of The Salvation Army, shone and burned their way through vice and ignorance, ridicule, and stubborn opposition. Multitudes have won their way and triumphed by the same burning.

How can we get this fire? Not by feasting, but by fasting. Not by playing, but by praying. Not by devouring the latest news, but by searching the Scriptures. Not by slothfulness, but by watching and by diligently seeking God and the souls that wander from Him.

*RLP,* 13

## Shine like the Sun

*Keep your eyes on the LORD! You will shine like the sun.*
(Psalm 34:5, CEV)

When Moses came down from Sinai, where he had met with God, "the Israelites could not gaze at Moses' face because of its glory" (2 Corinthians 3:7). And we read of Stephen, "Everyone in the high council stared at Stephen, because his face became as bright as an angel's" (Acts 6:15, NLT).

A Chicago multimillionaire once said that the one thing which always most impressed him about Salvationists was the light in their faces. (May that light never go out!) I know a Salvation Army officer who burns his way to victory in every appointment. He is an ordinary-looking man, with but slender gifts, but he has the fire. He burns.

What is this fire? It is love. It is faith. It is hope. It is passion, purpose, and determination. It is utter devotion. It is a divine discontent with formality, ceremonialism, lukewarmness, indifference, sham and noise, parade and spiritual death. It is singleness of eye and a consecration unto death. It is that which emboldened David to run out to meet the insolent giant and Esther to face the king and plead for her people, saying, "If I perish, I perish" (Esther 4:16). It is God the Holy Spirit burning in and through a humble, holy, faithful man or woman.

*RLP, 13*

## The Grace and Gift of Faith

*Without faith it is impossible to please God.*
(Hebrews 11:6, NIV)

There is an important difference between the grace of faith and the gift of faith, and I fear that confusing the two has led many people into darkness, possibly even to cast away all faith and to plunge into the black night of skepticism. The grace of faith is that which is given to everyone to work with, and by which he or she can come to God. The gift of faith is that which is bestowed upon us by the Holy Spirit, at the point where we have made free use of the grace of faith.

Exercising the grace of faith, I say, "I believe God will bless me," and I seek God wholeheartedly. I pray. I search the Bible to know God's will. I talk with Christians about the ways of God's dealings with the soul. I take up every cross.

At last, by some word of Scripture, testimony, or inward reasoning, God bestows upon me the gift of faith, by which I am enabled to grasp the blessings I have been seeking. Then I no longer say, "I believe God *will* bless me," but joyfully exclaim, "God *does* bless me!" Then the Holy Spirit witnesses that it is done, and neither any person nor any devil can rob me of my assurance.

*HH, 14*

## The Witness of Faith

*I wait for the LORD, my soul waits, and in his word I hope.*
(Psalm 130:5)

There is a danger in claiming the gift of faith before fully exercising the grace of faith. Suppose a brother believes God will give him the blessing of a clean heart. He should at once seek it from God, and if he perseveres, he will surely find. But if someone gets him to claim it before he has by the grace of faith fought through doubts and difficulties, and before God has bestowed the gift of faith, he will probably drift along for a time and then fall back, concluding that there is no such blessing. He should be warned, instructed, and encouraged to seek till he gets the assurance.

Should we not urge seekers to believe that God does the work? Yes, if you feel sure they have exercised the grace of faith fully and yielded all, then urge them tenderly and earnestly to trust Jesus; but if you are not sure, beware of urging them to claim a blessing God has not given them. The Holy Spirit will notify a person when he or she is to be blessed. Beware not to attempt the work of the Holy Spirit yourself. If you help seekers too much, they may die on your hands. But if you walk closely with God in humility and prayer, He will reveal to you a way to help them through.

*HH, 14*

## The Obedience of Faith

*The mystery that was kept secret for long ages . . . has been made known to all nations, according to the command of the eternal God, to bring about the obedience of faith.*
(Romans 16:25-26)

One day ten lepers met Jesus. "And they lifted up their voices and said, 'Jesus, Master, have mercy on us!' So when He saw them, He said to them, 'Go, show yourselves to the priests'" (Luke 17:13-14, NKJV). These poor fellows might have objected and said to Jesus, "But look at us! We are not different since you spoke to us. We would be fools to go in this plight, and we would not be received if we did go. Heal us, make us feel different, then we will go."

But they did not talk that way. They did not heed doubts and fears. Jesus had spoken the word and it was theirs to trust and obey, so they hobbled off, I imagine, as fast as they could go. "And it came to pass, that, as they went, they were cleansed" (Luke 17:14, KJV). That was cleansing through "the obedience of faith" (Romans 16:26).

Do you want the blessing of a clean heart? Give yourself fully to God right now. Ask for it, believe for it, and patiently and expectantly wait for it. Remind God of His promises. Don't give Him any rest till He comes and sanctifies you. Tell Him you will not let Him go till He blesses you (Genesis 32:26), then stay there expecting till you know the work is done.

*HTH, 3*

## The Coming of the Comforter

*The dove found no resting place . . . because water covered the surface of the whole earth.* (Genesis 8:9, HCSB)

The Comforter is ever coming to men and women, but He finds them so preoccupied with their own affairs that He cannot abide with them. The floods of worldliness, pleasure, passion, and business so overflow them that, like Noah's dove when sent out from the ark (Genesis 8:8-9), He can find no place to rest. But when He finds a troubled soul whose pleasures have dried up, whose passion is stilled, whose business is secondary to the needs of the Spirit, and who hungers and thirsts for God, then He can find a resting place. Then He will abide.

This coming of the Comforter is a holy event, a solemn act. It must be preceded by an intelligent and sincere covenant between the soul and God. It is a marriage of the soul to the Redeemer, and is not rushed. It is carefully considered. It is based on complete separation and consecration, the most serious pledges and vows. So if the Comforter is to come to abide, to be with us and in us evermore, we must come out and be separate for Him (2 Corinthians 6:17). The soul that is thus truly dedicated to Him becomes His, and He will come to that soul to abide forever, to be a shield and an "exceeding great reward" (Genesis 15:1, KJV).

*RLP, 20*

## Becalmed in Christ

*He calms the storm, so that its waves are still.*
(Psalm 107:29, NKJV)

A venerable Episcopal archdeacon came to see me about his soul. He is probably as well versed in theology as I, or better. He believes the truths I believe, and is grounded in sound doctrine, yet he was restless and uncertain and afraid. He had no peace. But as we prayed, and he looked unto Jesus, peace came to his heart; and some days later, he wrote to me: "Yesterday and today are days of heaven upon earth. I am possessed by a holy stillness, a blessed quietness. I am becalmed in Christ. I seem to grow by leaps and bounds in the things of God. I can now see His hand in every hour and every event. I am looking up trusting, resting, enswathed in His presence!" He had found that which is fundamental.

It is not acceptance of certain doctrines, but penitent and childlike faith in a divine Savior and loving loyalty to Him that save the soul and give it peace and purity and power. And those who thus yield themselves will have a revelation of Christ in their own souls. God will be unveiled to their understanding, and they will come to that knowledge of God and of Jesus Christ which is life eternal.

*RLP, 6*

## The Never-Ending Blessing

*We are being changed into his image with ever-increasing glory. This comes from the Lord, who is the Spirit.*
(2 Corinthians 3:18, GW)

I knew a man, educated, thoughtful, earnest, but without the knowledge of Christ in his heart. He took much offense at my testimony. Then, having met another with a similar testimony, he came to me with great frankness. "In the mouths of two witnesses this thing is established. How can I get this revelation for myself?"

He asked me to go with him to a meeting. When we arrived at the hall, everyone else was on the street conducting an open-air meeting. We took a front seat inside, and soon I heard the man whispering to himself. Turning, I found him with an upward look that was transfigured as he whispered, "Blessed Jesus, blessed Jesus!" I rejoiced, and in my heart I prayed for him. Nearly forty years later, I remember that prayer, one of the simplest I ever prayed: "O Lord, bless him so that he will never get over it in this world or the world to come!" When the opportunity was given for testimonies, the man stood and said, "No one can conceive what God has been doing in my soul this last half hour. Jesus Christ has come to my heart and revealed Himself." On the way home he praised God every step of the way. Afterward, everyone who knew him remarked at the transformation.

*RLP, 7*

## The Ever-Recurring Revelation

*"You refuse to come to me that you may have life."*
(John 5:40)

I have a half-brother, a man of the strictest integrity—clean-living, high-minded, honorable, faithful in his friendships, and elected on several occasions to positions of trust by his fellow citizens. But he is not a Christian. I love him with a great and tender love. I have prayed with him and for him. Once he was at the penitent-form [place of prayer] in my meeting, and with all earnestness I have entreated him, but he remains an agnostic.

Recently he sent me an article concerning an old clergyman who, after fifty years, has declared his unbelief. My half-brother seems to think that the apostasy of this old preacher is an argument against faith in Christ and the authority of the Bible. But people have been declaring their unbelief for ages. Ministers have fallen from faith again and again, yet men and women still believe in Jesus and prove their faith by transformed lives of utter self-sacrifice and lifelong devotion. What is the secret of this persistent faith? The ever-recurring revelation of Christ by the Spirit in penitent, obedient, believing souls.

There is a simple way to test whether an electrical wire is dead or alive. Touch it. So there is a simple way to prove whether or not Jesus Christ is Lord. Do what He bids.

*RLP, 7*

## The Vision and the Voice

*"My sheep hear my voice, and I know them, and they follow me."* (John 10:27)

Those who live in the Spirit and dwell in constant closeness with God have confidence in the report of their spiritual senses. When God gives them a vision, they obey. When God speaks, they rise up and follow. They know the voice of their Shepherd, and that voice leads them on (John 10:27).

The modern physiologist would say this is only some overwrought brain cell, or the activity of the endocrine glands. But the follower of Jesus can say with Paul, "I know whom I have believed" (2 Timothy 1:12).

It was the word sounding in the depths of his soul, "The just shall live by faith" (Romans 1:17, KJV), that liberated Martin Luther. It was the word of the Lord in his own heart that sent David Livingstone to darkest Africa and held him there through long and painful years, until on his knees he died praying for its redemption. It was the divine messages she heard, and the spiritual visions he followed, that made Catherine and William Booth the founders of The Salvation Army.

It is the vision and the voice that has called lads and lasses of every walk into Salvation Army ministry, and sent them into all the earth to save the lost. And the vision and the voice still appeal to the understanding heart.

*RLP, 8*

## Children of Light

*Do you not know that friendship with the world is enmity with God?* (James 4:4)

The unregenerate world is in darkness. We ourselves "at one time . . . were darkness" (Ephesians 5:8), and the darkness blinded our eyes. "But now [we] are light in the Lord," and bidden to walk as children of light.

Unregenerate men and women "think it is strange that [we] do not do the many wild and wasteful things they do" (1 Peter 4:4, NCV). They are mystified that we decline to join in their feasts. The world offers its friendship to the saints—ease and good success, riches and popularity—but on its own terms. The devil promised Jesus the kingdoms of the world if He would fall down and worship Satan. Self-denial and cross-bearing are wholly inconsistent with worldly alliances and entanglements.

Wherever the children of God have been seduced by the world's glitter and flattery, spiritual decay has begun and spiritual vision has blurred. But every great spiritual movement—the Reformation, the rise of Puritanism, the Quakers, Methodism, and The Salvation Army among them—as well as every local revival has been accompanied by a call for people who would be saved and purified and empowered by the Spirit to come out and be separate (2 Corinthians 6:17). We must answer that call, hold fast to that principle, and steadfastly maintain that practice, if we wish to retain spiritual power.

*RLP, 9*

## The Sense of Duty

*"Didn't you know that I had to be here, dealing with the things of my Father?"* (Luke 2:49, *The Message*)

Holiness increases our sense of duty and personal responsibility. It was the holiness of His heart that led the twelve-year-old Jesus to say to His mother, "Didn't you know that I had to be here, dealing with the things of my Father?" (Luke 2:49, *The Message*). To Him the world was not a playground only, but a field of labor. His Father had given Him work to do, and He must do it before the night came, when no one can work (John 9:4).

By this I do not understand that He was continually engaged in ceaseless, grinding toil, with no hours of recreation and rest. We know that in later years He went away with His disciples to rest. But He neglected no duty; He did not slight or shirk His work; He was no trifler. And this spirit always accompanies true holiness of heart.

Do not, however, be anxious about receiving a reward. This is largely deferred into the next world. It is your duty and mine to be faithful, to be faithful unto death. If reward is delayed, it will be all the greater when it comes, be assured of that. God will see to it that your treasure which you lay up with Him bears compound interest.

*WH, 12*

# The Goodness and Severity of God

*Therefore consider the goodness and severity of God.*
(Romans 11:22, NKJV)

It is life eternal to know God and Jesus Christ whom He has sent (John 17:3); but it must be the true and holy God, as He is, and not some false god who conforms to our poor little warped human desires and opinions.

Some misrepresent God by making Him utterly savage and cruel, and thus people are embittered against God. Others make Him appear as a sort of goody-goody God, who fawns upon sinners with mawkish sympathy and looks upon triflers and lukewarm Christians with weak, sentimental pity.

The truth lies between these extremes. There is mercy in God, but it is mingled with severity. There is wrath in God, but it is tempered with mercy.

When Dr. Samuel Johnson lay dying, he was much concerned about his soul. A friend said to him, "Sir, you seem to forget the merits of the Redeemer." "No," replied Dr. Johnson, "I do not forget the merits of the Redeemer, but I remember that He said He would place some on His right hand, and some on His left."[28]

Our only hope is in the wounds of Jesus, and the shelter of His blood. There, and only there, shall we find mercy, since we have sinned; but there, mercy is boundless and free.

*LS, 6*

## Killing Time

*My times are in your hand.* (Psalm 31:15)

It is so easy to kill time—to let it slip through one's fingers like sands of the seashore, or to fritter it away doing some good thing, or *better* thing, instead of the *best* thing. One of the snares of this age is its exceeding busyness—and it is a snare set especially to trap the servants of God. It makes us too busy to wait patiently on God in secret prayer, too busy to read the Bible quietly for personal soul food, too busy for meditation, too busy to speak to a caller about his or her soul and lead him or her to the Savior, too busy to give time to self-examination and solemn, secret worship and adoration of the Lord. It makes us so busy about the Lord's work that God Himself is forgotten or only dimly remembered, and crowded into the corner and background of our thoughts, affections, time, and work.

And yet how easy it is to redeem the time if we but rouse ourselves into spiritual wakefulness and set ourselves with quiet, steady purpose of heart to do so. "Let us not sleep, as others do," wrote Paul, "but let us keep awake and be sober" (1 Thessalonians 5:6).

*RLP,* 10

## In Season or Out of Season

*Never lose your sense of urgency, in season or out of season.* (2 Timothy 4:2, *Phillips*)

A big policeman sat in front of me on the streetcar. As I rose to leave, I laid my hand on his shoulder and said, "God bless you today!" He glanced up with grateful surprise, and my own heart was warmed.

I dined with six others in the home of a stranger. With a little watchfulness and without any effort, the conversation turned to spiritual things, after which we prayed. The time that might have been lost in profitless small talk was redeemed and given to the Master.

I began to read my Bible on the train. "You have something good there, haven't you?" inquired a vibrant voice. I looked up into the clear eyes of a gray, but vigorous, strong-faced man. "Yes," I replied. And for hundreds of miles we talked about the things of God.

I encountered a lady who was rejoicing in the Lord. She asked me if I did not remember speaking to her on the streetcar about her soul, some months before. I did not. "Well," said she, "that set me thinking, and I found no rest till I found Jesus and knew I was born again."

It is enough to make one weep and shout for joy to see how unfailingly God works with those who constantly and unselfishly and in faith work for Him.

*RLP,* 10

## Your Allies in Soul-Winning

*The LORD is on my side as my helper.* (Psalm 118:7)

There are difficulties in the way of reaching souls today. There is the drift away from organized religion. The church is no longer attractive to masses of people. But we must not magnify this difficulty. It was not so different in Paul's day, or Wesley's, or when General Booth began his work.

Oh, to shake men and women out of complacency and make them realize how deadly is their peril and how deep is the love of God in Christ. And while we face difficulties, we also have allies.

The human heart is an ally. In every human heart, conscience sits in judgment. Amid passion, pleasure, and business, its voice may not be heard, but if we can silence the clamor till conscience is heard, we will have gone a long way.

Funerals and open graves are our allies. Through these, men and women glimpse eternity. Let us appeal to the realities of eternity and press them home with earnestness.

God the Holy Spirit is our ally. He is before and behind and all about us. He is ever whispering to people's hearts, quickening their consciences. Let us cooperate with Him and work in glad and bold confidence, since He is our Helper. He will help us to pray, believe, and win souls.

*RLP*, 11

## Unanswerable Proofs

*O Lord God, you are God, and your words are true.*
(2 Samuel 7:28)

How can I prove the inspiration of the Bible? By the way it answers to the human heart. The key that fits an intricate lock was evidently made for that lock. The Bible meets me at every point of my moral and spiritual need. It fits my heart's intricate needs, and I exult to know that the divine Hand that fashioned me pours itself with fathomless comforts into my heart through the Book. But I cannot prove to you the truth of the Book any more than I can prove that the sun is shining, that honey is sweet, that the song of the bird is melodious.

The inspiration of the Bible is proved by experience, not logic. "Meditate on it day and night" (Joshua 1:8), and you shall taste its sweetness, behold its wonders, and hear in its words the whisperings of the everlasting Father.

How shall I prove that the Bible is a God-given, God-inspired Book? Shall I go to history, science, archaeology for proof? Yes, at the proper time and to the right people. But the most convincing proof is a redeemed life of joy and peace and patience, full of good works and testifying to the saving, sanctifying, keeping power and ever-living presence of the Lord Jesus.

*AP, 15*

## He Walked with God

*Enoch lived a total of 365 years. Enoch walked
with God; then he was gone because God took him.*
(Genesis 5:23-24, GW)

We are prone to look upon past ages and distant places as
peculiarly favorable to godliness. But really this is not so,
and especially is it not so of Enoch's age and place. The
age was most ungodly, and people had very little religious
light. They had no gospel, with Jesus revealed as a loving
Savior.

We have a whole Bible, a finished revelation. We have
the gospel. We have Jesus, crucified, buried, and raised to
glorious life again for our justification, and ascended on
high to the right hand of God to intercede for us, to pour
out the Holy Spirit upon us in rich measure, to live in us
through the Spirit. Yet we, in our trembling, pitiful, shameful unbelief, wonder how Enoch could walk with God!

I imagine Enoch made up his mind that it was possible to walk with God. He then made up his mind that
he *would* walk with God. He put his will into this matter. I
also think Enoch took such steps as were necessary to walk
with God. He separated himself in spirit from the ungodly
people about him, raised his voice against their evil ways,
and became not only a negatively righteous man, but a
positively holy man.

*HTH, 7*

## Faith Works Wonders

*Whoever says to this mountain, "Be lifted up and thrown into the sea"—and doesn't waver but believes that what is said will really happen—it will happen.* (Mark 11:23, CEB)

True faith is the most wonderful thing in the world. It makes a beggar act like a king, for he knows he is a child of the King. Faith makes the sorrowful to rejoice. I saw a devoted young wife and mother, whose husband had suddenly died, smile through her tears as she believed God. Her face was a benediction. Faith lightens the load of the heavy-laden. Paul fairly reveled in this fact. He wrote, "I can do all things through him who strengthens me" (Philippians 4:13).

Faith empowers one to do the impossible. Peter walked on the sea while he believed. Faith may see difficulties, but it does not magnify them; it takes no account of them. It looks at God's power and love and resources, and casts itself on Him, and through Him it triumphs.

Faith may be sore tempted, but it does not yield to discouragement. When we yield to discouragement, we at that moment cease to believe. Faith assures us that God is with us and will in His own way and time deliver us.

Finally, faith obeys. It does not sit in dreamy idleness but works as it has opportunity. Real faith obeys when there is no sign.

*RLP,* 12

## The Sacred and the Secular

*Whatever you do, do it from the heart for the Lord and not for people.* (Colossians 3:23, CEB)

Most people divide the work of the world into what they call sacred and secular work. Preaching, praying, reading the Bible, and the like, they consider sacred; but washing clothes, schooling, making shoes, practicing law, working in mines and shops—that they call secular work. But why make such a distinction? It is not the work, but the heart and purpose behind the work, that God looks at. The minister or missionary who works for the salary, or for social position, or for an opportunity for study and travel has a secular heart, and makes the work secular. But the farmer, lawyer, cook, or secretary who has a holy heart and does good work as unto the Lord makes his or her work sacred.

One poor woman used to say, "I am a scrubbing woman and a missionary by the grace of God." She went to the homes of the rich to clean, and she testified of Jesus everywhere she went. She scrubbed to pay expenses, and preached the gospel, and she scrubbed well that the gospel might not be despised.

We know not what part of our work God is going to use in His plans for saving the world. Therefore, let it all be good and true.

*WH, 12*

## The Axe and the Gimlet

*In everything . . . adorn the doctrine of God our Savior.*
(Titus 2:10)

We are God's tools. He is the Workman. I took an axe to cut down a tree, but I took a tiny gimlet to bore a hole in a piece of furniture I wished to mend. I could not cut down the tree with the gimlet, nor bore the hole with the axe, and yet both pieces of work were important. So the Lord has different kinds of work, for which He must have different kinds of workers.

Do not despise your work or be discouraged. You are as important to God as the gimlet was to me. Do your duty. Do it as though Jesus were in the class you teach, by the bench where you work, in your kitchen, office, store, or factory. Do it gladly, and He may take it up, and make it a part of His great plan, long after you have laid it down.

If you are true, you will "adorn the doctrine of God our Saviour in all things" (Titus 2:10, KJV). You will have the sweet approval of your own conscience, and you will someday hear the Master say, "Well done, good and faithful servant. You have been faithful over a little; I will set you over much. Enter into the joy of your master" (Matthew 25:21).

*WH, 12*

## In Times of Peril

*Let us hold fast the confession of our hope without wavering, for he who promised is faithful.* (Hebrews 10:23)

In times of peril, we must hold fast our faith—faith in God, faith in His care, faith in His superintending providence, in His pity and love despite all contrary appearances. We must hold fast our faith in His unalterable purpose to establish righteousness in the earth.

In times of trial, distress, and perplexity, faith must be fought for. A weak and flabby will and nerveless purpose will let faith slip. It is a priceless treasure which must be held fast. It was this deathless grasp of faith—or grasp of God by faith—that sustained the saints and soldiers of God in ages past. It was at a time when everything was swept away by invading armies, and famine was stalking through the land, that Habakkuk cried out, "Though the fig tree should not blossom, nor fruit be on the vines, the produce of the olive fail and the fields yield no food, the flock be cut off from the fold and there be no herd in the stalls, yet I will rejoice in the LORD; I will take joy in the God of my salvation" (Habakkuk 3:17-18).

He believed God. He held fast in the darkest hour when all the foundations on which people of the world build their hopes were ruthlessly swept away.

*RLP, 17*

## Cultivate Joy

*In your presence there is fullness of joy.* (Psalm 16:11)

Joy can be cultivated and should be, as is faith or any other fruit of the Spirit. How can this be?

1. By appropriating by faith the words that were spoken and written for the express purpose of giving us fullness of joy. "May the God of hope fill you with all joy and peace in believing" (Romans 15:13).

2. By meditating on these words and holding them in our minds and hearts as we would hold honey in our mouths, until we have gotten all the sweetness out of them.

3. By exercise, even as faith or love or patience is exercised. This we do by rejoicing in the Lord and praising God for His goodness and mercy, and shouting when the joy wells up in our souls.

Who can estimate the power there must have been in the joy that filled the heart of Peter and surged through the souls and beamed on the faces and flashed from the eyes of the 120 fire-baptized disciples, while he preached that sermon which won three thousand enemies to the Cross of a crucified Christ?

O Lord, flood the world with Your mighty joy!

*SWS,* 1

## The Soul-Winner's Secret

*A winner of souls is wise.* (Proverbs 11:30, GW)

"I was not disobedient to the heavenly vision," said Paul (Acts 26:19), and in that saying he reveals the secret of his wonderful success as a soul-winner: courageous obedience will surely lead to success.

This obedience must be prompt. If I speak when the Spirit moves me, I can usually introduce the subject of God's claims to anyone with happy results. But if I delay, the opportunity slips by.

This obedience must be exact. "Whatever He says to you, do it," said Mary to the servants at the wedding in Cana (John 2:5, NASB), and when they obeyed Him, Jesus wrought His first miracle. And so He will work miracles today if His chosen people will do whatever He says.

This obedience must be courageous. "Don't be afraid of a soul," said the Lord to Jeremiah (Jeremiah 1:8, *The Message*). Soul-winners must recognize that they are on picket duty for heaven, and rest in the assurance of their heavenly Father's care and do their duty courageously.

The obedience must be glad. The command is, "Serve the LORD with gladness!" (Psalm 100:2). Once we are wholly His and the Comforter abides in us, we shall not find it irksome to obey, and by obedience we shall save both ourselves and others to whom the Lord may send us.

*SWS, 2*

## The Way of Approach

*When you pray, go into your room and shut the door and pray to your Father who is in secret. And your Father who sees in secret will reward you.* (Matthew 6:6)

Prayer is the way of approach to God, and the soul-winner keeps it open by constant use. It is the channel by which all spiritual blessings and power are received, and therefore the soul-winner's life must be one of ceaseless prayer. It is the breath of the soul.

What an amazing statement is this: "Whatever you ask in prayer, believe that you have received it, and it will be yours" (Mark 11:24). And this: "If you abide in me, and my words abide in you, ask whatever you wish, and it will be done for you" (John 15:7). Amazing as they are, there they stand.

The soul-winner must pray *in secret*. He or she must get alone with God and pour intercessions and pleadings and arguments into the Father's ear to have success. There is no substitute for much wide-awake, expectant, secret waiting upon God for the outpouring of the Holy Spirit, the gifts of wisdom, strength, courage, hope, faith, and discernment. If we fail at this point, we will soon fail at every point.

Here, then, is one secret of success—communion and counsel and conversations in the closet with God. I say it reverently: He cannot turn away from us, but will surely reward us, and that openly, because He said He would, and He cannot lie.

*SWS, 3*

## What Prayer Must Be

*This is the confidence that we have toward him, that if we ask anything according to his will he hears us.* (1 John 5:14)

Prayer must be definite. Once, when Jesus was leaving Jericho, blind Bartimaeus sat by the wayside begging, and when he heard Jesus was passing by, he cried out, "Jesus, Son of David, have mercy on me!" That prayer was not definite—it was altogether too general. Jesus knew what Bartimaeus wanted, but He said, "What do you want me to do for you?" Then the blind man prayed a definite prayer: "Rabbi, let me recover my sight," and the definite prayer received a definite answer (Mark 10:46-52).

Prayer must be persistent. We are to hold on in prayer till we get an answer. Prayer must be for the glory of God and according to His will. If we ask things simply to gratify our own desires, God cannot grant them. Prayer must be believing prayer. "Whatever you ask in prayer, believe that you have received it, and it will be yours" (Mark 11:24).

Finally, prayer must be in the name of Jesus. He said, "Whatever you ask in my name, this I will do" (John 14:13). As children of God, we may approach with unabashed boldness into the presence of our heavenly Father and claim all the resources of heaven in our effort to save sinners and build up the Kingdom of God.

*SWS, 3*

## The Zeal of the Lord

*Do not be slothful in zeal, be fervent in spirit, serve the Lord.* (Romans 12:11)

It is said that Civil War general Philip Sheridan went to battle with all the fury of a madman. He claimed he never went into a battle from which he cared to come back alive unless he came as a victor. If he became so desperate in killing people, how much more desperate, if possible, should we become in our effort and desire to save them!

It was written of Jesus, "Zeal for your house will consume me" (John 2:17), and so it can be of every great soul-winner.

Not until a person can say with Paul, "I am ready . . . to die . . . for the name of the Lord Jesus" (Acts 21:13), can he or she hope to be largely used in winning souls. Those who are anxious about their dinner, and eager to get to bed at a reasonable hour, and concerned about their salary, and querulous about their reputation, and afraid of weariness and pain and headache and heartache will not make great soul-winners.

True zeal is from above. Its source is in the mountains of the Lord's holiness, and its springing fountains in the deep, cool valleys of humility. It is born of the Holy Spirit and flows from a knowledge of "the truth that is in Jesus" (Ephesians 4:21, NIV).

*SWS*, 4

## Kinds of Zeal to Avoid

*They have a zeal for God, but not according to knowledge.*
(Romans 10:2)

There are various kinds of zeal which should be avoided as deadly evils.

First: partial zeal. God sent Jehu to destroy the wicked house of Ahab and the worship of Baal, and he did so with fury. "But Jehu was not careful to walk in the law of the LORD, the God of Israel, with all his heart" (2 Kings 10:31). This kind of zeal is frequently seen in those who violently attack one sin, while indulging in some other sin.

Second: partisan zeal like that of the Pharisees and Sadducees. In these days it takes the form of excessive sectarian and denominational zeal, and makes bigots of people. Such zeal is from beneath and not from above.

Third: the zeal of ignorance. Paul said of his kinsmen, the Jews, "My heart's desire and prayer to God for them is that they may be saved. For I bear them witness that they have a zeal for God, but not according to knowledge" (Romans 10:1-2). True zeal issues from the knowledge of the dread condition of the sinner without Christ and of the inexpressible gift of God, of the possibilities of grace for the vilest sinner, of cleansing through the blood, sanctification by the Holy Spirit, and a life of blessed service and fruit-bearing.

*SWS*, 4

## True Zeal

*I toil and struggle, using the mighty strength which Christ supplies and which is at work in me.* (Colossians 1:29, GNT)

True zeal makes one faithful to Jesus and the souls for whom He died. It led Paul to keep back no truth that was profitable for the Ephesians, but to show them and teach them "in public and from house to house, testifying both to Jews and to Greeks of repentance toward God and of faith in our Lord Jesus Christ" (Acts 20:20-21). He was not content simply to get sinners to accept Jesus as their Savior, but taught them that "Christ in you [is] the hope of glory. Him we proclaim, warning everyone and teaching everyone with all wisdom, that we may present everyone mature in Christ. For this I toil, struggling with all his energy that he powerfully works within me" (Colossians 1:27-29).

True zeal is sacrificial. Jesus, consumed with zeal for the glory of God in the saving and sanctifying of people, was led "like a lamb to the slaughter" (Isaiah 53:7, NIV). He poured out His soul unto death for us, and gave His life a ransom for all. And the gift of His Spirit kindles and sustains this same sacrificial zeal in the hearts of all true soul-winners.

*SWS, 4*

## Spiritual Leadership

*The LORD was with Joseph.* (Genesis 39:2)

Spiritual leadership is a thing of the Holy Spirit, and not of birth, rank, title, education, or circumstances.

Joseph was a youthful prisoner in an Egyptian dungeon, but God was with him. And one day he reached his rightful place next to Pharaoh's throne.

Paul was a prisoner under Roman guards on board ship. But one day God's winds made the sea to boil, and winds and waves smote the ship, so that the hearts of all the others on board failed them for fear. Then Paul, by right of spiritual kingship, became the master of all in the ship (Acts 27).

I knew a Salvation Army lieutenant, a quiet, prayerful, faithful, humble, holy young man of moderate ability. The captain and his wife (who were his superiors) sat at his feet for spiritual counsel, though the lieutenant knew it not. They hung on his God-wise words, and treasured his spirit, and talked about his Christlikeness. They were in charge, but he held spiritual supremacy because he walked with God, and God was with him and in him.

Spiritual leadership comes by self-surrender, a courageous sacrifice of every idol. It is not gained by seeking great things for ourselves (Jeremiah 45:5). Therefore let those who aspire to this leadership pay the price, and seek it from God.

*SWS*, 5

## Don't Be Set Aside

*Keep yourselves in the love of God.* (Jude 1:21)

I hear people complaining and expressing fear that when they get old, they will be set aside and superseded by younger people without a tenth of their experience, forgetting that it is not long service and experience that makes spiritual leaders, but vigorous spiritual life, and that if they are set aside, it will be because they have neglected the divine life, the Holy Spirit in them.

Nothing can make leaders acceptable to people if they have lost the spirit of prayer and faith and fiery-hearted love, and the sweet simplicity and trustfulness and self-sacrifice of their youth, and are now living on past victories and revelations and blessings. But fresh anointing of the Spirit and present-day experiences will make them acceptable, though their eyes be dim and their backs bent and their voices husky with age. It was so with Charles Finney and George Whitefield and John Wesley, and so it may be with you.

A man or woman full of God cannot be thrust aside. If he is put into a desert place, then all will flock to the desert place, as they did to Jesus and John the Baptist. And if she is thrust into a corner, then the world will stop and bend its ear to her corner to hear the latest message from God.

*SWS, 5*

## The Wise Use of Time

*Make the best possible use of your time.*
(Colossians 4:5, *Phillips*)

The difference between wise people and fools, rich and poor, saints and sinners, the saved and the damned does not usually result so much from difference of circumstances as from the difference in their use of time. One redeems it for the purpose in view; the other squanders it. The one is ever up and doing, packing into every hour some search for truth, some prayer to God, some communion with Jesus, some service to others, some counsel to a saint, some warning or entreaty to a sinner; the other is ever neglecting the opportunity of the present, but full of vague purposes and dreams for an ever-receding will-o'-the-wisp future. The one plods patiently and surely to "glory and honor and immortality . . . [and] eternal life"; the other drifts dreamily but certainly into the regions of "wrath and fury, . . . tribulation and distress," and finally lands in hell (Romans 2:7-9).

To redeem time one does not want feverish hurry, but a prompt, steady, quiet use of the minutes. It was said of John Wesley that he was always in haste, but never in a hurry. "Make haste slowly" is a wise old adage.

*SWS*, 6

## The Soul-Winner's Studies

*The good hand of his God was on him. For Ezra had set his heart to study the Law of the LORD.* (Ezra 7:9-10)

Oh, that everyone who sets out to be a soul-winner might faithfully give a little time each day to those studies that will enlighten the mind and encourage fitness for the work to which God has called him or her.

1. Study the Bible. A doctor who knows all about law and art, history and theology, but is unacquainted with medical books, is a failure as a doctor. So the worker for souls must become full of the thoughts of God. Eat the Word and digest it and turn it into spiritual blood and bone and muscle, until you become, as someone has said, "a living Bible, bound in human skin."

2. Lay out a course of reading and stick to it, a few pages each day. Ten pages a day will mean from ten to fifteen books a year. It is well to carry a notebook and make notes.

3. Study people and methods. I know of no better method of acquainting oneself with the human heart and the way the Holy Spirit works than by a private conversation about the religious experiences of fellow Christians. Study the human heart, the Christian life, and religious experience wherever you can find a human being to talk with you.

*SWS, 7*

## The Soul-Winner's Bible

*Is not my word like fire, declares the LORD, and like a hammer that breaks the rock in pieces?* (Jeremiah 23:29)

No man or woman need hope to be a permanently successful soul-winner who is not a diligent student of the truth, of the will and ways of God, of people, and of methods.

A doctor must think and study, diligently and continuously, if she would understand the delicate human organism and the subtle diseases to which it is subject and the various remedies by which these diseases are to be healed. How much more then should the soul-winner study in order to understand the diseases of the soul and the application of the great remedy God has provided to meet all its needs. I have sometimes read or quoted the Word of God to people, and it fitted their case so pat that it smote them like a lightning bolt.

However, the soul-winner must not study the Bible simply in order to declare it, but rather to live by it—to be strengthened, corrected, and made wise by it. It must pass through your own soul and become a part of your own spiritual life before you can apply it effectually to the saving of others. And to do this you must be filled with the Holy Spirit. Only then will you be able to get much benefit from the Word of God or have much love for it.

*SWS*, 7

## The Christian's Armory

*A person lives not on bread alone, but by everything God says.* (Matthew 4:4, NCV)

Diligent attention to the Word of God is a command. God said to Joshua, "This Book of the Law shall not depart from your mouth, but you shall meditate on it day and night" (Joshua 1:8).

Catherine Booth read her Bible through a number of times before she was twelve years old. No wonder God made her a "mother of nations." She was full of truth, and she could never open her mouth without saying something that was calculated to overthrow the devil's kingdom of lies and build up God's Kingdom of righteousness and truth in people's hearts.

Again and again I have read the Bible through on my knees, and it is ever new and, as David said, "sweeter also than honey and the honeycomb" (Psalm 19:10, KJV). And like Job I can say, "I have esteemed the words of his mouth more than my necessary food" (Job 23:12, KJV).

John Wesley in his old age called himself "a man of one book." It is from this armory that the Christian is to draw weapons with which to fight all hell. It is here that we may study the mind and heart of God, the truth about Jesus Christ, sin and the way of escape from it, and the facts about heaven and hell, a Judgment Day and eternity.

*SWS, 7*

## The Care of the Body

*Your body is a temple of the Holy Spirit.*
(1 Corinthians 6:19)

We must take the best possible care of our bodies, yet without coddling and petting and pitying ourselves. This is our sacred duty. The body is the instrument through which the mind and the soul work in this world. A good body is as essential to the Christian as is a good instrument to the musician, or a staunch boat to the strong rower, and should be no more despised and neglected than the hunter's gun or the woodsman's axe. "Do you not know," said Paul, "that your body is a temple of the Holy Spirit within you?" (1 Corinthians 6:19), and "If anyone destroys God's temple, God will destroy that person" (1 Corinthians 3:17, NCV). As the most skillful musician is dependent upon his or her instrument, so we, in every walk of life, are in a large measure limited by and dependent upon the quality of the body.

Those who desire good health, long life, and a cheerful old age should live simply and regularly; they should seek enough sleep and at the same time be careful not to take too much sleep. Exercise is also very necessary for health. Work heartily, but don't work yourself to death. Court the fresh air day and night. Don't overeat. Don't starve. "Let your moderation be known unto all" (Philippians 4:5, KJV).

*SWS, 8*

## The Renewal of Power

*Wait on the LORD . . . and He shall strengthen your heart.*
(Psalm 27:14, NKJV)

To do God's work we must have God's power. We receive this power when we are sanctified wholly and filled with the Spirit, and we need never lose it. But while the Holy Spirit abides with the believer, there yet seems to be need for frequent renewals of the power He bestows. And, thank God, He has made ample provision to meet this need. "They that wait upon the LORD shall renew their strength," said Isaiah (Isaiah 40:31, KJV). "Wait on the LORD; be of good courage, and He shall strengthen your heart," cried David (Psalm 27:14, NKJV).

Years ago, Asa Mahan wrote of his old friend, Charles Finney, who succeeded him as president of Oberlin College: "The reason why he is bringing forth such wondrous fruit in his old age is that while his whole ministry has been under the power of the Spirit, his former baptisms have been renewed with increasing power and frequency during a few years past."

My own strength is usually renewed by the opening up of some new truth, or the powerful application of some promise or portion of the Word of God to my soul. There is abundant reserve power in God. He has not exhausted His resources, and I often comfort and encourage myself with the assurance of James: "He giveth more grace" (James 4:6, KJV).

*SWS*, 9

## No Discharge in This War

*Unite my heart to fear your name.* (Psalm 86:11)

The person who thinks to succeed in the infinite business of saving souls with a heart that is divided as yet knows nothing compared with that which he or she ought to know concerning the matter.

That someone may by personal magnetism, power or persuasiveness of speech, and a certain skill in playing upon people's emotions create an excitement that fairly simulates a revival, and yet have a divided heart, I admit. But that such a person can bring others to a thorough repentance and renunciation of sin, a hearty embrace of the Cross, an affectionate surrender to Jesus as a personal Savior and Master who requires deep humility and meekness and tender love as the marks of His disciples is yet to be proved.

As certainly as like begets like, so certainly will the soul-winner put the mark of his or her own spirit and consecration upon the people who are influenced. One who is not more than half won to the cause of our lowly Master will not more than half win others.

Soul-winners must abandon themselves to the Lord and to the Lord's work and, having put their hand to the plow, must not look back. They must love their work, and stick to it through all difficulties and discouragements, for there is no discharge in this war.

*SWS,* 10

## Separate from the World

*"They do not belong to the world, just as I do not belong to the world."* (John 17:16, WNT)

We are to be like Jesus in separation from the world. He took no pleasure in its wicked ways. He was not spoiled at all by its proud, sinful, selfish spirit. While He worked and associated with bad people to do them good, He was always separate from them in spirit.

One of our dear, pure Salvation Army rescue officers went to a house of prostitution to see a sick girl. While she was there, the health authorities declared the girl's sickness to be smallpox, and they sealed up the place. The officer was shut in for weeks among those poor lost women. She was in an evil place, but she was not of it. Her pure spirit was utterly opposed to the spirit of sin that ruled there.

So Jesus was in the world, but not of it. And in the same way, holy people are so changed that while they are in the world, they are not of it. They belong to heaven, and are but strangers and pilgrims doing all the good they can while passing through this world to their Father's house, their heavenly home.

*WH, 1*

## Burn the Bridges

*Cultivate these things. Immerse yourself in them. The*
*people will all see you mature right before their eyes!*
(1 Timothy 4:15, *The Message*)

If those engaged in secular pursuits are given up to their
work and consumed with their purpose, how much more
should the soul-winner be, who is fighting for righteousness
and holiness, for the Kingdom of love upon earth, rescu-
ing souls from the power of sin and the danger of eternal
burnings?

If God has set you to win souls, "make no provision for the
flesh, to gratify its desires" (Romans 13:14). Burn the bridges
behind you. Remember Paul's words to Timothy: "Give your
complete attention to these matters. Throw yourself into your
tasks so that everyone will see your progress" (1 Timothy 4:15,
NLT). Let your eye be single, make no plan for retreat, allow
no thought of it. Like Jesus, set your face steadfastly toward
your Jerusalem, your cross, your Kingdom, your glory, when,
having turned many to righteousness, you shall shine as the
stars forever and ever (Daniel 12:3).

You may be ignorant, your abilities may be limited, you
may have a stammering tongue and be utterly lacking in culture, but you can have an undivided, perfect heart toward
God and the work He has set you to do; and this is more
than all culture and education, all gifts and graces of person
and brain. Be not dismayed; it is not the perfect head, but the
perfect heart, which God blesses.

*SWS*, 10

## Fear and Finances

*Who among you by worrying can add a single moment to your life?* (Matthew 6:27, CEB)

Christians must not be overanxious about finances, but must laugh at the devil and all their fears, and trust God to supply all their needs.

When I was a little fellow, I never worried about where my next pair of shoes or my next meal was to come from. My mother did all that worrying, and I trusted her. Jesus says we are not to be anxious about what we shall eat or what we shall wear. "Is not life more than food, and the body more than clothing? Look at the birds of the air: they neither sow nor reap nor gather into barns, and yet your heavenly Father feeds them. Are you not of more value than they? . . . Therefore do not be anxious, saying, 'What shall we eat?' or 'What shall we drink?' or 'What shall we wear?' For . . . your heavenly Father knows that you need them all" (Matthew 6:25-26, 31-32).

Jesus would have me trust my heavenly Father as I did my mother. Then I can be a child again, and all I have to do is to pray and obey and trust the Lord, and He will supply my needs. Yes, that is what He means, for He says, "Seek first the kingdom of God and his righteousness, and all these things will be added to you" (Matthew 6:33).

*SWS*, 11

## The Sparrow and God's Child

*Your heavenly Father already knows all your needs.*
(Matthew 6:32, NLT)

Faith—simple faith, unmixed faith in God's promise—can no more exist in the same heart with worry than can fire and water, or light and darkness consort together; one extinguishes the other. Faith in the plain, unmistakable promise of God, begotten by the Holy Spirit, so links the believer to Jesus that the burden and care is the Lord's. He would have His child trust Him, walk the waves with Him, never doubt Him, shout the victory, and triumph over all fear.

God's supply depot is abundantly full and runs on schedule, but the worried and anxious unbeliever wants Him to run ahead of schedule. No, no! He may, in order to test and strengthen faith, not provide the second suit until the first one is ready to be laid aside. He may allow you to go to bed not knowing where breakfast is to come from, but it will come at breakfast time. Trust your heavenly Father, as does the sparrow. The wee thing tucks its tiny head under its little wing and sleeps, not knowing where it will find its breakfast. And when the day dawns, it chirps its merry note of praise, and God opens His great hand and feeds it. And "you are of more value than many sparrows," said Jesus (Matthew 10:31).

Trust Him! He will not fail you.

*SWS*, 11

## Truth That Saves

*Sanctify them by the truth; Your word is truth.*
(John 17:17, HCSB)

Some time ago I read that "there were over three thousand churches in two of the leading denominations of this country that did not report a single member added by profession of faith last year." Well may the writer add, "Think of more than three thousand ministers preaching a whole year, and aided by deacons and Sunday school teachers and Christian parents and prayer meetings and helps and helpers innumerable, and all without one conversion!"

Why this stupendous failure? These preachers and teachers and parents were orthodox, cultured, and skilled in biblical lore. No doubt they preached and taught truth, but it was not *the truth*—the truth that saves, the truth that first smites the conscience, lays bare the secrets of the heart, and arouses the slumbering soul until conviction has wrought its purpose, and penitence is complete, then whispers of forgiveness and peace, and offers mercy and salvation full and free through the bleeding Lamb of God.

Such truth preached faithfully and constantly in these pulpits and churches—with power, like thunderbolts from the cannon's mouth—might have set the nation in a blaze of revival fire. O Lord, evermore give to Your people leaders and teachers filled with the Spirit and clothed with His wisdom!

*SWS*, 12

# Deal Gently

*"Deal gently for my sake with the young man Absalom."*
(2 Samuel 18:5)

Absalom was in rebellion against David the king, his father, and had driven him forth from his throne, had outraged his father's marital ties, had sacrificed filial affection and trampled upon duty, and was now seeking his father's life. But David knew him only as his wayward boy, loved him still, and commanded his warriors to deal gently with him in the coming battle. He would have the rebellion crushed, but the rebel saved; the sin destroyed, but the sinner rescued.

How like Jesus that is! Does not His heart yearn over each sinner with unutterable tenderness? And does He not say to us, "Deal gently for My sake"?

But how shall one who has not this Spirit of perfect gentleness secure it? There is but one way. It is a fruit of the Spirit, and is to be had only down at Jesus' feet. Ask Him to give you His mind (Philippians 2:5). And as you ask, believe. You must walk in the footsteps of Jesus and feed on His words. Only to those who seek Him day by day with the whole heart, and that with joy, is it given to be like Him in these heavenly dispositions.

*SWS, 16*

## The Middle of the Way

*A bruised reed he will not break, and a faintly burning wick he will not quench; he will faithfully bring forth justice.* (Isaiah 42:3)

Sanctification floods the soul with great light and love, and thus subjects the possessor to two great and opposite dangers.

If we lean to the side of light, we are likely to become critical and impatient with others, too severe in our judgments. And thus we may break the bruised reed that Jesus would not break, or quench the smoking wick which Jesus would fan into a flame, and so fail to "faithfully bring forth justice" (Isaiah 42:3). It will be helpful to us to remember "the quarry from which [we] were dug" (Isaiah 51:1) and to be as merciful and patient with others as our Lord has been with us.

On the other hand, if we lean to the side of love, we are likely to be too lenient, too easy (as was Eli with his sons), using soothing ointments when we should wield a sword. Many a work of God has come to naught that might have been saved by a timely, courageous rebuke and faithful dealing.

To keep in the middle of the way, to walk in a blaze of light without becoming critical and harsh, and in fullness of love without being soft and weak, is the problem every sanctified soul must solve in order to keep the blessing and be increasingly useful.

*SWS*, 19

## The Coming of the Word

*Now the word of the LORD came to Jonah.* (Jonah 1:1)

Human beings cannot by searching find out God, but God can and does reveal Himself to them. In spite of the doubts and denials of agnostics and skeptics, God can and does make Himself known to His creatures. He does communicate with them. He opens their ears. He speaks to their hearts. He tells them His secrets. He shows them things to come. He reveals to them His will.

"Now the word of the LORD came to Jonah" (Jonah 1:1). Happy man! Men and women of force and spirit like to be brought into confidential relations with their rulers; to be entrusted with responsibility and sent on high missions. And here is an unknown, undistinguished man singled out from the crowd by the Lord God Almighty and made an ambassador of heaven. What dignity and honor!

It is an awesome thing for the word of the Lord to come to a man or woman. It means that person's hour has come. And from that hour, if we hush and listen and humble ourselves to obey this voice, we will cease to be of the common herd, and become sons and daughters of God and workers with Him.

*SWS*, 20

# When God Speaks

*After the fire there was a voice, a soft whisper.*
(1 Kings 19:12, HCSB)

The word of the Lord comes not with thunder crash that startles the world, but in stillest whispers to the heart of the one to whom it is addressed. The world hears no sound, but soon knows to whom God has spoken—knows by the love-lit eye, the shining face, the elastic step, the ringing voice, the positive message, the humble, patient devotion to duty, if the word is gladly received. Or it knows by the darkening countenance, the downcast, averted, or defiant eye, and the shrinking form that drops to the rear seats or flees if the word is not gladly received.

Mighty transformations are wrought by the coming of the word of the Lord to human hearts! They can never be the same as before. It will either exalt them to the place of partners and coworkers with God, and give them a seat with Jesus on His throne, or it will banish them from His presence and doom them to hell. If obedient to the word, they will be saved, empowered, brought into closest fellowship with God, into confidential relations with Him, and they will be transformed into the likeness of His Son. But if disobedient, they will shrivel as Judas did, and in the end become as devils.

*SWS*, 20

## Hear and Obey

*Then the word of the LORD came.* (Haggai 1:3)

When the word of the Lord comes to a person, it means honor and dignity and joy, but it also may mean sorrow and trial and long and sore discipline, which, if willingly embraced, will mean final and eternal and inexpressible honor, dignity, and joy.

It is a joyous thing to hear God's word, and through it to become a man or woman with a mission, even though to flesh and blood it proves a grievous thing. It is the only way to true peace and highest usefulness here, and to endless glory and unfailing joy hereafter. It means toil and labor and conflict, but if our faith does not fail, it means final and eternal victory, too. After Elijah's struggle and long warfare, the heavenly chariot swung so low that he stepped in and swept to heaven in a whirlwind of fire without tasting death.

It is ever by "the word of the Lord" that God reveals Himself to His people. Happy will you be if you have an ear to hear, a heart to understand, and the will to obey the word of the Lord which comes to you and bids you rise and serve your King. You, too, may know God's secret.

*SWS, 20*

# Like Jesus

*Put on the new self, created after the likeness of God in true righteousness and holiness.* (Ephesians 4:24)

The Bible teaches that we can be like Jesus.

The apostle John, speaking of those who expect to see Jesus, says, "All who have this eager expectation will keep themselves pure, just as he is pure" (1 John 3:3, NLT). That is a lofty standard of purity, for there was no impurity in Jesus. We are to be like Him in our separation from the world, in purity, in love, and in the fullness of the Spirit.

This work was begun in you when you first experienced new life. You gave up your sins. You were in some measure separated from the world. The love of God was shed abroad in your heart, and you felt that God was with you. But unless you have been sanctified wholly, you also feel that there are yet roots of bitterness within: quickness of temper, stirrings of pride, too great a sensitiveness to praise or blame, shame of the Cross, love of ease, worldly-mindedness, and the like. These must be taken away before your heart can be made clean, love to God and others made perfect, and the Holy Spirit have all His way in you. When this is done, you will have the experience the Bible calls holiness.

*WH, 1*

## Prepare the Way

*Prepare the way of the LORD.* (Isaiah 40:3)

God never raises a crop without human help. He furnishes the sunshine and air and rain, and He gives life to the seed so that it may grow. People must prepare the ground, plant the seed, keep down the weeds, and gather in the harvest. They may think they are doing it all, but our loving heavenly Father has been preparing the earth for thousands of years for every potato that grows.

And so it is in matters that concern our souls. God and the individual must work together, both to save and to sanctify. Ages before we were born, God provided the means of salvation for all. Jesus came and died for our sins. The Holy Spirit was given, the Bible was written, and all things were made ready.

But the sinner must hear the truth and repent, must ask God for pardon and believe, before he or she can be saved. For a sinner to expect salvation without doing this would be as big a piece of folly as for a farmer to expect a crop of potatoes without having planted them.

Just so, to get the priceless gift of a clean heart we must work together with God. He waits and longs to give the blessing. But before He can do so, we must get ourselves ready.

*WH, 3*

## The Gift of a Clean Heart

*Blessed are the pure in heart.* (Matthew 5:8)

To get the priceless gift of a clean heart, you must do your part, which is very simple and easily within your power.

(1) You must see your need of the blessing; and to see this need, you must be clearly justified. Sinners are blind to these things. (2) You must not hide the need, but frankly confess it. If your heart is not clean, do not be afraid to say so. (3) You must believe that the blessing is for you. If you do not believe that you can be cleansed, you will not seek for it. But our heavenly Father offers His full salvation to all who will take it. (4) You must believe that it is for you *now*. It is astonishing how sinners wish to put off salvation, and it is even more astonishing how saved people put off seeking a clean heart. Nothing grieves the Holy Spirit and hardens the heart like this delay of unbelief. (5) You must come to Jesus for the blessing, giving your all to Him, that He may give His all to you. The Lord offers us the biggest blessing this side of heaven. But in exchange He asks us to give Him our little all.

*WH*, 3

## It Shall Be Done

*The man believed the word that Jesus spoke to him.*
(John 4:50)

A nobleman whose son was sick came to Jesus, saying, "'Sir, come down before my child dies.' Jesus said to him, 'Go; your son will live.' The man believed the word that Jesus spoke to him and went on his way" (John 4:49-50). The next day when he got home, he found his boy well. That is the kind of faith that walks off with the blessing.

Again and again I have seen people burst into the light when they have consecrated their all, and believed in this way. Some time ago in a holiness meeting, I asked one seeker, "Do you now give yourself and your all to God?"

"Yes, I do," said he.

"Well, whose man are you, then?" I inquired.

"I am the Lord's."

"Can you trust the Lord to sanctify His own man?"

"Yes, I can."

"When?"

"Now!" and he burst into the holy joy of faith, and began to praise the Lord at once. You too can have the blessing just now.

*WH, 3*

## A New and Living Way

*Christ's love compels us.* (2 Corinthians 5:14, NIV)

"I wish I knew the secret of Paul's piety," said Asa Mahan to Charles Finney one day.

Finney replied, "Paul said, 'The love of Christ constraineth us'" (2 Corinthians 5:14, KJV). Just then the glorious truth burst upon Mahan's mind that we are sanctified not by works, but by faith which works by love, and that the religion of Jesus is not one of vows and resolutions, and terrible struggle and effort, but of life and power and joyous love. He went out of Finney's room, saying, "I see it, I see it!" and from that hour his life was one of triumphant holiness.

Oh, that all would see that the way of holiness is a "new and living way" (Hebrews 10:20), not an old, dead, tiresome, heart-aching, heartbreaking way of forms and ceremonies that leaves the soul still baffled and unsatisfied, and with a sense of failure and defeat! It is a way of victory and joy.

The simple secret of this new and living way is the constraining love of Christ. When we realize that He loves us and died for us, and that He wants a service of love, and then give ourselves up heartily, in faith, to such a love service, the secret becomes ours.

*WH, 5*

## Out of Very Love

*Christ's love . . . has the first and last word in everything we do.* (2 Corinthians 5:14, *The Message*)

"Will I have to go and tell Mother, and my brothers, and my church, how inconsistent I have been?" asked a young woman with whom I was talking about the blessing. "I don't feel that I can ever do that."

She had been defeated again and again by fits of temper, and I felt she ought to confess to those whom she had probably hindered by her inconsistency. But I saw that she would not get the blessing by doing it because she *must*, but because she *wanted to*, out of very love for Jesus and others. So I replied that the Lord did not want a slavish service from her, but a love service. I assured her that if she did it in that spirit, she would find it a joy.

Have you been serving the Lord blindly and slavishly, simply because it is your duty, and yet with a constant feeling of unrest and unfitness? Oh, how He loves you, and wants to catch your ear, and win your heart, and draw you into a glad love service!

Let this love constrain you. "We love Him because He first loved us" (1 John 4:19, NKJV). Trust Him. Give yourself wholly and heartily to Him, and be sure you serve Him for love, and you will have learned the secret of a holy, happy life.

*WH, 5*

## Offer Your Body

*Present your bodies as a living sacrifice, holy and acceptable to God.* (Romans 12:1)

Many people think that sanctification, or holiness, has to do only with the soul. But the truth is that it has to do with every part of our nature and every article of our possession. The body is to be sanctified as well as the soul. Paul wrote to the Thessalonians as follows: "May the God of peace himself sanctify you completely, and may your whole spirit and soul and body be kept blameless at the coming of our Lord Jesus Christ" (1 Thessalonians 5:23). By this he means that the body is to be set apart and kept as a holy thing for the Lord.

We are to make a present of our bodies to the Lord. Paul says, "I appeal to you . . . to present your bodies as a living sacrifice, holy and acceptable to God, which is your spiritual worship" (Romans 12:1). Just as the soldier surrenders his personal liberty and gives his body to his country for hard campaigns, toilsome marches, weary sieges, and—if need be—death, so we are to present our bodies to the Lord. Jesus gave His body for us, and we are to give our bodies to Him.

*WH, 6*

## Stand Up Straight!

*Stand up straight! Stop your knees from shaking and walk a straight path.* (Hebrews 12:12-13, CEV)

The whole body is to be given to the Lord, and kept and used for Him. Since Jesus ascended to heaven, He has no body upon earth. So, will you prove your love to Him by letting Him have yours? If so, no sexual impurity is to be allowed, no unclean habit is to be indulged, no appetite is to be permitted to gain mastery, but the whole body is to be kept under control and made the servant of the soul.

Young people are likely to squander their health in all sorts of useless and careless ways, and are tempted to laugh and sneer at their elders when they lift a warning voice. But they will someday find that advance in holiness, progress toward heaven, and happiness and usefulness are more dependent on the right care of the body than they supposed.

*Let my hands perform His bidding,*
*Let my feet run in His ways,*
*Let mine eyes see Jesus only,*
*Let my lips speak forth His praise.*
*All for Jesus! All for Jesus!*
*Let my lips speak forth His praise.*[29]

*WH, 6*

## The Sanctification of the Body

*Every athlete in training submits to strict discipline.*
(1 Corinthians 9:25, GNT)

The sanctification of the body is both a glorious privilege and an important duty.

Athletes, when in training, are exceedingly careful about their health. They select their food with care and eat nothing that would disagree with them. They abstain from strong drink and tobacco. They go to bed and get up at regular hours. They sleep with open windows and, of course, have plenty of fresh air and systematic exercise. This they do for months, and sometimes for years, simply that they may beat some other athletes in contests of strength and skill. Now they do it, says Paul, "in order that they may receive a perishable crown, but we an imperishable one" (1 Corinthians 9:25, LEB). And then he adds, "I discipline my body and bring it under strict control, so that after preaching to others, I myself will not be disqualified" (1 Corinthians 9:27, HCSB).

I know a man who noticed that when he ate too much, he became irritable and was subject to various temptations from which a careful diet freed him. He had to control his appetite in order to keep a clean heart.

"Dear friend, I am praying that all is well with you and that your body is as healthy as I know your soul is" (3 John 1:2, NLT 1996).

*WH, 6*

## Instruments of Righteousness

*Offer the parts of your body to him as instruments of righteousness.* (Romans 6:13, NIV 1984)

Not only are we to present our bodies as a whole to the Lord, but each member as well.

Our eyes are to be turned away from impure things. General William Booth told of a holy man who kept his eyes straight before him as he walked, not even looking into shop windows, lest worldly, covetous thoughts fill his mind.

Our ears are to be sanctified too. "Take care what you listen to," said Jesus (Mark 4:24, NASB). As the body can be poisoned or nourished by the things we eat, so can the soul be poisoned or nourished by the things we hear.

Neither should we speak evil. While we cannot control the tongues of others, we must control our own.

Let the feet also be given to the Lord, no longer to walk in the ways of sin, but to walk in the path of duty and to run on errands of mercy.

Likewise the hands are to be used for holy service and no longer to smite and pilfer.

Finally, we must not forget that the heart is the fountain from which flows all else. Therefore, "keep your heart with all vigilance, for from it flow the springs of life" (Proverbs 4:23).

*WH, 6*

## The Unconscious Power of Holiness

*The words of the wise heard in quiet are better than the shouting of a ruler among fools.* (Ecclesiastes 9:17)

Two sanctified Salvationists, a man and his wife, were followed home from their meetings several nights by a nurse from the hospital nearby. She could not get away from her duties long enough to attend the meetings, but she said to herself, *I will walk home behind them, and maybe I shall get something for my soul.*

She did. All unconscious that a hungry heart was feeding upon their words, the Salvationists talked about Jesus and His uttermost salvation, and the nurse was so filled with desire to glorify God and save souls that she left her work, became a missionary, and is now in the Far East. This strange story came back from Korea to the two Salvationists, after many days, to surprise and gladden them, and fill them with wonder at the unconscious power of holy conversation.

"You are the salt of the earth," said Jesus. "You are the light of the world" (Matthew 5:13-14). Such lives are full of healing, cleansing, helping, comforting power. And so may your life be, if you will seek, ask for, and receive the Holy Spirit as your Sanctifier.

*WH, 7*

## Holiness and Humility

*If you put yourself above others, you will be put down.*
*But if you humble yourself, you will be honored.*
(Luke 14:11, CEV)

Those who oppose holiness often say that the doctrine tends to spiritual pride. But holy people are those who have found themselves out, and pronounced judgment against themselves, and come to Jesus to be made every whit whole. And so long as they keep the blessing, they are deeply humble.

God said to Israel by the prophet Ezekiel, "Then you will remember your evil ways, and your deeds that were not good, and you will loathe yourselves for your iniquities and your abominations" (Ezekiel 36:31).

This is a certain effect of entire sanctification. The sinful heart apologizes for itself, excuses inbred sin, favors it, argues for it. Not so those who are holy. They remember their former pride, and long and pray to sink deeper and deeper into the infinite ocean of the Savior's humility, until every trace and stain of pride are forever washed away.

Those who have thus seen the plague of their own hearts may be cleansed in the precious blood, and may now have holy hearts, but they will never say to another, "Stay away! Don't touch me! I'm holier than you are" (Isaiah 65:5, GW). Rather, remembering their own former condition, they will point others to the Lamb of God, who takes away the sins of the world.

*WH, 8*

## Marks of Humility

*Be clothed with humility.* (1 Peter 5:5, KJV)

"Do you wish to be great?" asked Augustine. "Then begin by being little."[30] Here are some marks of truly humble people:

1. They do not take offense easily, but are "first pure, then peaceable, gentle, open to reason, full of mercy" (James 3:17).

2. They are not jealous of their position and dignity. A man was casting out devils in the name of Jesus, and the unsanctified disciples took offense, and forbade him. But Jesus said, "Do not stop him" (Mark 9:39).

3. They do not seek great things for themselves, but agree with Solomon when he says, "Better to be lowly of spirit with the humble than to divide plunder with the proud" (Proverbs 16:19, HCSB).

4. They are modest in dress. They desire "the beauty that comes from within, the unfading beauty of a gentle and quiet spirit" (1 Peter 3:4, NLT).

5. They are also plain and simple in speech. They seek to speak the truth in the power of the Holy Spirit, but never with "great swelling words" (2 Peter 2:18, KJV) that will arouse admiration for themselves. They speak not to be applauded, but to feed hungry hearts; not to be admired by people, but to be approved by God.

*WH, 8*

## Let Him Keep You

*All glory to God, who is able to keep you from falling away.* (Jude 1:24, NLT)

Do you ask, "How can I keep the blessing?"

Do not let your poor heart be burdened with the thought that you have to do it all yourself. In this, as in all else, you are only a worker together with God. He loves you more than a mother loves her little child, and He is going to help you to keep the blessing. Remember that the blessing is simply the result of His indwelling in your heart, and you are not to think so much about keeping the blessing as about keeping Him.

It will not be a hard matter to keep Him in your heart if you are in earnest, for He wanted to get there when you were a sinner, and He certainly desires to stay there as long as you will let Him. And if you will let Him, He will keep *you*.

Oh, how it rested me and comforted my heart one day when, sore tempted by the devil, I read these words: "Now to him who is able to keep you from stumbling and to present you blameless before the presence of his glory with great joy" (Jude 1:24). I saw that He was able to keep me, and I knew that He was willing, and my heart rested on the promise.

*WH*, 9

## Stick to Jesus

*Hold on to what you have, so that no one will take your crown.* (Revelation 3:11, NIV)

To keep the blessing of holiness, you must keep all upon the altar.

The devil will try to get you to come down from the cross. The world will allure you, the flesh will cry out against you, your friends may tease and torment or threaten you. But you must stick to Jesus, and take nothing back that you have given to Him. There is usefulness and peace and God's smile and a crown and a Kingdom before you, but only condemnation, ruin, and hell behind.

A little boy in Africa heard of Jesus' tender dying love and saving power, and he gave himself fully to the Lord. Enraged, his unsaved father said, "I'll beat this Jesus out of him." And he beat the little fellow most cruelly.

But the boy was still true. Then the father said, "I'll smoke this Jesus out of him." So he shut the boy within a hut and nearly smothered him with smoke. Then he tried starvation. All persecution failed, however, and the little fellow remained true. He had given all to Jesus, and he would have nothing back. When asked how he had endured all the terrible trials he had passed through, he quietly said, "I just stuck to Jesus."

*WH, 9*

## Be Quick to Obey

*I will be quick to obey your commands.* (Psalm 119:60, NIrv)

If you would keep the blessing of holiness, you must be quick to obey God. I do not mean by this that you are to forgo thinking and praying about all that you do. God wants you to take time to speak to Him and consider and find out His will; but once you have found it, you must not delay, but obey at once.

Oh, the losses of peace and power and joy and sweet communion with God that people suffer through hesitation! Like the Roman governor Felix, they wait for "a convenient season" (Acts 24:25, KJV), which never comes! And, like Felix, they lose all. "Strike while the iron is hot." "Make hay while the sun shines." "Put out to sea while the tide is in."

Do as Abraham did. God told him to sacrifice Isaac as a burnt offering—Isaac, the light of his eyes, the hope of his old age, the treasure of his heart! He did not parley and delay, but "got up early the next morning and . . . left with Isaac . . . for the place where God had told him to go" (Genesis 22:3, CEV).

If you have lost the blessing through a failure to promptly obey, do not be utterly discouraged, but begin over again, and the Lord will restore you.

*WH, 9*

## Stand by Your Facts

*You, however, are not in the flesh but in the Spirit, if in fact the Spirit of God dwells in you.* (Romans 8:9)

To keep the blessing of holiness, do not depend upon your feelings. As a friend of mine used to say, "Stand by your facts."

Young Christians are very likely to be betrayed by their feelings. When they are happy, they are in danger of thinking themselves better than they are, and of not watching and praying as they should. And when they are not happy, they are likely to get discouraged and conclude that it is useless for them to try to be holy. Pay attention to your facts, and let your feelings take care of themselves.

If people are kind to you, and your digestion is good, and your sleep sound, you will probably feel well. But if people are unkind, and your supper lies heavy in your stomach, and your sleep is broken by horrid dreams, you will probably not feel well. But in neither case is your relation to God changed. Your facts are just the same. If you have given yourself to God, and have taken nothing back, but can say, "My all is on the altar, and I trust in You," then you are His, and your business is to stand by that fact, and trust that the blood of Jesus keeps you clean (1 John 1:7).

*WH, 9*

## Keep the Fire Burning

*Each one helps the other, and says to another, "Take courage!"* (Isaiah 41:6, HCSB)

One of the greatest helps for keeping the blessing of holiness is to meet together as often as possible with others who possess it, in order to read the Bible, pray with each other, and encourage one another. This can usually be done just before or between the opportunities for Sunday worship. This practice helped me more than anything else, I think, when I first got the blessing. Put a burning coal by itself, and the fire will go out, and it will be cold and black. But put several coals together, and they will burn brightly. And so it is with hearts full of holy fire.

At such meetings it is good to unite in prayer for others whom you are eager to see converted or to enter into the blessing, and as you see them getting saved and sanctified, this will add mightily to your own faith and love. As the Bible says, "Each one helps the other, and says to another, 'Take courage!'" (Isaiah 41:6, HCSB).

Wholehearted and continued consecration and self-denial, earnest prayer, joyful and diligent study of God's Word, deep humility before the Lord, aggressive work for others, and humble, definite testimony to the blessing will surely establish us in holiness, and keep us from falling.

*WH*, 9; *LS*, 15

## Fishing for People

*"Follow me, and I will make you fish for people."*
(Matthew 4:19, NRSV)

When Jesus saves a soul, that soul wants to see others saved. There are two things to remember:

1. Most sinners hope someone will speak to them about their soul. People often smile and laugh when their hearts are breaking, and they are only waiting for someone to point them to Jesus.

2. When God moves us to speak to people, we may be sure that He has been dealing with their hearts and preparing the way. When the Lord sent Philip to speak to the Ethiopian, He had the Ethiopian all ready for Philip's message.

A friend of mine used to meet a certain railroad conductor almost every day. One day my friend felt he ought to speak to that conductor about his soul. But he trembled and ran away like Jonah. After three weeks of agony he saw that conductor again. He could stand it no longer. He braced himself and said, "Lord, help me! I will speak to him." Then he spoke, and to his surprise, the big man burst into tears and said, "I have really been wanting someone to speak to me about my soul for three weeks."

God is faithful; He had been to that man before He sent my friend to him. And there are hungry souls all around us like that one.

*WH*, 10

## The Zeal of a Clean Heart

*The fruit of a righteous person is a tree of life, and a winner of souls is wise.* (Proverbs 11:30, GW)

Holiness increases the desire to see people saved and makes it burn with a quenchless flame. The zeal of others blazes up, burns low, and often dies out; but the zeal of those with clean hearts, full of the Holy Spirit, increases year by year. Others do not grieve if souls are not saved, but they feel that they must see souls saved, or die. Others run away from a prayer meeting and are zealous for social events, suppers, and musical festivals; but nothing pleases the clean-hearted so much as a meeting where souls are crying to God for pardon and cleansing, then shouting for joy.

And the zeal of these clean-hearted people for the salvation and sanctification of others leads them to do something to reach them. They let their light shine. They speak to needy souls wherever they find them. Holiness makes it easy for them to do this. They love to do it. They find that as they follow the Spirit, the Lord fills their mouths with truth and gives them something to say. I have never known anyone to get the blessing without this desire following.

*WH*, 10

## The Sin of Worry

*Do not worry about tomorrow, for tomorrow will worry about itself. Each day has enough trouble of its own.*
(Matthew 6:34, NIV)

Worry is a great foe to holiness, and perfect trust puts an end to worry.

Most people do not see this to be a sin, but it is. It dishonors God, blinds the eyes to His will, and deafens the ears to His voice. Worrying prevents quiet thought and earnest, believing prayer.

First, we should not worry over things that we can help, but work to put them right. Sir Isaac Newton, one of the greatest of humankind, had labored for eight years preparing the manuscript of one of his great works. One day he came into his study, and found that his dog had knocked over a candle and burned all his papers. Without a sign of anger or impatience, Newton quietly remarked, "Little do you know the labor and trouble to which you have put your master!" and without worrying, he sat down to do that vast work over again.

Second, we should not worry over the things we cannot help, but quietly and confidently look to the Lord for help. There is no possible evil that may befall us from which God cannot deliver us, if He sees that that is best for us, or give us grace to bear, if that is best. Holiness of heart enables us to see this.

*WH*, 11

## The Secret of Peace

*Give all your worries to him, because he cares about you.*
(1 Peter 5:7, NCV)

The heart realization of heavenly help, of God's presence in time of trouble, is the secret of a life of perfect peace, in which anxious care is not shunned, but joyously and constantly rolled on the Lord, who bids us cast our care on Him. Such trust is not a state of lazy indifference, but of the highest activity of heart and will. It is an unfailing fruit of the Holy Spirit dwelling in a clean heart. And we can only keep this trust by obedience to the Holy Spirit, strict attention to daily duty, watchfulness against temptation, much believing, persevering, unhurried prayer, and by nourishing our faith on God's Word daily.

Has someone talked unkindly or falsely about you? Don't worry, but pray, and go on loving him or her and doing your duty. Are you sick? Don't worry, but pray. The Lord can raise you up (James 5:15) or make the sickness work for good (Romans 8:28). Have your own wrongdoings brought you into trouble? Don't worry, but repent, trust in Jesus, walk in your present light, and the blood will cleanse you, and God will surely help you. Are you troubled about the future? Don't worry. Walk with God today in obedient trust, and tomorrow He will be with you. He will never fail you nor forsake you.

*WH, 11*

## The Blessing Lost

*"Anyone who chooses to do the will of God will find out whether my teaching comes from God or whether I speak on my own."* (John 7:17, NIV)

A letter from a Salvation Army officer reached me with an anguished cry for spiritual help. She tells how she "entered Army work as a girl of seventeen, definitely sanctified, full of zeal and ambition for the Kingdom." But she came into contact with some people to whom she looked for spiritual counsel who were, to her mind, "scarcely saved." Through looking too much at the unfaithfulness of others, her own zeal lessened. Instead of having continued victory, she has had defeat ever since. She closes her letter with the cry, "Oh, if I only knew someone who has really reclaimed that blessing for which my soul yearns!"

When people lose the experience of full salvation, they will never get it again if they spend their time in vain regrets over lost emotions. The look must be forward, not backward; outward, not inward; and upward, not downward. They must look not to other people, but to Jesus, who said, "Anyone who chooses to do the will of God will find out whether my teaching comes from God or whether I speak on my own" (John 7:17, NIV). He emphasized the exercise of the will, not the influence of emotions. We must give our whole attention to willing and doing, not feeling. Comfortable feelings will follow right willing and doing if we have faith.

*RLP, 16*

## The Blessing Regained

*O you of little faith, why did you doubt?* (Matthew 14:31)

A Salvation Army officer told me that for ten years she had not had the blessing and that her soul was drying up. I discovered that she had been bitterly criticizing an officer under whom she had worked and pointed out that this was a violation of the Lord's commands. I told her she must ask the officer's forgiveness, but she said she could not.

On Sunday morning, she said to me, "I feel as though I have been in hell all night!" I replied, "You have not been in hell; you have only been in the vestibule of hell!" I felt confident that she was facing a crisis, and that the Holy Spirit was making, possibly, a final appeal to her.

That night we had a great meeting. Thirty souls were seeking the Lord at the penitent-form. She sat halfway down the hall, a picture of despair. I urged her to settle it, and she came forward at once. At last she promised God she would ask forgiveness, and peace began to nestle in her heart.

The next morning she came to me with a radiant face and said, "God has come back to my heart! I feel as though I have been in heaven!"

If you have lost the blessing, God waits to bless you again if, with penitent heart and full consecration, you will now believe.

*RLP,* 16

# Whisper in the King's Ear

*"Abide in me, and I in you."* (John 15:4)

Prayer is a puzzle to unbelievers, but a sweet privilege to us. A stranger will hesitate to approach a king, but the king's child will climb on the king's knee, whisper in the king's ear, and ask all sorts of favors—and get them too. That is the secret of prayer.

When we have repented of sin, given ourselves to God, and been born again, we are His dear children, and we have a right to come to Him in prayer. The devil will try to hinder us, and if our faith is weak, we may doubt and hesitate; but God wants us to come, with all our wishes, burdens, perplexities, everything.

Nothing that is of interest to us is too small to interest Him. Many people think God is interested only in big things. But the same God who made the flaming suns and mighty worlds made the tiny insect, fashioned the lenses of its little eye, and painted with brightest colors its dainty wing. He is interested in the little quite as much as in the great. Therefore we may bring everything to Him in prayer.

*WH*, 13

# Dare to Ask

*The prayer of a righteous person has great power.*
(James 5:16)

For many days there had been no rain in Ohio. The fields were parched and brown, and everything cried out for water. One Sunday, before his sermon, evangelist Charles Finney prayed for rain. Finney told the Lord all about their great need, and among other things said, "We do not presume to dictate to Thee what is best for us, yet Thou dost invite us to come to Thee as children to a father, and tell Thee what we want. We want rain. Our pastures are dry. The cattle are lowing and wandering about in search of water. Unless Thou dost give us rain our cattle must die, for we shall have no hay for them for winter; and our harvests will come to naught. O Lord, send us rain, and send it now! Although to us there is no sign of it, it is an easy thing for Thee to do. Send it now, Lord, for Christ's sake!"

And the Lord sent it. Before the service was half over, the rain came in such torrents that the preacher's voice could not be heard.

Finney took God at His word, and dared to ask for what he wanted. Just so, we should be definite and pray for what we want.

*WH*, 13

## Pray with Lively Faith

*"I tell you, whatever you ask in prayer, believe that you have received it, and it will be yours."* (Mark 11:24)

Many people pray for things they want, but they do not get them because they seek "to satisfy [their] own desires" (James 4:3, *Phillips*).

The secret of prevailing prayer is this: that we are so in love with Jesus, so at one with Him, that we do not want anything to use or spend in any way that would grieve Him. I want a new suit of clothes. What for? That I may strut around in pride? No, but that I may be suitably clothed for my work for God. I want a clean heart. What for? That I may be happy, and get to heaven? No, not that alone, but that I may honor God, and help Him to win others. When I want things in that spirit, then the Lord can trust me with anything for which I ask Him, for I will not ask Him for anything that is not for His glory.

And we must pray in faith. It is heartbreaking, the way people doubt God, the cold, lifeless prayers they utter before Him! God is much more willing to give good things to us than we are to give good gifts to our own children. And we should come with lively faith that will not be denied.

*WH*, 13

## Persevere in Prayer

*Pray in the Spirit at all times and on every occasion.*
(Ephesians 6:18, NLT)

We must persevere in prayer, and not let go till the answer comes, or until God shows us why it does not come.

Sometimes the answer to prayer comes at once. One morning I prayed for a suit of clothes which I very much needed. A great peace came into my heart, and I got off my knees laughing, knowing that God had heard and answered. How and when the suit was to come I did not know. That same morning a man arrived at my home to take me to the tailor's, to be measured for the best suit in his shop. I knew absolutely nothing about this when I prayed, but God did.

But sometimes the answer is delayed. At such times we must not fold our hands and idly conclude that it is not God's will. Instead, we must search our hearts to make sure the hindrance is not in us, and still continue to plead with God, and in due time the answer will come.

A young man prayed for a friend for thirteen months, and finally died without seeing him saved. But God was faithful, and in due time that friend was converted.

Wrestle with God, give Him no rest, remind Him every day of His promise, and He must hear and answer you.

*WH*, 13

## Fact and Faith

*The grace of the Lord Jesus Christ and the love of God
and the fellowship of the Holy Spirit be with you all.*
(2 Corinthians 13:14)

In the ordinary affairs of life, we grasp facts without puzzling ourselves over *how*. Who can explain how light reveals material objects, how sound conveys ideas to our minds? We know and believe these facts, but the *how* we pass by as a mystery unrevealed. What God has revealed, we believe. We cannot understand how Jesus turned water into wine, how He multiplied a few loaves and fishes and fed thousands, how He opened blind eyes. But the facts we believe. Wireless telegraphic messages are sent over the vast wastes of ocean. That is a fact, and we believe it. But *how* they go need not be our concern.

So it is with the Trinity. While the Bible and reason plainly declare that there is but one God, the Scriptures reveal that there are three Persons in the Godhead—Father, Son, and Holy Spirit—as in Paul's benediction to the Corinthians: "The grace of the Lord Jesus Christ and the love of God and the fellowship of the Holy Spirit be with you all" (2 Corinthians 13:14).

But only the *fact* is revealed. *How* there can be three Persons in one Godhead is not revealed. The *how* is a mystery, and is not a matter of faith at all. But the *fact* is a matter of revelation, and therefore a matter of faith.

*HGC, 1*

OCTOBER 31

## The Spirit of Adoption

*Those who are led by the Spirit of God are the children of God.* (Romans 8:14, NIV)

Every child of God, every true follower of Jesus, has the Holy Spirit in some gracious manner and measure, else that person would not be a child of God; for it is only those "who are led by the Spirit of God" who "are the children of God" (Romans 8:14, NIV).

When we yield and trust, and are accepted of the Lord, and are saved by grace, it is the Holy Spirit who assures us of the Father's favor, and notifies us that we are saved. "The Spirit himself bears witness with our spirit that we are children of God." He is "the Spirit of adoption . . . by whom we cry, 'Abba! Father!'" (Romans 8:16, 15).

It is He who strengthens the new follower of Jesus to fight against and overcome sin, and it is He who begets within that person a hope of fuller righteousness through faith in Christ.

*And every virtue we possess,*
*And every victory won,*
*And every thought of holiness,*
*Are His alone.*[31]

*HGC, 2*

## Bold in Our God

*We were bold in our God to speak to you the gospel of God in much conflict.* (1 Thessalonians 2:2, NKJV)

Boldness is a fruit of righteousness, and is always found in those who are full of the Holy Spirit. They forget themselves, and so lose all fear. Fear is a fruit of selfishness. Boldness thrives when selfishness is destroyed. This was the secret of the martyrs when burned at the stake or thrown to the wild beasts.

Gideon fearlessly attacked one hundred and twenty thousand Midianites with but three hundred unarmed men. Jonathan and his armor-bearer charged the Philistine garrison and routed hundreds of the enemy. David faced the lion and the bear, and inspired all Israel by battling with and killing Goliath. The prophets were men and women of the highest courage, who fearlessly rebuked kings, and at the risk of life, denounced popular sins and called the people back to righteousness. They feared God, and so lost the fear of people. They believed God, and so obeyed Him, and found His favor, and were entrusted with His high missions and everlasting employments.

"Fear not, for I am with you," the Lord said (Isaiah 41:10). The apostle Paul believed this, and so was able to say, "We were bold in our God" (1 Thessalonians 2:2, NKJV). God was his high tower, his strength and unfailing defense, and so he was not afraid.

*HGC, 16*

## As David's Smooth Stones

*David took off [Saul's] armor. . . . He went out to a stream
and picked up five smooth rocks and . . . went straight
toward Goliath.* (1 Samuel 17:39-40, CEV)

An educated minister had a skeptical lawyer in his congregation, whom he wanted very much to see come to faith.
One day, to the minister's delight, the lawyer testified that
he had experienced new life in Christ, and wished to join
the church. After some conversation, the pastor rather
blushingly inquired, "May I ask which of my sermons led
you to Christ?"

Then the lawyer, with some little confusion, replied,
"Well, to tell you the truth, Pastor, it was not one of your
sermons at all. A few Sundays ago, the church steps were
very slippery, and old Auntie Blank was trying to descend
them. She was crippled and feeble and in danger of falling, when I took hold of her arm and assisted her to the
sidewalk. She looked up into my eyes and thanked me,
and with a bright smile on her face, asked, 'Do you love
my Jesus?' That led me to Christ." It was like the smooth
stone that killed the giant, when Saul's armor and sword
had failed!

Be a man or woman of much secret prayer. Take time
to listen to God's voice. Read your Bible; love it, pray over
it. Get your mind stored with truths that will be to you as
David's smooth stones, and God will surely use you and
make you a blessing.

*HTH, 26*

## Charitable Judgments

*If you feel inclined to set yourself up as a judge of those who sin, let me assure you, whoever you are, that you are in no position to do so.* (Romans 2:1, *Phillips*)

When the Holy Spirit comes in His fullness, He strips us of our self-righteousness and pride and conceit. We see ourselves as the chief of sinners, and realize that only through the stripes of Jesus are we healed; and ever after, as we live in the Spirit, our boast is in Him and our glory is in the Cross. Remembering the hole of the pit from which we were quarried, we are filled with tender pity for all who are not in the way. And while we do not excuse or belittle sin, our judgments are full of charity.

> *Judge not; the workings of his brain*
> *And of his heart thou canst not see:*
> *What looks to thy dim eyes a stain,*
> *In God's pure light may only be*
> *A scar, brought from some well-won field,*
> *Where thou wouldst only faint and yield.*[32]

True charity does not wink at iniquity, but it is as far removed from a sharp, condemning spirit as light is from darkness. It is quick to condemn sin, but is full of saving, long-suffering compassion for the sinner.

*HGC, 7*

## A Teachable Mind

*The heartfelt counsel of a friend is as sweet as perfume and incense.* (Proverbs 27:9, NLT)

A humble, teachable mind marks those in whom the Holy Spirit dwells. They submit themselves one to the other, welcome instruction and correction, and esteem "open rebuke . . . better than secret love" (Proverbs 27:5, KJV). They believe that the Lord has yet many things to say to them, and they are willing and glad for Him to say them by whomever He will, but especially by their leaders and their brothers and sisters.

But Satan seeks to destroy all this lowliness of spirit and humbleness of mind. Those in whom his deadly work has begun are wiser in their own conceit "than seven people who answer sensibly" (Proverbs 26:16, CEB). They are wiser than all their teachers, and no one can instruct them. It is this huge conceit that has led some to announce themselves as apostles and prophets to whom all must listen or fall under the wrath of God.

The Holy Spirit may lead to a holy rivalry in love and humility, and kindness and self-denial and good works, but He never leads His servants into such swelling conceit that they can no longer be taught by others. We cannot be too much on our guard against false spirits who would counterfeit the work and leadings of the Holy Spirit.

*HGC, 7*

## A Tolerant Attitude

*Foolish people are always fighting, but avoiding quarrels will bring you honor.* (Proverbs 20:3, NCV)

Those who are filled with the Spirit are tolerant of others who may differ from them in opinion or in doctrine. They are firm in their own convictions, but they do not condemn all those who differ. They are glad to believe that people are often better than their creed, and may be saved in spite of it. Like mountains whose bases are bathed with sunshine and clothed with fruitful fields and vineyards while their tops are covered with dark clouds, so human hearts are often fruitful in the graces of charity while their heads are yet darkened by doctrinal error.

But Satan, under guise of love for and loyalty to the truth, will introduce the spirit of intolerance. It was this spirit that crucified Jesus, burned John Huss at the stake, hanged Girolamo Savonarola, and inspired the horrors of the Inquisition. And the same spirit blinds the eyes of many professing Christians. They murder love to protect what they often blindly call truth. What is truth without love? A dead thing, an encumbrance, "the letter [that] kills" (2 Corinthians 3:6)!

Truth is precious, and sound doctrine to be esteemed more than silver and gold. But love can exist where truth is not held in its most perfect and complete forms, and love is the one thing needful.

*HGC, 7*

# NOVEMBER 6

## A Spirit of Unity

*How good and pleasant it is when God's people live together in unity!* (Psalm 133:1, NIV)

The presence of the Holy Spirit produces unity among Christians. People who have been sitting behind their sectarian fences in self-complacent ease, proselytizing zeal, or grim defiance are suddenly lifted above the fence and find sweet fellowship with each other when He comes into their hearts.

They esteem others better than themselves, and reflect the unity of Christians in the beginning in Jerusalem: "The whole group of those who believed were of one heart and soul" (Acts 4:32, NRSV). What an ideal is this! And since it has been attained once, it can be attained again and retained, but only by the indwelling of the Holy Spirit.

It was for this that Jesus poured out His heart in the garden of Gethsemane. And what was the standard of unity? Listen! "As you are in me and I am in you, I pray that they can also be one in us. Then the world will believe that you sent me" (John 17:21, NCV). Such unity has a wondrous power to compel the belief of worldly people. It is for this His blessed heart eternally yearns, and it is for this that the Holy Spirit works in the hearts of those who receive Him.

*HGC, 7*


310

## The Lowly Life

*"Take my yoke upon you, and learn from me, for I am gentle and lowly in heart."* (Matthew 11:29)

The Holy Spirit produces the same meekness of heart and lowly service that were seen in the Master. Ambition for rank and power and money and fame vanishes, and in its place is a consuming desire to accomplish in full the blessed, beneficent will of God.

Some time ago I met a woman who received pay that in a few years would have made her independently wealthy. But the Spirit of Jesus came into her heart, and she is now nursing the poor, and doing the most loathsome and exacting service for them, and doing it with a smiling face, for her food and clothes.

Do you have visions of glory and rapturous delight, and so count yourself filled with the Spirit? Do these visions lead you to virtue and to lowly, loving service? If not, watch yourself. Thank God for the mounts of transfiguration where we behold His glory! But down in the valley are suffering children, and to them He would have us go with the glory of the mount on our faces, and lowly love in our hearts, and clean hands ready for any service. He would have us give ourselves to them. And if we love Him, if we follow Him, if we are truly filled with the Holy Spirit, we will.

*HGC, 9*

NOVEMBER 8

## The God of Hope

*May the God of hope fill you with joy and peace in
your faith, that by the power of the Holy Spirit, your
whole life and outlook may be radiant with hope.*
(Romans 15:13, *Phillips*)

Are you ever cast down and depressed in spirit? Listen to
Paul: "May the God of hope fill you with all joy and peace
in believing, so that by the power of the Holy Spirit you
may abound in hope" (Romans 15:13). What cheer is in
those words! They ring like the shout of triumph.

God Himself is "the God of hope." There is no gloom,
no depression, no wasting sickness of deferred hope in
Him. He is a brimming fountain and ocean of hope eternally, and He is our God. He is our Hope.

Out of His infinite fullness He is to fill us. Not half fill
us, but fill us with joy—all joy—and peace.

And this is not by some condition or means that is so
high and difficult that we cannot perform our part, but it
is simply in believing—something the little child and the
aged philosopher, the poor and the rich, the ignorant and
the learned can do. And the result will be abounding hope
"by the power of the Holy Spirit" (Romans 15:13).

*HGC, 10*

## Hope in Affliction

*We rejoice in hope of the glory of God.* (Romans 5:2)

God's wisdom and ability to make all things work together for our good are not to be measured by our understanding, but by our faith. My child is in serious difficulty and does not know how to help himself, so I say, "Leave it to me." He may not understand how I am to help him, but he trusts me, and rejoices in hope. We are God's dear children, and He knows how to help us, if we will only commit ourselves to Him in faith.

Afflictions may overtake us, and yet "this light momentary affliction is preparing for us an eternal weight of glory beyond all comparison, as we look not to the things that are seen but to the things that are unseen" (2 Corinthians 4:17-18). But such a promise as that only mocks us if we do not believe. "In all their affliction he was afflicted, and the angel of his presence saved them; in his love and in his pity he redeemed them" (Isaiah 63:9). And He is just the same today. If we are tried "in the furnace of affliction" (Isaiah 48:10), we must nestle down into His will and, believing, "abound in hope by the power of the Holy Spirit" (Romans 15:13, NKJV).

*HGC, 10*

## No Time for Gossip

*"My servants will sing out of the joy of their hearts."*
(Isaiah 65:14, NIV)

Years ago the Lord gave me a blessed revival in a little village. One result was that the people now had no time for gossip. They were all talking about the things of the Lord. When they met each other, they praised the Lord and encouraged each other to press on in the heavenly way. If they met a person who had not experienced salvation, they tenderly urged him or her to be reconciled to God.

There was no criticizing of their neighbors, no fault-finding with their circumstances. Their conversation was joyous, cheerful, and helpful—the natural, spontaneous outflow of hearts filled with the Spirit.

People often fall into gossip and criticism not so much from ill will as from old habit, as a wagon falls into a rut. Or they drift into the current of conversation around them. But the Holy Spirit lifts us out of the old ruts, and we must follow Him with care lest we fall into them again.

This is the Holy Spirit's substitute for gossip and fault-finding and slander: "Be filled with the Spirit, addressing one another in psalms and hymns and spiritual songs, singing and making melody to the Lord with your heart, giving thanks always and for everything to God the Father in the name of our Lord Jesus Christ" (Ephesians 5:18-20).

*HGC, 11*

## An Eternal Sin

*Whoever blasphemes against the Holy Spirit never has forgiveness, but is guilty of an eternal sin.* (Mark 3:29)

Jesus was casting out devils, and the experts in Moses' law said, "Beelzebul is in him. . . . He forces demons out of people with the help of the ruler of demons." To this Jesus replied, "How can Satan force out Satan? If a kingdom is divided against itself, that kingdom cannot last" (Mark 3:22-24, GW).

Jesus did not rail against them, nor flatly deny their base assertion, but showed how logically false their statement must be. And then, with grave authority, He added, "Truly I tell you, people will be forgiven for their sins and whatever blasphemies they utter; but whoever blasphemes against the Holy Spirit can never have forgiveness, but is guilty of an eternal sin" (Mark 3:28-30, NRSV).

Jesus worked these signs and wonders by the power of the Holy Spirit, that He might win their confidence, and that they might believe and be saved. But they refused to believe, and in their malignant obstinacy heaped scorn upon Him. It was not so much one act of sin as a deep-seated rebellion against God that led them to choose darkness rather than light, and so to blaspheme against the Holy Spirit, who is ceaselessly striving to make God's love known in our hearts and transfigure our character by love.

*HGC, 12*

## The Unpardonable Sin

*Cast me not away from your presence, and take not your Holy Spirit from me.* (Psalm 51:11)

One night a gentleman arose during a revival in Canada and urged those present to accept Jesus as their Savior and receive the Holy Spirit. He said he had sinned against the Holy Spirit, and could nevermore be pardoned. With all earnest tenderness he exhorted them not to harden their hearts. Suddenly the scales of doubt dropped from his eyes, and he saw that he had not in his inmost heart rejected Jesus, and so had not committed the unpardonable sin. In an instant his heart was filled with light and love and peace, and sweet assurance that Jesus was his Savior.

John Bunyan was also afflicted with horrible fears that he had committed this sin. In *Grace Abounding to the Chief of Sinners*, he tells how he was delivered from his doubts and was filled once more with the joy of the Lord.

I once thought I had committed this sin, and for twenty-eight days was in a horrible pit of doubt and fear. But God drew me out, and showed me that this is a sin committed only by those who, in spite of all evidence, harden their hearts, and shield themselves in their sins in order to deny and blaspheme the Lord.

Those who fear they have committed this sin may generally be assured that they have not.

*HGC, 12*

## Grieving the Spirit

*Do not grieve the Holy Spirit of God.* (Ephesians 4:30)

One day, in a fit of boyish temper, I spoke hot words of anger against another person, and this deeply grieved my mother. She said little, but I can still see her look of grief across a third of a century. A stranger might have been amused or incensed at my words, but Mother was grieved to her heart by my lack of love.

We can anger a stranger or an enemy, but it is only a friend we grieve. The Holy Spirit is such a Friend; and shall we carelessly offend Him, and estrange ourselves from Him in spite of His love? He is grieved, as was my mother, by the unloving speech and spirit of God's children.

Paul teaches us (Ephesians 4:29-31) that it is not by some huge wickedness, some Judas-like betrayal, that we grieve the Holy Spirit, but by that which most people count little and unimportant: by talk that corrupts, by gossip, bitterness, and uncharitable criticisms and faultfindings.

There is a sense in which every sin is against the Holy Spirit. Of course, not every such sin is unpardonable, but the tendency of all sin is in that direction. Therefore, it is infinitely important that we beware of offenses against the Spirit, "that none of you may be hardened by the deceitfulness of sin" (Hebrews 3:13).

*HGC, 13*

## Have You Rejoiced Today?

*Rejoice before the Lord your God in all that you undertake.* (Deuteronomy 12:18)

Some years ago a sanctified woman went alone to keep her daily hour with God. But to her surprise, it seemed that she could not find Him, either in prayer or in His Word. She searched her heart for evidence of sin, but the Spirit showed her nothing contrary to God. She searched her memory for any breach of covenant, any broken vows, but could find none.

Then she asked the Lord to show her if there were any duty unfulfilled, any command unnoticed, and quick as thought came the often-read words, "Rejoice evermore" (1 Thessalonians 5:16, KJV). "Have you done that this morning?" She had not.

At once she began to count her blessings and thank the Lord for each one, and rejoice in Him for all the ways He had led her, and the gifts He had bestowed, and in a very few minutes the Lord stood revealed to her spiritual consciousness.

She had not committed sin, nor resisted the Spirit, but she had not turned on the main, and so her soul was not flooded with living waters. But that morning she learned a lifelong lesson, and she has ever since safeguarded her soul by obeying the many commands to "rejoice in the Lord."

*HGC, 13*

## Resisting the Spirit

*Must you forever resist the Holy Spirit?* (Acts 7:51, NLT)

Grieving and quenching the Holy Spirit may be done unintentionally by lack of thought and prayer and hearty devotion to the Lord Jesus, but they prepare the way and lead to intentional and positive resistance to the Spirit. To resist the Spirit is to fight against Him.

The ten plagues that came upon Pharaoh and his people were ten open doors into God's favor and fellowship, which they themselves shut by their stubborn resistance. And what on a large scale befalls nations and peoples, on a small scale also befalls individuals. Those who receive and obey the Lord are enlightened and blessed and saved. Those who resist and reject Him are sadly left to themselves and surely swallowed up in destruction.

Likewise, the professing Christian who, convicted of his or her need of the blessing of heart holiness and of God's desire and willingness to bestow it now, refuses to seek it in wholehearted affectionate consecration and faith, is resisting the Holy Spirit. Such resistance imperils the soul beyond all possible computation.

We must beware. We must watch and pray and walk softly with the Lord in glad obedience and childlike faith, if we would escape the darkness and dryness that result from grieving and quenching the Spirit, and the dangers that surely come from resisting Him.

*HGC, 13*

## Lightning in Our Darkness

*People who are unspiritual don't accept the things*
*from God's Spirit. They are foolishness to them.*
(1 Corinthians 2:14, CEB)

A horseman lost his way in a pitiless storm on a black and starless night. Suddenly his horse drew back and refused to take another step. He urged it forward, but it only threw itself back upon its haunches. Just then a vivid flash of lightning revealed a great precipice upon the brink of which he stood. It was but an instant, and then the pitchy blackness hid it again from view. But he turned his horse and anxiously rode away from the terrible danger.

Into the blackness of the sinner's night the Holy Spirit flashes a light that gives a glimpse of eternal things which, heeded, would lead to the sweet peace and security of eternal day. For when the Holy Spirit is heeded and honored, the night passes, the shadows flee away, "the Sun of Righteousness [arises] with healing in His wings" (Malachi 4:2, NKJV), and, saved and sanctified, men and women walk in His light in safety and joy. Doctrines which before were repellent and foolish—or a stumbling block—now become precious and satisfying to the soul. And truths which before were hid in impenetrable darkness, or seen only as through dense gloom and fog, are now seen clearly as in the light of broad day.

The great teacher of truth is the Spirit of Truth.

*HGC, 14*

## Earnest Prayer

*Pray in the Spirit in every situation.* (Ephesians 6:18, GW)

An important work of the Holy Spirit is to teach us how to pray, instruct us what to pray for, and inspire us to pray earnestly, without ceasing, and in faith for the things we desire and the things that are dear to the heart of the Lord.

Prayer is exceedingly simple. The faintest cry for help, a whisper for mercy, is prayer. But when the Holy Spirit comes and fills the soul with His blessed presence, prayer becomes more than a cry. It ceases to be a feeble request, and often becomes a striving for greater things, a wrestling with God (Romans 15:30; Colossians 4:12).

It was in this spirit and fellowship that Abraham prayed for Sodom (Genesis 18:23-32); that Moses interceded for Israel, and stood between them and God's hot displeasure (Exodus 32:7-14); and that Elijah prevailed to shut up the heavens for three years and six months, and then again prevailed in his prayer for rain (James 5:17-18).

God would have us come to Him not only as a foolish and ignorant child comes, but as an ambassador to the home office, as a full-grown son or daughter who has become of age and entered into partnership with his or her father, as a bride who is one in all interests and affections with the bridegroom.

*HGC, 15*

## Mighty Prayer

*Let us therefore come boldly to the throne of grace, that we may obtain mercy and find grace to help in time of need.*
(Hebrews 4:16, NKJV)

Three great obstacles hinder mighty prayer: selfishness, unbelief, and ignorance. The blessing of the Spirit sweeps away these obstacles.

1. Selfishness must be cast out by the incoming of love. When this is done, we shall not be asking for things to use for our own pleasures, to gratify our appetites, pride, ambition, or ease. We shall seek only the glory of our Lord and the common good of our fellow human beings.

2. Unbelief must be destroyed. Doubt paralyzes prayer. Only as the eye of faith sees our Father God upon the throne, inviting us to come without fear and make our wants known, does prayer cease to be a feeble, timid cry and become a mighty spiritual force, moving God Himself in the interests which it seeks.

3. Knowledge and wisdom must take the place of foolish ignorance. If my little child asks for a glittering razor, I refuse the request. But when my full-grown son asks for one, I grant it. So God cannot wisely answer some prayers, for they are foolish or untimely. Hence, we need not love and faith only, but wisdom and knowledge, that we may ask according to the will of God. We should think before we pray, and study that we may pray wisely.

*HGC, 15*

## As Friend with Friend

*"I have called you friends, for all that I have heard from my Father I have made known to you."* (John 15:15)

Spirit-filled men and women talk with God as friend with friend, and the Holy Spirit helps their infirmities and intercedes within them with unutterable groanings, according to the will of God (Romans 8:26-27; 1 Corinthians 2:11).

A young man felt called to mission work in China, but his mother offered strong opposition to his going. An agent of the mission, knowing the need of the work and vexed with the mother, one day laid the case before Hudson Taylor.

"Mr. Taylor gently suggested our praying about it," he said. "Such a prayer I have never heard before! It seemed to me more like a conversation with a trusted friend whose advice he was seeking. He talked the matter over from every point of view—the side of the young man, of China's needs, of the mother and her natural feelings, and also my side. It was a revelation to me. I saw that prayer did not mean merely asking for things—much less asking for things to be carried out by God according to our ideas—but that it means *communion*, fellowship, partnership with our heavenly Father. And when our will is really blended with His, what liberty we may have in asking for what we want!"

*HGC, 15*

## The Gentle Servant

*We were gentle among you, like a nursing mother taking care of her own children.* (1 Thessalonians 2:7)

The fierce hurricane that casts down the giant trees of the forest is not so mighty as the gentle sunshine, which, from tiny seeds and acorns, lifts aloft the towering spires of oak and fir on a thousand hills and mountains.

The wild storm that lashes the sea into foam and fury is feeble compared to the gentle yet immeasurably powerful influence which twice a day swings the oceans in resistless tides from shore to shore.

And as in the physical world the mighty powers are gentle in their vast workings, so it is in the spiritual world. The light that falls on the lids of the sleeping infant, and wakes it from its slumber, is not more gentle than the "still small voice" (1 Kings 19:12, KJV) that brings assurance of forgiveness or cleansing to them that look unto Jesus.

Oh, the gentleness of God! "Your gentleness made me great," said David (Psalm 18:35). "By the humility and gentleness of Christ, I appeal to you" (2 Corinthians 10:1, NIV), wrote Paul. And again, "The fruit of the Spirit is love, joy, peace, longsuffering, gentleness" (Galatians 5:22, KJV). And as the Father, Son, and Holy Spirit are gentle, so will be the servant of the Lord who is filled with the Spirit.

*HGC, 16*

## The Holy Spirit's Call

*The Holy Spirit said, "Appoint Barnabas and Saul to the work I have called them to undertake."* (Acts 13:2, CEB)

God chooses His own workers. The Holy Spirit calls men and women to many employments for His glory, and I doubt not would still more often do so, if they would but listen and wait upon Him to know His will.

Sometimes the call comes as distinctly as though a voice had spoken from the skies into the depths of the heart. It may come as a gentle conviction, as though a gossamer bridle were placed upon the heart and conscience. The suggestion gradually becomes clearer until it masters the one who is called.

The soul whom God calls cannot safely neglect or despise the call. We will find our mission on earth, our happiness and peace, our power and prosperity, our reward in heaven, and probably heaven itself, bound up with that call and dependent upon it. We may run away from it, as did Jonah, and find a waiting ship to favor our flight; but we will also find fierce storms and billowing seas overtaking us, and big-mouthed fishes of trouble and disaster ready to swallow us.

But if we heed the call and cheerfully go where God appoints, God will go with us; we shall nevermore be left alone. The Holy Spirit will surely accompany us, and we may be among the happiest souls on earth.

*HGC, 18*

## Keep the Blessing Current

*Above all else, guard your heart, for everything you do flows from it.* (Proverbs 4:23, NIV)

Keep your eyes on Jesus, and guard yourself against the beginnings of temptation and sin. Keep your mind pure. Fill it with clean thoughts, loving thoughts, and holy affections. Lift your thoughts above fleshly and low things to spiritual levels. Sing songs and make melody in your heart to the Lord.

Sin does not leap upon us fully armed. It steals in through a look, a swift, silent suggestion, or imagination. Deal promptly and sternly with your eyes and your ears. Turn away your eyes from beholding evil, and your ears from listening to evil. Make a covenant with your eyes as did Job. Stand on guard at Eye-gate and Ear-gate lest sin get into your heart through those gateways.

Often drop on your knees or lift your heart in secret prayer, and do not forget to mingle thanksgiving with your prayers. You do not praise God enough. Begin now. Thank Him now and praise Him, for He is worthy.

Finally, seek to pass some of your blessing on to another soul, as the widow of Zarephath (1 Kings 17:7-16) shared her bit of oil and handful of meal with Elijah and found it multiplying through the months of famine. So will you find your blessings multiplying as you share them with others.

*AP, 18*

## When the Comforter Is Come

*I am overwhelmed with joy despite all our troubles.*
(2 Corinthians 7:4, *The Message*)

A pastor went one morning to visit two women who were greatly afflicted. They had long been professing Christians and members of the church. He asked the first, "How is it with you this morning?" "Oh, I have not slept all night," she replied. "I have so much pain. It is so hard to have to lie here. I cannot see why God deals so with me." Evidently, she was not filled with the Spirit, but was in a controversy with the Lord about her sufferings and would not be comforted.

Leaving her, he called immediately upon the other woman, and asked, "How are you today?" "Oh, I had such a night of suffering!" Then there came out upon her a beautiful radiance. "But Jesus was so near and helped me so, that I could suffer this way and more, if my Father thinks best." On she went with cheer and triumph that made the sickroom a vestibule of glory. No lack of comfort in her heart, for the Comforter Himself, the Holy Spirit, had been invited and had come in.

Not all God's dear children thus triumph over their difficulties and sufferings, but this is God's standard, and they may attain unto it if, by faith, they will open their hearts and "be filled with the Spirit" (Ephesians 5:18).

*HGC, 20*

## The Spirit of Thankfulness

*Give thanks to him; bless his name!* (Psalm 100:4)

Nothing will keep the heart so young, and banish care so quickly, and make one's influence so fragrant and gracious, and shed abroad such peace and gladness as the spirit of thankfulness.

This spirit can and should be cultivated. There is much in the lot of each of us to be thankful for. We should thank Him for personal liberty and for the measure of health we have. We should thank Him for food, and the appetite to eat it, and the power to digest it. We should thank Him for clothes to wear and books to read. We should thank Him for the church, the Bible, the revelation of Jesus Christ, the Fountain opened for sin and uncleanness. We should thank Him for home and friends, and heaven bending over all.

Truly, we have much to thank God for, but if we would be thankful, we must set our hearts to do it with a will. We grumble and complain without thought, but we must *think* to give thanks. To murmur and repine is natural; to give thanks—to really give thanks—is supernatural. It is a spirit not earth-born, but heaven-sent, and yet, like all things from God, it can be cultivated.

*HTH, 19*

## Moving Heaven

*In every thing give thanks: for this is the will of God in Christ Jesus concerning you.* (1 Thessalonians 5:18, KJV)

Do you ask, "How can I pray in faith?" Hunt up God's promises, and go to Him with them, and say with David, "Remember your word to your servant, in which you have made me hope" (Psalm 119:49). That is what Charles Finney did. He wanted rain, and he went to God with the promise, "When the poor and needy seek water, and there is none, and their tongue is parched with thirst, I the LORD will answer them" (Isaiah 41:17).

And we should mingle thanks with our prayers, even before we see the answer. "In everything by prayer and supplication with thanksgiving let your requests be made known to God," wrote Paul (Philippians 4:6). A mother got gloriously sanctified at a Salvation Army penitent-form, and then began to pray in faith for the conversion of her daughter. For some time she prayed, but one day she said, "Lord, I am not going to pray for this any longer, but I am going to thank Thee for the salvation of my child." Within a week the girl was saved.

Holy people are in vital union and partnership with God, and their prayers inspired by the Holy Spirit move all heaven in their behalf.

*WH, 13*

## Overcome Evil with Good

*Do not be overcome by evil, but overcome evil with good.*
(Romans 12:21, NIV)

A Russian peasant named Sutajeff could get no help from the religious teachers of his village, so he learned to read, and while studying the Bible he found the narrow way, the gospel of Jesus, and walked gladly in it. One night neighbors of his stole some of his grain, but in their haste or carelessness they left a bag. He found it, and ran after them to restore it, "For," said he, "fellows who have to steal must be hard up." And by this Christlike spirit he saved both himself and them, for he kept the spirit of love in his own heart, and they were converted and became his most ardent disciples.

A beggar woman to whom he gave lodging stole the bedding and ran away with it. She was pursued by the neighbors, and was just about to be put in prison when Sutajeff appeared, became her advocate, secured her acquittal, and gave her food and money for her journey.

He recognized the law of his new life and gladly obeyed it, and so was not overcome by evil, but persistently and triumphantly overcame evil with good (Romans 12:21).

*HGC, 19*

## The Spirit and Method of Jesus

*If anyone wants to sue you and take your shirt, hand over your coat as well.* (Matthew 5:40, NIV)

A Salvation Army officer [pastor] went to a hard corps [church], and found that his predecessor was sending back to friends, asking for money which his own corps much needed. Losing sight of the Spirit of Jesus, he made a complaint about it, and the money was returned. But he became lean in his soul. He had quenched the Spirit. He had not only refused to give his coat, but had fought for the return of the shirt, and his poor heart was sad and heavy.

He came to me with anxious inquiry as to what I thought of his action. I had to admit that the other man had transgressed, and that the money ought to be returned. But I felt that the officer should have been more grieved over the unChristlike spirit of his brother than over the loss of the money, and that like Sutajeff, the Russian peasant, he should have said, "Poor fellow! He must be hard up; I will send him money myself." When I told him that story, he came to himself very quickly, and was soon back in the narrow way and rejoicing in the smile of Jesus once again.

This is the spirit and method of Jesus; and by men and women filled with this spirit and following this method, He will yet win the world.

*HGC, 19*

## Put Your Sword Away

*Jesus said, "Put your sword back where it belongs."*
(Matthew 26:52, *The Message*)

When you are reviled, demeaned, and slandered, and are tempted to retort, Jesus says to you, "Put your sword away" (Matthew 26:52, CEV). When you are wronged and ill-treated, and people ride roughshod over you, and you feel it would be simple justice to smite back, He says, "Put your sword away." "Live peaceably with all" (Romans 12:18). Your weapons are not carnal, but spiritual, now that you belong to Him, and have your citizenship in heaven.

"But will not people walk over us, if we do not stand up for our rights?" you ask. I argue that you are to stand up for your higher rather than your lower rights, the rights of your heavenly life rather than your earthly life. Stand up for your rights in the way and spirit of Jesus rather than in the way and spirit of the world.

"By mercy and truth iniquity is purged," wrote Solomon (Proverbs 16:6, KJV). Take mercy and truth for your weapons, and God will be with you and for you, and great shall be your victory and joy.

*HGC, 19*

## From the Flinty Rock

*We rejoice in our sufferings, knowing that suffering produces endurance, and endurance produces character, and character produces hope.* (Romans 5:3-4)

Sin is present, with its contradictions and falsehoods, its darkness, its wars, brutalities, and injustices, producing awful harvests of pain and sorrow, yet God, in wonderful wisdom and loving-kindness, turns even these into instruments by which to fashion beautiful graces in us.

Storm succeeds sunshine, and darkness the light. Pain follows hard on the heels of pleasure, while sorrow peers over the shoulder of joy. Gladness and grief, rest and toil, peace and war, interminably intermingled, follow each other in ceaseless succession in this world. We cannot escape suffering while in the body. But we can receive it with a faith that robs it of its terror and extracts from it richest blessing; from the flinty rock will gush forth living waters, and the carcass of the lion will furnish the sweetest honey (Exodus 17:1-7; Judges 14:5-9).

This is so even when the suffering is a result of our own folly or sin. It is intended as a teacher, a corrective, a remedy, a warning. And it will surely work for good if, instead of repining and vainly regretting the past, we steadily look unto Jesus and learn our lesson in patience and thankfulness.

*HGC, 20*

## Triumph over the Worst

*My flesh and my heart may fail, but God is the strength of my heart and my portion forever.* (Psalm 73:26)

It is not by hypnotizing the soul, nor by blessing it into ecstatic insensibility, that the Lord enables the Spirit-filled believer to triumph over suffering. Rather it is by giving the soul a sweet, constant, and unshaken assurance through faith:

1. that it is freely and fully accepted in Christ;
2. that whatever suffering comes, it is measured, weighed, and permitted by love infinitely tender, and guided by wisdom that cannot err;
3. that however difficult it may be to explain suffering now, it is nevertheless one of the "all things" which "work together for good to them that love God" (Romans 8:28, KJV);
4. that though foes may have formed against us sharp weapons, yet they cannot prosper, for the Lord's shield and buckler defend us; though all things be lost, and though "my flesh and my heart may fail, . . . God is the strength of my heart and my portion forever" (Psalm 73:26).

This is faith's triumph over the worst the world can offer through the blessed fullness of the indwelling Comforter.

*HGC, 20*

## The Overflowing Blessing

*There shall be showers of blessing.* (Ezekiel 34:26, KJV)

The children of Israel were instructed by Moses to give tithes of all they had to the Lord, and in return God promised to richly bless them. But they became covetous and unbelieving, and began to rob God by withholding their tithes, and then God began to withhold His blessing from them.

But still God loved and pitied them, and spoke to them again and again by His prophets. Finally, by the prophet Malachi, He said, "'Bring the whole tithe into the storehouse, that there may be food in my house. Test me in this,' says the LORD Almighty, 'and see if I will not throw open the floodgates of heaven'" (Malachi 3:10, NIV). He promised to make their barns overflow if they would be faithful.

Now, this overflow of granaries is a type of overflowing hearts and lives when we give ourselves fully to God, and the blessed Holy Spirit comes in. The blessing is too big to contain, but just bursts out and gladdens and refreshes and purifies wherever it goes.

Do you ask, "How can I get such a blessing?" You will get it by bringing in all the tithes, by giving yourself in wholehearted, joyous consecration. Do not try to bargain with the Lord, but wait on Him, and He will give it to you.

*HGC, 21*

## Rivers of Living Water

*"If anyone believes in me, rivers of living water will flow out from that person's heart."* (John 7:38, NCV)

When we give ourselves fully to God, and the blessed Holy Spirit comes in, "rivers of living water" (John 7:38) begin to overflow our lives.

There is an overflow of *love*. Sin brings in an overflow of hate, but this blessing causes love to overflow, making us to love all—strangers, and even our enemies.

There is an overflow of *peace*. It settles old quarrels and grudges. Kindly words and sweet goodwill take the place of bitterness and strife.

There is an overflow of *joy*. It makes the face to shine; it glances from the eye, and bubbles out in thanksgiving and praise.

There is an overflow of *patience* and *long-suffer*ing. A man got this blessing, and his wife was so enraged that she left him to live with his unmarried brother. He was terribly tempted to kill them both. But the Lord gave him the patience and long-suffering of Jesus, enabling him to treat them with utmost kindness, until all his neighbors believed in his religion.

There is an overflow of *goodness* and *generosity*. I read the other day of a poor man who supports eight missionaries. When asked how, he replied that he denied himself, and managed his affairs in order to do it.

When the Comforter comes, great blessing fills the heart and overflows through all of life. *HGC, 21*

# Success in Spiritual Leadership

*For the sake of your servant and according to your will, you have done this great thing and made known all these promises.* (1 Chronicles 17:19, NIV)

A mighty man or woman inspires and trains others to be mighty. We wonder and exclaim often at the slaughter of Goliath by David, and we forget that David was the forerunner of a race of fearless, invincible warriors and giant-killers.

Moses inspired a tribe of cowering, spiritless slaves to throw off the iron bondage of Pharaoh. He fired them with a national spirit, and welded and organized them into a people that could be hurled with resistless power against the walled cities and trained warriors of Canaan.

But what was the secret of David and Moses? Doubtless, they were cast in a finer mold than most people; but their secret was not in themselves. Their secret is an open one. It is the secret of every truly successful spiritual leader from then till now, and there is no other way to success in spiritual leadership.

Joseph Parker declared that great lives are built on great promises, and so they are. These men had found God. They got close to Him, and He spoke to them. He gave them promises. He revealed His way and truth to them, and as they trusted Him, believed His promises, and fashioned their lives according to His truth, everything else followed.

*HGC, 22*

## The Tempered Temper

*Cease from anger and forsake wrath.* (Psalm 37:8, NASB)

Two letters recently reached me, inquiring if I thought it possible to have temper destroyed. Evidently this question perplexes many people, and yet the answer seems to me simple.

Temper, in the sense the word is generally used, is not a faculty or power of the soul, but is rather an irregular, passionate, violent expression of selfishness. When selfishness is destroyed by love—by the incoming of the Holy Spirit, creating within us a clean heart—such evil temper is gone, just as the friction and consequent wear and heat of two wheels is gone when the cogs are perfectly adjusted to each other.

We do not destroy the wheels to get rid of the friction, but we readjust them. That is, we put them into right relations with each other, and then they do their work noiselessly and perfectly. So, strictly speaking, sanctification does not destroy self, but it destroys selfishness—the abnormal and mean and disordered assertion of self. The people of God are to be sanctified, rectified, purified, brought into harmony with God's will as revealed in His Word, and united to Him in Jesus, so that His life of holiness and love flows continually through all the avenues of their being, as the sap of the vine flows through all parts of the branch.

*HGC, 23*

## As Oak Trees Begin

*Unless a grain of wheat falls into the earth and dies,*
*it remains alone; but if it dies, it bears much fruit.*
(John 12:24)

Great revivals and awakenings never begin in a great way. They begin as oak trees begin. There is nothing spectacular about the beginning of an oak tree. In darkness, in loneliness, an acorn gives up its life; and the oak, at first only a tiny root and a tiny stem of green, is born. So revivals are born, so the Kingdom of God comes. Someone, no longer trying to advance his or her own interests, dies—dies to self, to the world, to praise, position, and power—and lives unto Christ, lives to save others. And the awakening of sinners comes; souls are born into the Kingdom of God, and in turn become soul-winners.

"Anyone who wants to be my disciple must follow me" (John 12:26, NLT), said Jesus. Such a one must lose his or her old life, old ambitions, and old values for His sake, His cause, and the souls for whom He died.

That is the price that must be paid. He can show no easier way to us. It is costly. But shall we wish to win eternal and infinite values cheaply? We do not really win souls until we constrain them to follow us, as we follow Christ, through death—death to sin, death to the flesh and the world—into newness of life unto holiness.

*AP, 3*

# The Day of Small Things

*Do not despise these small beginnings.* (Zechariah 4:10, NLT)

The soul-winner must not despise the day of small things. It is better to speak to a small company and win a half dozen of them, than to speak to a thousand and have no one saved or sanctified, though they all go away exclaiming, "Wasn't the meeting grand!"

Some years ago I went to a large city, where I thought we had a flourishing Salvation Army corps [church]. The officer had unusual ability, but had become stale and spiritually lifeless. Where hundreds should have greeted me, fifty tired, listless people were present. I was fiercely tempted to leave the place, telling the officer I would not spend my strength helping a man with no more spirit and interest than he manifested.

Then I looked at the poor, wearied people before me, and my heart was swept with a great wave of pity for them—"sheep without a shepherd" (Matthew 9:36). And I set myself with full purpose of heart to bless and feed them, to save them, and in the next six days the big hall was crowded and we rejoiced over ninety souls seeking the Savior.

True soul-winners count not their lives dear unto themselves (Acts 20:24, KJV). They give themselves desperately to their task, and there are times when they sob and cry, "Give me souls, or I die."

*AP, 3*

## The Purpose of Pain

*The LORD disciplines those he loves.* (Hebrews 12:6, NLT)

For days I have been an amused observer of one of my little grandsons. One of his chief joys is to get into his bath. It is perfectly delicious to watch as he coos and gurgles, and splashes water all over, and blinks when water pops into his eyes. But how he loathes being undressed and redressed! He kicks and cries and objects in all manner of baby ways, while his insistent mother ignores all his objections, not asking what he likes, and dresses him as she thinks best.

All this is gentle and wise, but to him much of it is "painful." "For the moment all discipline seems painful rather than pleasant, but later"—let us note this "but later"—"it yields the peaceful fruit of righteousness to those who have been trained by it" (Hebrews 12:11). The child will learn slowly, but surely, that all this "painful" insistence of his unyielding mother was but the expression of wise, thoughtful, sacrificial love.

This is God's way. Happy shall we be when we come to look upon the perplexing and harassing things of life, the "painful" things, as instruments in the hands of our heavenly Father for the polishing of our character.

*AP, 5*

## Chastening's Triumph

*God's discipline is always good for us, so that we might share in his holiness.* (Hebrews 12:10, NLT)

My sweet mother, after my father's death, was left alone with me, her tiny boy, and often when she should have been firm and unbending, she yielded to melting tenderness, of which I was quick to take advantage. I do not remember it, but she herself told me that I would have been spoiled had she not married again and found in my stepfather a counterpoise to her tenderness. He was firm and unbending, and I stood in awe of him, much to my profit. I have no quarrel in my memory with his dealings, but only gratitude and affection.

But it is to my darling mother I owe my deepest debt of love and gratitude. As I grew older, her gentleness and tenderness became the most powerful instrument of discipline to my wayward spirit, just as grace is more mighty to break and refashion hard hearts than law, and Mount Calvary more influential for redemption than Mount Sinai.

There was a time when Jesus turned and rebuked Peter with sharp, incisive words (Matthew 16:23). But at last the character and spirit of Jesus had so far mastered Peter that a look sufficed to break his heart (Luke 22:61-62). This is the final triumph of all the chastenings of God's love. Once He has thus broken us, He can henceforth guide us with His eye.

*AP, 5*

## Spiritual Gangrene

*The thing which I greatly feared is come upon me, and*
*that which I was afraid of is come unto me.* (Job 3:25, KJV)

Some years ago, two or three officers [ministers] at a
Salvation Army headquarters became suspicious about
their future in the Army, and lost their joy and power.
The miserable spiritual gangrene spread to the corps officers (pastors), and they lost their joy and trust in straining
their poor eyes to look into the future, for which God commanded them to trust Him without an anxious thought.

Subsequently, the light and glory fled from the meetings, and the whole work languished, withered, and almost
died. Those poor, foolish, fearful doubters could not see
that their anxiety was producing the conditions that would
bring all their fears upon them like an avalanche. Not
until men and women full of faith, joy, and the Holy Spirit
rejoiced and prayed and shouted and rallied the doubting
ones did the work recover.

The soul that doubts and fears and murmurs is walking
right into the jaws of trouble. If we begin to be anxious
about the future, it saps our joy and robs us of our trust in
God. But to the man or woman who keeps glad in God,
who rejoices and prays and trusts in the teeth of hell, the
path grows brighter unto the perfect day. God has pledged
Himself to stand by such a person as that.

*RLP,* 18

## God-Permitted Opportunities

*The temptations in your life are no different from what others experience.* (1 Corinthians 10:13, NLT)

As the storm and whirlwind, which twist the roots and toughen the fibers of an oak, also help in its development, so temptation is a part of our lot. Our moral character is being fashioned and tested, and one of the most important factors in the formation of right character is temptation.

An unchaste woman tempted Joseph, and he began the ascent to sublime heights of holy character and influence by resisting and overcoming the temptation.

Moses, doubtless, was tempted to remain in the luxury of Pharaoh's court. But he resisted and overcame, "choosing rather to suffer affliction with the people of God, than to enjoy the pleasures of sin for a season" (Hebrews 11:25, KJV).

Daniel was tempted by Nebuchadnezzar's table, and peculiar strength was added to the temptation by the fact that he was a captive slave. But he "resolved that he would not defile himself with the king's food, or with the wine that he drank" (Daniel 1:8). And he received at last the highest honors the king could bestow.

These temptations were part of their discipline. They were God-permitted opportunities. And we, in turn and according to our strength and duties, must be tempted. We cannot evade it, but—thank God—we, as they, can overcome it and rise by means of our fellowship with Jesus.

*RLP, 19*

## For Those Who Are Tempted

*Because Jesus experienced temptation when he suffered,*
*he is able to help others when they are tempted.*
(Hebrews 2:18, GW)

The Bible is teeming with encouragements to tempted
souls. Scripture assures us:

1. "No temptation has overtaken you except what is common to humanity" (1 Corinthians 10:13, HCSB). Others have
gone this way before us triumphant, and so may we.

2. "God is faithful, and . . . with the temptation he will
also provide the way of escape, that you may be able to
endure it" (1 Corinthians 10:13). God will not allow any
trial to exceed our strength, if we will promptly look to
Him and seek His help.

3. Jesus is able "to sympathize with our weaknesses,"
for He is "one who in every respect has been tempted as
we are, yet without sin" (Hebrews 4:15). And "because he
himself has suffered when tempted, he is able to help those
who are being tempted" (Hebrews 2:18).

4. "Blessed are those who persevere under trial, because
when they have stood the test, they will receive the crown of
life" (James 1:12, TNIV). How can the oak have the crown of
life, strength, and lordly beauty unless it stands the storm?

God will not fail us. He will bless us, walk with us, teach
and comfort us, strengthening us until He could pile cares,
perplexities, and mountain-like responsibilities upon us
without a tremor of doubt or complaint on our part.

*RLP,* 19

## All of Heaven Is on Our Side

*God is faithful, and he will not let you be tempted beyond your ability.* (1 Corinthians 10:13)

What are we to do since we know we will be tried by temptation?

1. "Watch and pray that you may not enter into temptation" (Matthew 26:41). If we run carelessly into temptation, we may find it more difficult than we supposed to get out. If David had watched and prayed, as he should, he would not have brought such shame and reproach to the cause of God as he did.

2. If temptation which we cannot escape comes upon us, then we are to do like Roosevelt's Rough Riders: rush forward with a shout and fight to a finish. James says, "My brothers and sisters, when you have many kinds of troubles, you should be full of joy, because you know that these troubles test your faith, and this will give you patience" (James 1:2-3, NCV). Face each temptation as it comes. Fight it out.

It is good for us to consider that all of heaven is on our side. Our heavenly Father is pledged to give us more grace. Jesus "knows our frame; he remembers that we are dust" (Psalm 103:14). He would have us come to Him with all confidence (Hebrews 4:16), and He will not fail us, but will with the temptation also make a way to escape, that we may be able to bear it.

*RLP,* 19

## Perfect Obedience of the Heart

*Be perfect, therefore, as your heavenly Father is perfect.*
(Matthew 5:48, NIV)

My little boy, with his heart beating high to help his papa, goes into the garden to pull the weeds from among the vegetables. But he comes to the corn, and he doesn't know the difference between corn and weeds, and while pulling up the weeds he also pulls up my corn.

When I come home, he runs to me with eyes dancing, bursting to tell me how he has helped me by weeding the garden. I go out and find that, while he has weeded the garden, he has also pulled up my sweet corn. But I see that he has done it with a heart full of desire to please his father, and that the trouble has not been with his heart, but with his ignorant little head. And seeing his perfect little heart, I press him to my breast and call him my little man. This is the kind of perfection God wants in us—perfect obedience of the heart.

Now let me ask you, what kind of heart do you have? Have you submitted to Him? Have you consecrated yourself wholly to Him? Have you let Him have all His way with you? How anger and pride and selfishness and uncleanness must grieve Him! The perfect-hearted person has put all these things away.

*GS, 5*

## Keeping Sweet

*Salt is good, but if the salt has lost its saltiness, how will you make it salty again? Have salt in yourselves.*
(Mark 9:50)

"Do tell me how to keep cool!" I implored of the secretary as I walked into a New York office on a recent roasting, steaming-hot day.

"I wish someone would tell me how to keep sweet!" she replied, with a pathetic look on her anxious face.

The Scriptures never tell us to keep sweet, but the Savior bids us, "Have salt in yourselves" and then adds what may stand for sweetness: "be at peace with one another" (Mark 9:50). And Paul writes, "Let your speech always be gracious, seasoned with salt" (Colossians 4:6). Possibly the "grace" in this text stands for the sweetness so longed for by that secretary, but the saving power of salt was uppermost in the mind of Paul.

Nevertheless, her longing to be kept sweet was a heavenly desire. And God was, and is, waiting to fulfill that desire. Unfortunately, too many are quite content to be sour, grouchy, ill-tempered, impatient, angry, hasty, and hurtful in speech and temper.

The love of God is the great sweetener of all life. It is both a fountain and a fire. Be filled with His love, and you shall know the secret of keeping sweet.

*RLP, 22*

## Let It In

*If anyone hears my voice and opens the door, I will come in.* (Revelation 3:20)

"Let the peace of Christ rule in your hearts," writes Paul (Colossians 3:15). He does not seem to think it a difficult matter. All we have to do is *let it*. It is at hand. We do not have to ascend into heaven to get sunshine; it pours itself in boundless floods all about us. All we need to do is open wide our doors and windows and let it in.

"*Let* the word of Christ dwell in you richly" (Colossians 3:16, emphasis added). Some people turn as naturally and instantly to the Word of God for instruction, guidance, comfort, and courage as the magnetic needle turns to the pole. When they go, it leads them. When they sleep, it keeps them. When they awake, it talks with them (Proverbs 6:22, KJV).

Again, "*Let* this mind be in you, which was also in Christ Jesus" (Philippians 2:5, KJV, emphasis added). Jesus sought nothing for Himself. He came not to be served, but to serve, and give His life. Anyone among us can let the lowly mind of the Master live in him or her.

Finally, "*Let* mutual love continue" (Hebrews 13:1, NRSV, emphasis added). If the fires of love are fed with fresh fuel every day, they will burn on and on until they are caught up and commingled with the very heart of God Himself.

*RLP, 22*

## Unwaveringly Sure

*Consider it pure joy, my brothers and sisters, whenever you face trials of many kinds.* (James 1:2, NIV)

"I feel that my sense of security and faith are waiting to be tried before I can be quite sure of myself." So wrote an exceptionally bright young woman to me in a recent letter, and in those words are revealed a halting and mixed faith and a subtle temptation of the Accuser.

Of course, our "faith and sense of security" are always being tried, and we should quietly and confidently welcome such trial, for it is by the trial of faith that our character is perfected. James says, "Consider it pure joy, my brothers and sisters, whenever you face trials of many kinds, because you know that the testing of your faith produces perseverance. Let perseverance finish its work so that you may be mature and complete, not lacking anything" (James 1:2-4, NIV).

So it is reasonable and normal to expect trials, but this young comrade's phrase—"before I can be quite sure of myself"—reveals the work of the tempter, slyly turning her eyes from Jesus to herself.

We are never to be sure of ourselves, but quietly, unwaveringly sure of our Redeemer. We shall be tried, but we shall not be left alone. As He was with the three young men in Nebuchadnezzar's furnace (Daniel 3:24-25), so He will be with us.

*AP, 13*

## Follow the Real Jesus

*False christs and false prophets will appear . . . to
deceive, if possible, even those whom God has chosen.*
(Matthew 24:24, CEB)

Truly, many "false christs" have gone out into the world.

There are dreamy, poetical christs, whose words are
"more soothing than oil, yet they are drawn swords" (Psalm
55:21, NIV). There are fashionable christs, "lovers of pleasure
rather than lovers of God, having the appearance of godliness, but denying its power" (2 Timothy 3:4-5). There are
mercantile christs, who make God's house "a den of thieves"
(Matthew 21:13, KJV). There are feeding christs, who would
catch people by feeding the stomach rather than the heart
and head (Romans 16:18). There are learned, philosophical
christs, who take people captive "by philosophy and empty
deceit, according to human tradition" (Colossians 2:8).
There are political-reform christs, who forget their Father's
business in an all-absorbing effort to govern this world, who
travel halfway across the continent to deliver a speech on
some current issue, while a hundred thousand sinners are
going to hell at home.

Seek to know and follow in the footsteps of the true, real
Jesus. They wanted to make Him a king one day, but He
wouldn't be a king, save of people's hearts. He "made himself
of no reputation" (Philippians 2:7, KJV). He became a Servant
of all, that He might make us "partakers of the divine nature"
and let us "share his holiness" (2 Peter 1:4; Hebrews 12:10).

*HH, 20*

## For This We Were Born

*It's in Christ that we find out who we are and what we are living for.* (Ephesians 1:11, *The Message*)

Jesus came as a lowly stranger into the iron furnace of this sin-cursed, devil-enslaved world. He toiled with its toiling millions, suffered their sorrows and sicknesses and even their death . . . and then rose again and ascended "far above all rule and authority and power and dominion" (Ephesians 1:21). From that place of power He pleads our cause, guides our steps, strengthens our hearts, illuminates our minds, and secures for us boundless gifts and graces.

He desires that we should sustain the same relation to Him now that He sustained to His heavenly Father in the days of His humanity. This being so, I am under as much obligation now to be holy, to be empowered by the Spirit, and to be about my Lord's business, as I shall be in heaven. And this is not only an obligation, but an inspiration!

Having caught a glimpse of this high and holy purpose, how could I be content ever again to grope in the malarial fogs of unbelief, and grovel on the dunghill of this world's poor little pleasures? How can I not deny myself and even sacrifice my life in order to "know him and the power of his resurrection" (Philippians 3:10)? It was for this we were born, and to fall short of this will be infinite and eternal loss.

*HTH, 22*

## Abounding in Hope

*May the power of the Holy Spirit fill you with hope.*
(Romans 15:13, CEV)

God's people are a hopeful people. In the darkest night and the fiercest storm they still hope in God, though it may be feebly. But He would have His people "abound in hope" so that they should always be buoyant, triumphant.

But how can that be in a world such as this? We are surrounded by awful, merciless forces that at any moment may overwhelm us. The fire may burn us, the water may drown us, the hurricane may sweep us away, friends may desert us, foes may master us. There is the depression that comes from failing health, from poverty, from overwork and constant care, from thwarted plans, disappointed ambitions, slighted love, and base ingratitude.

Under some blessed outpouring of the Spirit the work of God revives, vile sinners are saved, Zion puts on her beautiful garments, and the waste place becomes a fruitful field; and then the spiritual tide recedes, the forces of evil again sweep over the heritage of the Lord, and the battle must be fought all over again.

How can one be always abounding in hope in such a world? It is possible "by the power of the Holy Spirit" (Romans 15:13, NKJV), but only through His power. And this power will not fail so long as we fix our eyes on eternal things and believe.

*HGC, 10*

## Perfect Peace

*You will keep in perfect peace all who trust in you, all whose thoughts are fixed on you!* (Isaiah 26:3, NLT)

I confess it is no easy matter for most people to keep their minds stayed on our Lord. They would rather think about business, about pleasure, about the news of the day, about politics, education, music, or even the work of the Lord, than about the Lord Himself.

Now, these matters must take some of our thought. But just as a young couple in love, in all their work and pleasure, think each of the other though they may be far apart, so we should in everything think of and commune with Jesus, and let our hearts fully trust His wisdom, love, and power, and then we shall be kept in "perfect peace."

Ten thousand times I have been at my wits' end, but, oh, how it comforted me to know that Jesus saw the end from the beginning and was making all things work together for my good because I loved and trusted Him! "In him lie hidden all the treasures of wisdom and knowledge," and we, in our ignorance and foolishness, "are complete through [our] union with Christ" (Colossians 2:3, 10, NLT). We may not understand, but He understands. We may be perplexed, but He is not perplexed. Then we ought to trust Him if we are His, and we shall be kept in "perfect peace."

*HH*, 21

## The Best Gifts

*Earnestly desire the best gifts.* (1 Corinthians 12:31, NKJV)

"Earnestly desire" not the highest promotions, not the best positions, but "the best gifts" (1 Corinthians 12:31, NKJV)—those gifts which God bestows upon the people who diligently seek Him.

Nero sat upon the throne of the world; but a poor, despised Jew in a dungeon in Rome, whose head Nero cut off, possessed the best gifts. And while Nero's name rots, Paul's name and works are a foundation upon which the righteous have built for centuries.

There were venerable churchmen in England, some hundreds of years ago, who held high places and power. But a poor, despised tinker in the filthy Bedford jail had earnestly desired and received "the best gifts." And while these church dignitaries are forgotten by and large, the world knows and loves the saintly tinker, John Bunyan, and is ever being made better and lifted nearer to God by his wise works and words.

You and I should seek these "best gifts" with all our hearts, and we should be satisfied with nothing short of them. What are these gifts? There is one which in a sense includes them all, and the germ of them all is in that—the gift of the Holy Spirit. Have you received the Holy Spirit? Is He dwelling in your heart? Desire Him. Live not a day without His blessed presence in you.

*LS*, 11

## Past Thrones and Palaces

*The Word was made flesh, and dwelt among us.*
(John 1:14, KJV)

Peter the Great, perhaps the mightiest monarch of his day, used to make shoes like a common cobbler, that he might enter into sympathy with his people and help them to realize that labor is honorable and full of dignity. It was a great stoop from the throne of Russia to a cobbler's bench, but I will tell you of a greater.

We are told that God "made the worlds" by His Son, and that the Son upholds "all things by the word of his power" (Hebrews 1:2, 3, KJV). He is the Master Workman, stretching forth the heavens as a curtain, creating worlds and hurling them into space and causing them to move, not in chaotic confusion, but in clock-like harmony.

But John tells us, "The Word was made flesh, and dwelt among us" (John 1:14, KJV). And when He clothed Himself with our flesh, He took a lowly place in a peasant's home. He might have stopped at a throne, or among the rich and lordly. But instead He went down past thrones and palaces, and was born among the cattle. He came to a life of poverty and of toil, and He who made the worlds and upheld them by the word of His power learned to be a carpenter.

*HTH, 17*

## Heavenly Things First

*Glory to God in the highest, and on earth peace among those with whom he is pleased!* (Luke 2:14)

When the heavenly host appeared over the plain of Bethlehem, the first note of their song was, "Glory to God in the highest." God was foremost in their thought, then His glory. Afterwards they sang, "Peace on earth to people He favors" (Luke 2:14, HCSB).

As citizens of heaven, we too must put heavenly things first. Thus, the Christmas song of the angels becomes a guide to us in these days. Our chief business is to give glory to God and put Him first in our lives.

This spirit of seeking God's glory first will make us hate sin, because it robs God of His glory, and we will wax hot with holy indignation when we see God dishonored.

This spirit will lead us out to warfare for God, to go out and plead with others to turn from their evil ways, yield their hearts to God, and love and serve Him.

This spirit makes sacrifice a joy and service a delight. Everything we have is at God's disposal; we surrender all for the glory of our Lord.

Blessed are we when this spirit of heaven fills us and we put heavenly things first, and sing, "Glory to God in the highest!"

*LS,* 5

## Peace on Earth

*On earth peace to those who have his good will!*
(Luke 2:14, GW)

The gospel is but the spirit of heaven projecting itself into this world. It is only in proportion as this spirit possesses people and takes possession of the earth that the second note of the Christmas song of the angels becomes possible: "on earth peace" (Luke 2:14).

How shall we do this? How can I, a poor, weak, short-sighted man, help to fill the world with peace?

In the first place, by keeping my own heart with all diligence and letting the peace of God rule in it. I must also be a man of peace in my own family and community, in my church or corps, remembering that "a soft answer turns away wrath, but a harsh word stirs up anger" (Proverbs 15:1).

Most importantly, though I cannot enter into the councils of kings and queens and presidents, and in such high places work for peace among the nations, I can enter into my closet and pray for these leaders with their heavy burdens, asking God to guide and help them to rule the world in peace.

Let us exalt our calling to be peacemakers, and let us pray with faith and great gladness, and God will hear and give us peace.

*LS, 5*

## The Great Unveiling

*His name shall be called Wonderful, Counselor, Mighty God, Everlasting Father, Prince of Peace.* (Isaiah 9:6)

We look into the Bethlehem manger, and see that that Child is our help, and that "the government shall be upon his shoulder" (Isaiah 9:6). Then, repenting and believing on Him, we find pardon, peace, and cleansing in His blood, and we cry out, "Wonderful!"

Life is a labyrinth, the universe is a riddle. The wisest philosophers cannot solve the problems of evil, pain, and death. But we discover that in Him "are hidden all the treasures of wisdom and knowledge" (Colossians 2:3). He resolves our riddles. We rest in Him as our "Counselor."

We are oppressed with our utter littleness and weakness, and in our despair we look again, and we see Him stilling the storm, raising the dead, calming people's fierce, wild passions, and we cry out, "The mighty God!"

Bereft and lonely, we cry like an orphaned child in the night. There is none to help, and no one understands. Then He draws nigh with fathomless consolations of love. And we nestle close and whisper, "The everlasting Father! The Prince of Peace!"

This is Jesus. We saw Him first as a helpless Child. But oh, how He has grown as we have looked! Yet He stooped to our lowly condition and humbled Himself, and suffered and died for us, and made atonement for our sins.

*GS, 1*

## Spiritual Songs

*Speak to each other with psalms, hymns, and spiritual songs, singing and making music in your hearts to the Lord.* (Ephesians 5:19, NCV)

One day at a camp meeting I sat alone under great trees with a Salvation Army officer who had just lost his wife. He quoted Charles Wesley's "Wrestling Jacob":

*Come, O thou Traveler unknown,*
    *Whom still I hold, but cannot see!*
*My company before is gone,*
    *And I am left alone with Thee;*
*With Thee all night I mean to stay*
    *And wrestle till the break of day.*[33]

And as in deep and quiet tones he spoke the words of that noble hymn, the power and value of our songs as devotional helps (when spoken or read, apart from singing) burst upon me as never before.

Let me exhort you to "sing psalms, hymns, and spiritual songs, as you praise the Lord with all your heart" (Ephesians 5:19, CEV). Keep hymns and spiritual songs by your bedside with your Bible and carry them with you to read. They will enrich your faith, invigorate your hope, and keep warm and tender your love.

*RLP, 27*

## Evidences of Inspiration

*Your word is a lamp to my feet and a light to my path.*
(Psalm 119:105)

The sun does not need learned astronomical treatises to prove its existence. All it needs is that we should have eyes to see. What the sun is in the world of material things, the Bible is in the world of spiritual things. It carries in itself its evidences of inspiration.

Does the Bible offer hope to the soul who has turned his or her back on light and goodness and God? It, and it alone, tells of a Savior and of a loving heavenly Father who waits to welcome sinners.

Does the Bible have any word for the burdened, perplexed, and careworn? "Come to me, all who labor and are heavy laden, and I will give you rest" (Matthew 11:28). Has it any word for the oppressed, the afflicted? "He has not ignored or belittled the suffering of the needy. He has not turned his back on them, but has listened to their cries for help" (Psalm 22:24, NLT). A word for those whose eyes are dim with tears? "God will wipe away every tear from their eyes" (Revelation 7:17). For those who are in pain? "Neither shall there be mourning, nor crying, nor pain anymore" (Revelation 21:4).

While others debate the inspiration of the Word, let us eat it, drink it, proclaim it, and live it.

*AP*, 15 and 12

## When the Way Is Rough

*It is good for one to bear the yoke in youth.*
(Lamentations 3:27, NRSV)

Men and women who do things for God usually in the beginning find their way rough. "It's a good thing when you're young to stick it out through the hard times," wrote Jeremiah (Lamentations 3:27, *The Message*), and this is their lot and their portion. Their hearts are encouraged not by favorable circumstances and applauding crowds, but by a stern sense of duty, a whisper of faith and hope, and a hidden fire of love which "laughs at impossibilities and cries: 'It shall be done!'"[34]

It was doubtless so with Noah through those long years of waiting and working, while the faith was being fashioned and tried which made him heir of the world. It certainly was so with Joseph, through those years of slavery and imprisonment before he was lifted up and made ruler of Egypt. It was so with Moses and David and Daniel and Paul. It was so with William Booth. They struggled on against ridicule, reproach, and persecution, when to human vision it seemed that God Himself, if not against them, was indifferent to them.

Do as they did, dear soul. Persevere. "Hold on, so you can do what God wants and receive what he has promised" (Hebrews 10:36, NCV).

*RLP, 26*

## Thrown Back on God

*"Here on earth you will have many trials and sorrows.*
*But take heart, because I have overcome the world."*
(John 16:33, NLT)

From infancy my life has been punctuated by tragic losses, surprises, and pains.

My earliest recollections are of my bereaved and weeping widowed mother. In my adolescence, I was away at school when I received my first telegram: "Mother is dying." For the next twelve years I had no home.

At the beginning of my Salvation Army ministry, a ruffian hurled a brick at my head and laid me up for eighteen months. I was later stricken with an agonizingly painful sickness, and I lay at death's door among strangers for weary weeks, returning home a mere shadow of a man. Some years after that, lying helpless in a hospital with a great surgical wound that threatened my life, I received word that my sweet wife, the darling of my life, was dying.

I do not argue, though in fact it may be so, that these are the best things that could have befallen me. But I do testify that by God's grace, they have all worked together for my good. They have worked in me to humble my proud and wayward nature. They have thrown me back on God. And they have been rigorous and unsparing, but also compelling teachers of fortitude, sympathy, and understanding.

*RLP, 28*

## When the Enemy Whispers

*They overcame him by the blood of the Lamb, and by the word of their testimony; and they loved not their lives unto the death.* (Revelation 12:11, KJV)

A dear brother wrote, "I do not seem to enjoy the blessing as I should. I am sure I strive with all my heart to live close to God, but there is something in the way. Please pray for me!"

What can be the trouble? Perhaps the enemy whispers, "You do not feel as you ought to feel; there is something in the way," and instead of resisting the devil, our brother has unwittingly agreed with the devil. And that something is a tiny root of practical unbelief, which frustrates the grace of God.

Revelation 12:10 (NIV) says, "The accuser of our brothers and sisters, who accuses them before our God day and night, has been hurled down." How was he hurled down? Note the next verse: (1) "they triumphed over him by the blood of the Lamb." That is, they trusted the efficacy of the blood; (2) "and by the word of their testimony." That is, they dared to testify in the face of a mocking and accusing devil that "the blood of Jesus . . . cleanses us from all sin" (1 John 1:7); and (3) "they did not love their lives so much as to shrink from death." That is, they were prepared to die for their testimony.

These three conditions, firmly and fully met, will lead one into the enjoyment of the blessing and, maintained, will make the blessing permanent.

*RLP, 21*

## "I Recommend Him to the World"

*For God alone, O my soul, wait in silence, for my hope is from him.* (Psalm 62:5)

What has God not done for me? What has He not been to me? I recommend Him to the world. He has taught me that sin is the only thing that can harm me, and that the only thing that can profit me is "faith working through love" (Galatians 5:6). He has taught me to hang upon Jesus by faith, and to show my love by obeying Him in all things and by seeking in all ways to lead others to obey Him.

I praise Him! I adore Him! He can do with me as He pleases, for I am His. He is too wise to make mistakes and too good to do me evil. I trust Him, I trust Him, I trust Him! "My hope is from him" (Psalm 62:5), not from others, not from myself, but from Him. He will never fail me.

For the past ten years God has enabled me to keep a perfect, unbroken purpose to serve Him with my whole heart. No temptation has swerved that steadfast purpose. "HOLINESS TO THE LORD" (Exodus 28:36, KJV) has been my motto.

My heart pants after Him and, as I seek Him in fervent, patient, believing prayer and in diligent searching of His Word, He is deepening the work of grace in my soul.

*HH, Intro*

**THE SALVATION ARMY**, an international movement, is an evangelical part of the universal Christian church. Its message is based on the Bible. Its ministry is motivated by the love of God. Its mission is to preach the gospel of Jesus Christ and to meet human needs in His name without discrimination.

The Salvation Army ministers in more than 120 countries. The Army's doctrine follows the mainstream of Christian belief, and its articles of faith emphasize God's saving purposes. To learn more, visit www.salvationarmy.org.

**BOB HOSTETLER** is an award-winning writer, editor, and speaker from southwestern Ohio. His books, which include the award-winning *Don't Check Your Brains at the Door* (co-authored with Josh McDowell) and the novel *The Bone Box*, have sold over three million copies. He has won two Gold Medallion Awards, four Ohio Associated Press awards, and an Amy Foundation Award. He served as an officer in The Salvation Army (1980–1992) and is the founding pastor of Cobblestone Community Church in Oxford, Ohio. He and his wife, Robin, have two grown children, Aubrey and Aaron, who have given them four beautiful grandchildren.

# ACKNOWLEDGMENTS

Thank you to Steve Laube of the Steve Laube Agency for representing this project, and for going above and beyond the call of duty in making this dream a reality.

Thank you to Linda Johnson and the Salvation Army's Eastern Territorial leaders for believing in this book and its message, and for the expertise that made it better at every point in the process.

Thank you also to Jan Long Harris, Sharon Leavitt, and the Tyndale Momentum team, for their vision and enthusiasm for this project.

Thank you to Dr. Lynell Johnson of The Salvation Army and Caleb Sjogren of Tyndale House Publishers for the tireless work of breathtaking insight and editorial genius they contributed to this work. I am grateful to have had them as coworkers, cocreators, and coeditors of this devotional.

Thank you also—and most of all—to the lovely Robin, my wife, without whose love and support I could never have begun, let alone finished, this project.

# SCRIPTURE PERMISSIONS

Unless otherwise noted, all Scripture quotations are from *The Holy Bible*, English Standard Version® (ESV®), copyright © 2001 by Crossway, a publishing ministry of Good News Publishers. Used by permission. All rights reserved.

Scripture quotations marked ASV are from *The Holy Bible*, American Standard Version. Public domain.

Scripture quotations marked CEB are taken from the Common English Bible®, CEB®, copyright © 2010, 2011 by Common English Bible.™ Used by permission. All rights reserved worldwide. The "CEB" and "Common English Bible" trademarks are registered in the United States Patent and Trademark Office by Common English Bible. Use of either trademark requires the permission of Common English Bible.

Scripture quotations marked CEV are taken from the Contemporary English Version, copyright © 1991, 1992, 1995 by American Bible Society. Used by permission.

Scripture quotations marked GNT are from the Good News Translation in Today's English Version—Second Edition, copyright © 1992 by American Bible Society. Used by permission.

Scripture quotations marked GW are taken from GOD'S WORD®, © 1995 God's Word to the Nations. Used by permission of Baker Publishing Group.

Scripture quotations marked HCSB are taken from the Holman Christian Standard Bible®, copyright © 1999, 2000, 2002, 2003, 2009 by Holman Bible Publishers. Used by permission. Holman Christian Standard Bible®, Holman CSB®, and HCSB® are federally registered trademarks of Holman Bible Publishers.

Scripture quotations marked KJV are taken from the *Holy Bible*, King James Version. Public domain.

Scripture quotations marked LEB are from the *Lexham English Bible*. Copyright © 2012 Logos Bible Software. Lexham is a registered trademark of Logos Bible Software.

Scripture quotations marked *The Message* are taken from *The Message* by Eugene H. Peterson, copyright © 1993, 1994, 1995, 1996, 2000, 2001, 2002. Used by permission of NavPress Publishing Group. All rights reserved.

Scripture quotations marked NASB are taken from the New American Standard Bible,® copyright © 1960, 1962, 1963, 1968, 1971, 1972, 1973, 1975, 1977, 1995 by The Lockman Foundation. Used by permission.

Scripture quotations marked NCV are taken from the New Century Version.®
Copyright © 2005 by Thomas Nelson, Inc. Used by permission. All rights
reserved.

Scripture quotations marked NIrV are taken from the Holy Bible, *New
International Reader's Version,*® *NIrV.*® Copyright © 1995, 1996, 1998 by
Biblica, Inc.™ Used by permission of Zondervan. All rights reserved worldwide.
www.zondervan.com.

Scripture quotations marked NIV are taken from the Holy Bible, *New International Version,*® *NIV.*® Copyright © 1973, 1978, 1984, 2011 by Biblica, Inc.™
Used by permission of Zondervan. All rights reserved worldwide.
www.zondervan.com.

Scripture quotations marked NIV 1984 are taken from the 1984 edition of
the Holy Bible, *New International Version,*® *NIV.*® Copyright © 1973, 1978,
1984 by Biblica, Inc.™ Used by permission of Zondervan. All rights reserved.
www.zondervan.com.

Scripture quotations marked NKJV are taken from the New King James
Version.® Copyright © 1982 by Thomas Nelson, Inc. Used by permission.
All rights reserved.

Scripture quotations marked NLT are taken from the *Holy Bible*, New Living
Translation, second edition, copyright © 1996, 2004, 2007 by Tyndale House
Foundation. (Some quotations may be from the NLT, first edition, copyright ©
1996.) Used by permission of Tyndale House Publishers, Inc., Carol Stream, IL
60188. All rights reserved.

Scripture quotations marked NRSV are taken from New Revised Standard
Version Bible, copyright © 1989, Division of Christian Education of the
National Council of the Churches of Christ in the United States of America.
Used by permission. All rights reserved.

Scripture verses marked *Phillips* are taken from *The New Testament in Modern
English* by J. B. Phillips, copyright © J. B. Phillips, 1958, 1959, 1960, 1972. All
rights reserved.

Scripture quotations marked TNIV are taken from the Holy Bible, *Today's New
International Version,*® *TNIV.*® Copyright © 2001, 2005 by Biblica, Inc.™ Used by
permission of Zondervan. All rights reserved worldwide. www.zondervan.com.

Scripture quotations marked WBT are from the Webster Bible translation.
Public domain.

Scripture quotations marked WNT are from the Weymouth New Testament.
Public domain.

# NOTES

1. R. David Rightmire, *Sanctified Sanity: The Life and Teaching of Samuel Logan Brengle* (Alexandria, Virginia: Crest Books, 2003), 156.
2. Rightmire, 85-86.
3. John Stott, *The Incomparable Christ* (Downers Grove, IL: InterVarsity Press, 2001), 155.
4. Robert J. Morgan, *The Promise: God Works All Things Together for Your Good* (Nashville: B & H Publishing, 2010), 134.
5. John Morley, *The Life of William Ewart Gladstone, Volume 1* (London: Macmillan and Company, Ltd., 2006), 634.
6. Attributed to J. Wilbur Chapman in *The Art of Soul-Winning* by J. W. Mahood (Cincinnati: Jennings and Pye, 1901), 77–78.
7. "O When Shall My Soul Find Her Rest," Bramwell Booth, public domain.
8. Revised from "Not Death, but Love," the first sonnet in *Sonnets from the Portuguese*, by Elizabeth Barrett Browning. Public domain.
9. James Russell Lowell, "The Present Crisis," line 40, http://www.bartleby .com/42/805.html.
10. "Come, O Thou Traveler Unknown," Charles Wesley, public domain.
11. Robert Browning, *The Poems of Robert Browning*, "Christmas Eve," part XX, lines 52–53 (London: Wordsworth Editions, 1994), 408.
12. "When You Feel Weakest, Dangers Surround," Lucy Booth–Hellberg, *The Salvation Army Songbook*.
13. "I Knew That God in His Word Had Spoken," F. C. Baker, public domain.
14. William Bramwell, *Memoir of the Life and Ministry of the Reverend William Bramwell* (London: Simpkin, Marshall, and Co., 1848), 191.
15. Quoted in Howard Agnew Johnston, *Scientific Christian Thinking* (New York: George H. Doran Company, 1922), 224.
16. "Take My Life and Let It Be," Frances Ridley Havergal, public domain.
17. "Come, Holy Ghost, All-Quickening Fire," Charles Wesley, public domain.
18. John Fletcher, *The Works of the Reverend John Fletcher* (London: John Mason, 1859), 166.
19. "From My Soul Break Every Fetter," Elizabeth MacKenzie, public domain.
20. "Sovereign of All the Worlds on High," Philip Doddridge, public domain.
21. "Give Me a Heart Like Thine," copyrighted in 1919 by Homer A. Rodeheaver.
22. "Father of Jesus Christ, My Lord," Charles Wesley, public domain.
23. Francis Bacon, *Essays*, XXXIV (Of Riches).
24. St. Francis de Sales, *Letters of Spiritual Direction*, Letter 51.
25. St. Augustine, quoted by Rufus M. Jones, *Fundamental Ends of Life* (n. p.: Kessinger Publishing, 2003), 115.

26. David Shibley, *Great for God: Missionaries Who Changed the World* (Green Forest, AR: New Leaf Press, 2012), 49.

27. In the author's testimony given June 19, 1919, this quote is attributed to Victor Hugo. See http://www.raptureready.com/resource/brengle/slaves18 .html.

28. Roy B. Zuck, ed., *Vital Biblical Issues: Examining Problem Passages of the Bible* (Grand Rapids, MI: Kregel Publications, 1994), 139.

29. "All for Jesus," Mary D. James, public domain.

30. Quoted in Jacque Marsollier, *The Life of St. Francis of Sales*, trans. W. H. Coombes (London: Shepton-Mallet, 1812), 501.

31. "Our Blest Redeemer, Ere He Breathed," Harriet Auber, public domain.

32. Adelaide A. Procter, "Judge Not," public domain.

33. "Come, O Thou Traveler Unknown," Charles Wesley, public domain.

34. "Father of Jesus Christ, My Lord," Charles Wesley, public domain.

The Salvation Army, an international movement, is an evangelical part of the universal Christian church. Its message is based on the Bible. Its ministry is motivated by the love of God. Its mission is to preach the gospel of Jesus Christ and to meet human needs in His name without discrimination.

CP0656